General Psychology

About the Authors

DOUGLAS H. FRYER (1891–1960) received the degree of Doctor of Philosophy from Clark University in 1923. He held the rank of Adjunct Professor of Psychology in New York University, where he served as chairman of the Psychology Department from 1924 to 1940. He was vice-president and secretary of Richardson, Bellows, Henry, & Co., industrial psychological consultants. His record includes service as president of the American Association for Applied Psychology and of the Association of Consulting Psychologists, and he was elected vice-president of the American Association for the Advancement of Science. Among his published books on psychology are *The Measurement of Interests* and *Vocational Self-Guidance.*

EDWIN R. HENRY received the degree of Doctor of Philosophy from Ohio State University in 1931. He succeeded Dr. Fryer as chairman of the Psychology Department at New York University from 1940 to 1945, and now holds the rank of Adjunct Professor of Psychology. He is presently Personnel Research Advisor for the Standard Oil Company of New Jersey. Dr. Henry is joint editor (with Douglas H. Fryer) of the two-volume *Handbook of Applied Psychology.*

CHARLES P. SPARKS completed his graduate studies in psychology at Tulane University. For some years he was associated with the Indianapolis Public Schools as Director of Psychological Services. At present he is a regional director for Richardson, Bellows, Henry, & Co., in charge of its New Orleans office.

COLLEGE OUTLINE SERIES

General Psychology

Fourth Edition

DOUGLAS H. FRYER

EDWIN R. HENRY

CHARLES P. SPARKS

New York
BARNES & NOBLE, INC.
Publishers · Booksellers · Founded 1873

©

Fourth Edition, 1954

Copyright, 1936, 1937, 1950, 1954
By BARNES & NOBLE, INC.
All rights reserved

Reprinted, 1964

L. C. catalogue card number: 54–5725

Preface to the Fourth Edition

This outline of General Psychology does not represent any single "school" of psychological theory. Rather, it is objective in the sense that facts and theories are allowed to speak for themselves. Concise summaries of these facts and theories are presented, epitomizing the essentials of psychology in its present stage of development.

The new edition represents a drastic revision of preceding editions. The entire book has been thoroughly reorganized and completely rewritten. All the principal findings of contemporary research on General Psychology have been culled to meet the growing need among college students for information in this field.

The usual features of the College Outline Series are included, the Tabulated Bibliography and the Quick Reference Table, which key the outline to standard textbooks in psychology. For more intensive reading by the student, selected references are listed by chapters, beginning on page 251. For summaries of related knowledge, students may consult companion volumes of the College Outline Series, as follows:

> Coville *et al.*: *Abnormal Psychology*
> Crow and Crow: *Readings in General Psychology*
> Crow and Crow: *Child Psychology*
> Pintner *et al.*: *Educational Psychology*

A comprehensive series of tests is provided, beginning on page 257. Scoring keys are given which enable the student to review his knowledge, to correct his misconceptions, and to acquire new information through use of the tests.

Table of Contents

Tabulated Bibliography
of Standard Textbooks

This *College Outline* is keyed to standard textbooks in two ways.

1. If you are studying one of the following textbooks, consult the cross references here listed to find which pages of this *Outline* summarize the appropriate chapter of your text. (Roman numerals refer to the textbook chapters, Arabic figures to the corresponding pages of this *Outline*.)

2. If you are using this *Outline* as your basis for study and need a fuller treatment of a topic, consult the pages of any of the standard textbooks as indicated in the Quick Reference Table on pp. xiii–xix.

Brennan. *General Psychology*, rev. ed., 1952, Macmillan.

II (1–16); VII (7–10); VIII (27–42, 45–53); IX (54–60); X (106–113); XI (103–107); XII (90–101); XIII (68–89); XIV (60–67); XV (65–66); XVI (145–167); XVIII (191–201); XXVII (60–63).

Bugelski. *Introduction to Principles of Psychology*, 1960, Rinehart.

I, II (1–16); III (43–53, 131–144); IV (17–26, 68–113); V (27–42); VI (114–130, 217–245); VII, VIII (43–50, 145–167); IX, X (168–178); XI (179–190); XII (191–201); XIII, XIV (202–216).

Gagné and Fleishman. *Psychology and Human Performance*, 1959, Holt.

I (1–16); II (17–26, 67–113); III (54–67, 145–167); IV (17–26, 179–190); V (114–130, 217–245); VI (145–167); VII (54–67); VIII (228–230); IX (168–178); X (185–190); XI (217–235).

Garrett. *General Psychology*, 2nd ed., 1961, American Book Co.

I (1–16); II, III (131–144); IV (17–42, 68–113); V (54–67); VI (191–201); VII (179–190); VIII, IX, X (145–167); XI (168–178); XII (114–130); XIII (217–235); XIV (236–245); XV (202–216).

Geldard. *Fundamentals of Psychology*, 1962, Wiley.

I (1–16); II (179–190); III (191–201); IV (43–49, 145–167); VI (17–26, 54–60); VII (68–102); VIII (103–113); IX, X (185–190); XI, XII (145–167); XIII (168–

178); XIV, XV (60–67); XVI (131–144); XVII (217–245); XVIII, XIX (202–216).

Hebb. *A Textbook of Psychology*, 1958, Saunders.

I (10–16); II (56–67); III (17–26, 43–53); IV (27–38); V (38–42); VI (131–144); VII (145–167); VIII (179–201); IX (56–113); X (168–178); XI (114–130); XII (217–235); XIII (1–16, 246–249).

Hilgard. *Introduction to Psychology*, 3rd ed., 1962, Harcourt, Brace.

I (1–16); II (17–42); III, IV (131–144); V (179–190); VI (191–201); VII (54–67); VIII (68–113); IX–XI (43–53, 145–167); XII (168–178); XIII (114–130); XIV (217–245); XVI, XVII (206–216).

Johnson. *Psychology: A Problem-Solving Approach*, 1961, Harper.

I (1–16); II, III (179–201); IV (17–26, 68–113); V (54–67); VI, VII (43–50, 145–167); VIII (168–178); XI (217–245); XII, XIII (202–216).

Kendler. *Basic Psychology*, 1963, Appleton-Century-Crofts.

I, II, III (1–16, 17–26); IV (119–127); V (27–42); VI (68–102); VII (43–53); VIII (54–67); IX (179–190); X (145–167); XIII (202–216); XVI (217–235).

Kimble and Garmezy. *Principles of General Psychology*, 1963, Ronald.

I, II (1–16); III (119–130); IV (217–235); V (236–245); VI (45–53); VII (159–167); VIII (168–178); IX (156–159); X (27–42); XI, XII, XIII (54–67, 68–89, 90–102, 103–113); XIV (179–190); XV (131–144); XVI (202–216).

Krech and Crutchfield. *Elements of Psychology*, 1958, Knopf.

I (1–16); II–VI (54–67); VII (68–113); VIII–XI (179–201); XII (27–42, 199–200); XIII–XIV (168–178); XV–XVIII (43–49, 145–167); XIX (114–130); XX (217–242); XXI (131–137, 242–245); XXII (137–144); XXIII–XXIV (202–216).

Lewis. *Scientific Principles of Psychology*, 1963, Prentice-Hall, Inc.

I (7–10); II (1–7); III (121–129); IV (220–235); V (117–118); VI (45–50); VII, VIII, IX (50–53); X (43–45); XI (179–190); XII (63–67); XIII (169–178); XIV (199–201); XV (185–189); XVI, XVII (202–216); XVIII (131–144); XIX (68–101); XX (54–62); XXI (27–42).

Lindgren and Byrne. *Psychology*, 1961, Wiley.

I (1–16); II, III (131–144); IV (17–53, 68–113); V (145–167); VI (54–67); VII (179–201); VIII (114–130); IX (217–235); X (202–215).

Morgan. *Introduction to Psychology*, 2nd ed., 1961, McGraw-Hill.

I (1–16, 246–249); II (131–144); III (17–26, 179–190); IV (191–201); V (43–53, 145–167); VI (168–178); VII (54–67); VIII (114–130); IX (202–210); X (210–216); XV (217–245); XVIII (68–89); XIX (90–113); XXI (27–42).

Munn. *Introduction to Psychology*, 1962, Houghton Mifflin.

I, II (1–16, 114–130); III (121–122, 236–245); IV, V (217–235); VI (179–190); VII (191–201); IX (202–216); X, XI (145–167); XII (168–178); XIII (17–26, 27–42, 68–113); XIV (54–67).

Munn. *Psychology*, 1961, Houghton Mifflin.

I, II (1–16); III (27–42); IV (131–143); V (119–130); VI (217–235); VII, VIII (236–245); IX, X (202–216); XI, XII (179–190); XIII (191–201); XV (17–26); XVI (43–53); XVII, XVIII (145–167); XIX (168–178); XX (68–89); XXI (90–113); XXII (63–67).

Ringness, Klausmeier, and Singer. *Psychology in Theory and Practice*, 1955, Houghton Mifflin.

I (2–6); II (172–193); IV (154–158); V (187–193); VI (175–181); VII (181–183); VIII (183–187); IX (6–13); X (117–132); XI (136–169); XII (204–229); XIII (257–262); XIV (232–257); XV (376–385, 388–392); XVI (265–273); XVII (274–280).

Ruch. *Psychology and Life*, 1963, Scott, Foresman.

I (1–16); II (131–144); III, IV, V (145–167); VI (179–190); VII (191–201); X (68–113); XI (54–67); XII (168–178); XIII, XIV (202–216, 217–235); Section I (27–42); Section II (114–130).

Sanford. *Psychology*, 1961, Wadsworth.

I, II (1–16); III (131–144); IV (217–235); V (114–130); VI (236–245); VII (179–185); VIII (185–190); IX (191–201); X (17–26, 54–60); XI (68–113); XII (60–67); XIII (43–53, 145–148); XIV (148–167); XV (168–178); XVI–XVIII (202–216); XX (27–42).

Sartain *et al.* *Psychology: Understanding Human Behavior*, 2nd ed., 1962, McGraw-Hill.

I (1–16); II (131–134); IV (179–190); V (191–201); VI (202–216); IX (17–42); X (68–113); XI (54–67); XII (43–53); XIII (145–167); XIV (168–178); XV–XVII (217–245).

Sells. *Essentials of Psychology*, 1962, Ronald.

I (1–16); II (145–167); III (17–26, 68–113); IV (54–67); V (179–190); VI (191–201); VIII (217–245); IX, X (202–216).

Smith and Smith. *The Behavior of Man*, 1958, Holt.

I (3–26); II (94–108); III (109–113); IV (103–106, 266–270); V (201–204, 233–250); VI (204–207, 250–264); VII (207–212); VIII (212–218); X (126–139); XI (265–296); XII (319–344); XIII (145–172); XIV (173–200); XV (427–477); XVI (401–409); XVII (409–417).

Wickens and Meyer. *Psychology*, 2nd ed., 1961, Dryden.

I (1–26); II (422–502); III (503–524); IV (37–53); V (192–245); X (269–285); XI (27–36, 54–112); XII (246–268); XIII (113–161); XIV (162–191); XV (319–421); XVI (286–295, 311–318); XVII (296–311); XVIII (525–528).

Williams. *Psychology*, 1960, Harcourt, Brace.

I (1–16); II (152–159); III (131–144); V (68–102); VI (103–113); VII (17–42); IX (179–190); X (191–201); XI (43–53, 145–167); XII (217–245); XIII (54–67); XIV (168–178); XV (202–216).

Woodworth and Schlosberg. *Experimental Psychology*, rev. ed., 1954, Holt.

IV (541–581); V (72–106); VI (362–527); VII (323–361); VIII (267–322); XI (528–540, 582–813); XII (814–848); XIV (107–191).

Valentine and Wickens. *Experimental Foundations of General Psychology*, 3rd ed., 1949, Rinehart.

IV (226–231); V (131–134); VI (134–144); VII (220–226); VIII (236–245); X (179–190); XIII (191–201); XV (54–67); XVI (43–53); XVII (145–156); XVIII (156–159); XIX (168–178); XXI (202–216).

QUICK REFERENCE TABLE

All numbers

See preceding pages for

CHAP.	TOPIC	BREN-NAN	BUGEL-SKI	GAGNE	GARRETT	GELDARD
1	The Study of General Psychology	1–26 77–89	3–50	1–10	1–31	1–8
2	Stimulation, Integration, and Reaction		51–67	11–22		
3	Nervous Integration	90–94	139–167	23–29	122–134	
4	Development of Reaction	94–99	167–171	30–49		9–32
5	Sensation and Perception	100–107 159–181	95–138	178–218	135–171	83–99 245–288
6	Vision and Visual Phenomena	143–158		15–16 184–187	95–111	101–114
7	Audition and Auditory Phenomena	131–142		16–17 187–192	111–118	114–129
8	Our Other Senses	108–130		193–217	118–122	131–147
9	Collection and Interpretation of Data			90–140	383–408	
10	Birth, Growth, and Maturation	251–272	68–94		33–94	
11	Learning	194–211	197–281	142–177	245–350	53–82 181–223
12	Thinking and Problem-Solving		285–329	263–292	351–381	225–243
13	Motivation		330–377	50–89	209–230	149–179
14	Emotion	227–244	378–413	150–151	173–207	33–52
15	Personality and Personal Adjustment		414–539		230–244 495–623	329–414
16	Tests and Testing		172–196	340–368	409–428	
17	Individual Differences			90–141	428–493	
18	Concluding Formulation					

CHAP.	TOPIC	MUNN	RING-NESS, K. & S.	RUCH	SAN-FORD	SAR-TAIN et al.
1	The Study of General Psychology	1–28	2–6	5–13	3–57	1–27
2	Stimulation, Integration, and Reaction	29–49	172–193	13–29		
3	Nervous Integration	50–77		525–553	489–516	192–209
4	Development of Reaction	253–313	154–158	594–598 145–146 165–167	279–301	
5	Sensation and Perception	562–606	187–193	290–320 263–264	239–242 259–262	232–253
6	Vision and Visual Phenomena	507–531	175–181	264–277	242–246 262–271	214–218
7	Audition and Auditory Phenomena	532–550	181–183	277–282	246–250 271–277	218–222
8	Our Other Senses	551–561	183–187	282–289	251–257	222–231
9	Collection and Interpretation of Data		6–13	555–573	119–139	314–335
10	Birth, Growth, and Maturation	79–108	117–132	30–68	59–89	28–49
11	Learning	371–477	136–169	72–98	303–355	254–290
12	Thinking and Problem-Solving	478–506	204–229	322–349	357–375	291–313
13	Motivation	253–312	257–262	144–168	169–217	75–95
14	Emotion	313–343	232–257	170–198	219–237	96–117
15	Personality and Personal Adjustment	206–254	376–385 388–392	352–355 389–410	371–487	50–74 118–165 384–407
16	Tests and Testing	137–205	265–273	356–385	91–117	336–348
17	Individual Differences	109–136	274–280	381–382	141–167	348–383
18	Concluding Formulation	635–667		579–584		

TO STANDARD TEXTBOOKS

refer to pages.

complete titles of books.

SELLS	SMITH & SMITH	WICKENS	WILLIAMS	WOOD & S	VALENTINE
	3–26	1–26	1–35		1–40
	94–108	422–502			
	109–113	503–524	172–189		
	103–106 266–270	37–53	190–209	541–581	327–345
122–128 156–205	201–204 233–250	192–245	123–130 358–393	72–106	303–326
128–136	204–207 250–264		120–138	362–527	
136–142	207–213		138–147	323–361	
142–156	212–218		148–171	267–322	
	126–139	269–285	58–122		69–117
59–121	265–296	27–36 54–112	36–57 247–318	528–540 582–813	346–387
	319–344	246–268	394–426	814–848	388–432
206–246	145–172	113–161	210–241		185–230
247–286	173–200	162–191	242–273	107–191	231–302
287–321 358–381	427–477	319–421	427–626		433–461
325–357 382–417	401–409	286–295 311–318			41–68 119–133
325–357 382–417	409–417	296–311	319–357		134–156
		525–528			

1

The Study of General Psychology

A science is a unit of systematized facts or knowledge. The facts of relationships between living organisms and their environment constitute the science of psychology.

THE HISTORICAL BACKGROUND OF PSYCHOLOGY

Psychology has both a traditional and a scientific history, as has any other science. As an experimental science it dates only from about 1875, although experiments definitely psychological in nature were performed throughout the 19th century. Traditionally, psychology dates back to the earliest speculations concerning the relationships of man with his environment.

Primitive Notions of Mind and Soul. Earliest attempts to explain the relationship of events were in terms of hidden causal agents. Thus, spirits or gods were thought to direct the activities of lightning, rain, etc. and also the activities of men. The internal forces in man came to be called *mind* or *soul*. This form of interpretation was *animism*.

The Greek Philosophers. Beginning about 600 B.C., and for almost a thousand years thereafter, the Greek intellectuals observed, inferred, and discussed the ordering of the universe, including the relationship of man to the universe. A number of their concepts were (some still are) important to psychology.

Empedocles (*c.* 490–*c.* 435 B.C.) posited that the cosmos was composed of four elements—earth, air, fire, and water. Hippocrates (*c.* 460–*c.* 377 B.C.) translated these elements into four bodily *humors* and characterized the *temperament* of individuals as dependent upon a balance of these humors. Some researchers are still trying to establish *somatotypes* (body types related to temperaments).

1

Plato (427–347 B.C.) recognized two classes of phenomena: *things* and *ideas*. Ideas, he held, come from two sources: some are innate and come with the soul; others are the product of observations through the sense organs. The conception of a *mind-body problem* expressed in a theory of *psychophysical dualism* has recurred in philosophy and psychology.

The giant of the Greek theorists was Aristotle (384–322 B.C.). Among his many contributions were: (1) a great deal of knowledge concerning the anatomy and physiology of the body, (2) an explanation of learning in terms of association of ideas (i.e., because of contiguity, contrast, or similarity the reappearance of one element of a situation serves to recall ideas originally connected with the situation), (3) the concept that animals form one continuous series from lower to higher forms (evolution was not implied), and (4) a stress upon the development of knowledge based upon observation and thus upon the development of empirical science. Aristotle's point of view should be contrasted with that of Plato, who encouraged the rational deductive method and so the development of philosophy.

After Aristotle, the Greeks turned to ethics. Zeno, the Stoic (c. 336–c. 264 B.C.), taught that a wise man should be governed by reason, subdue all passions, and be indifferent to pleasure or pain. In direct contrast, Epicurus (c. 342–270 B.C.) taught that the final good is pleasure and that any act which gives happiness is good.

The work of the Greeks was significant, not only for its own excellence but also for the fact that it represented, in its end products, the philosophy and science which held sway for about fifteen centuries.

Developments during the Christian Era. After the birth of Christ, and the subsequent rise of the Church, considerations of science and philosophy were subordinated to promulgation and interpretation of religious and spiritual doctrines. St. Augustine (354–430) described conscious activity and stated his belief in its unifying and continuous development. He also introduced and made use of the *method of introspection* (self-observation of conscious activity) and produced the first definite development of what later became known as *faculty psychology* (see p. 4). St. Thomas Aquinas (1225?–1274?) attempted to harmonize science and religion. According to him, scientific truth is based upon observation and experimentation, whereas religious truth is based upon the divine authority of the Church.

The Revival of Science. During the 15th and 16th centuries Western civilization was stirring in many directions, but with difficulty—new forms in art, literature, and music arose; numerous geographical discoveries were made; the power of the Church was successfully questioned; and many notable scientific investigations were well under way. Among the more important of the latter were those of Copernicus (1473–1543) in astronomy, Kepler (1571–1630) in astronomy and vision, Galileo (1564–1642) in optics and astronomy, Newton (1642–1727) in physics and the psychology of vision, and Harvey (1578–1657) in physiology. Perhaps the chief contribution of these scientists to psychology was their emphasis upon objective study of facts in general.

Pre-experimental Psychology. The specific problem of how man gets along with his environment remained almost static from Aristotle to Descartes (1596–1650). Descartes produced two ideas of great import: (1) a *mechanistic* explanation of the way in which the body works, and (2) a *dualistic* interpretation of the mind-body problem, i.e., the mind and the body are separate entities but *interact* at one point in the body.

The mind-body problem was a very important one for the 17th and 18th century philosophers and in various ways has been carried down into very recent psychology. After Descartes came many explanations: (1) *occasionalism* (Geulincx, 1625–1699, and Malebranche, 1638–1715), according to which God intervenes between mind and body as the occasion demands; (2) *double aspect* (Spinoza, 1632–1677), in which mind and body are viewed as different aspects of the same substance; and (3) *psychophysical parallelism* (the German, Leibnitz, 1646–1716, and a group known as *English associationists, c.* 1700 ff.), according to which the mind and body are separate and do not interact, but are nevertheless parallel in their actions since the same causes affect both.

The associationists, or *empiricists* as they are sometimes called, were more important for another contribution. They advocated the doctrine of *association* to account for development of the individual through experience; that is, simple sensations and ideas become compounded in one way or another to form complex sensations and ideas. Thomas Hobbes (1588–1679) and John

Locke (1632–1704) initiated the movement, and a long line of philosopher-psychologists, though differing among themselves as to the source of ideas, advocated some form of associationism as the real explanation of mental activity. Among the more important of these men were: Berkeley (1685–1753), Hume (1711–1776), Hartley (1705–1757), James Mill (1773–1836), John Mill (1806–1873), Spencer (1820–1903), and Bain (1818–1903).

Opposed to association theory was the *doctrine of mental faculties* (the Germans, Wolff, 1679–1754, and Kant, 1724–1804, and a Scottish group, Reid, 1710–1796, Stewart, 1753–1828, and Thomas Brown, 1778–1820). In its most extreme form, the doctrine of mental faculties classified mind into departments, such as *intellect, emotions, will,* etc., which functioned independently. Two direct developments of faculty psychology cannot be overlooked: (1) *phrenology* (Gall, 1758–1828), in which the faculties were assembled, classified, and related to definite cranial areas, and (2) advocacy of the introduction of training materials into the schools for the avowed purpose of exercising the faculties and making them grow. Both are controverted by modern scientific evidence, but each persists in popular uncritical thought.

THE RISE OF EXPERIMENTAL PSYCHOLOGY

During the later part of the 18th century and in the early 19th, many notable discoveries were made in the fields of physiology, neurology, physics, and mathematics, all of which had a considerable effect on the development of experimental psychology. Haller (1759), Whytt (1750), Galvani (1792), Bell (1811), and Magendie (1822) made important discoveries concerned with functions of the nervous system and muscles. Bessel (1823), an astronomer, became interested in individual differences in speed of reaction and evolved the concept of the *personal equation* (an individual's pattern of deviations from the group norm). Flourens (1824) performed the first extirpation experiments (removal of all or parts of body organs, frequently parts of the brain), using animals as his subjects, and Marshall Hall (1832) studied the nervous basis of reflex behavior, sectioning the spinal cord of a snake and observing the responses. Johannes Müller (1826) developed the theory of the "specific energy of the nerves," the doctrine that each sensory nerve gives rise to a specific sensation regardless of the manner in which it is stimulated. Claude Bernard (1859) developed the basic ideas of present-day endocrinology and the concept of what later became called *homeostasis* (organism's tendency to maintain physiological equilibrium). Darwin (1859) gave biology, and animal psychology, an entirely new basis with his theory of evolution.

Psychology in Germany. Several of the men mentioned above performed experiments which might well come out of a psychological laboratory today. Their work became truly psychological when it was synthesized with that of the philosopher-psychologists. This was done by Lotze (1852), Bain (1856), and Wundt (1874).

E. H. Weber (*c.* 1830) had studied a definitely psychological topic, the relation between stimulation and the resulting sensitivity (sensation). Fechner (1860) further extended Weber's work, modified his conclusions, and reformulated on a mathematical basis the Weber law of the relation of stimulation to sensitivity.

Relying heavily on the theoretical formulations of Müller, Helmholtz developed theories of color vision (1852) and audition (1863) based upon experimental work, theories which are still basic in psychology, physiology, and physics.

Experimental psychology is usually said to date from 1879, when Wilhelm Wundt founded the first recognized laboratory of psychology at Leipzig, Germany. Wundt's chief experimental interest was in conscious activity and in determining the *structure of the mind,* although he also wrote much of a speculative nature, as in his *Folk Psychology.* Psychologists from many countries, and especially from the United States, went to study with Wundt.

Though Wundt was the leader of the "new" psychology, not everyone agreed with him. Simultaneous with Wundt's book on physiological psychology (1874) was a text by Brentano, *Psychology from an Empirical Point of View.* Brentano's "act" psychology contributed little during the early period, but the point of view became highly important in the psychologies known as *functionalism, behaviorism,* and *Gestalt psychology,* which are described later in this chapter.

Psychology in England. There was no real counterpart in England of the laboratory psychology of Wundt. Under the direct influence of Darwin's theories of evolution, Sir Francis Galton (1869) initiated study in the field of individual differences. He developed new methods, such as the case history, the genetic approach, and the use of twins. He also developed the concept of a "test" as a measure of a particular trait being considered, and started the use of correlation technique as a statistical method of analyzing data. Galton was followed by such men as Karl Pearson (1857–1936) and Spearman (1863–1945), giving England a leadership in the development of statistical methods which has not been relinquished.

Psychology in France. The French early became interested in abnormal mental behavior. In 1792 Pinel took the mental cases out of chains and dungeons in a Paris hospital, and in 1801 he published a treatise on mental alienation. Esquirol (1817), Charcot (1872), Bernheim (1875), Ribot (1881), and Janet (1906) are all great names in the history of abnormal psychology and psychiatry.

The French were also much interested in what is now known as *hypnosis,* developed by Mesmer (1779) as "animal magnetism."

Seguin (1848) utilized techniques both of testing and of teaching mentally retarded children. Alfred Binet (1857–1911) and Théodore Simon (1873–   ) developed a test of intelligence which has set the pattern for work from 1905 to the present day.

Psychology in America. Three main lines of influence are manifest in the activities of American psychologists: (1) the experimental laboratory emphasis of Wundt, (2) the Darwinian theory of evolution, and (3) the mathematical concept of the normal probability curve (Gauss, 1809). All are reflected in the laboratory experiments, the genetic studies, and the statistical techniques of American psychology.

The American pioneers, with exceptions to be noted later, were likely to show a marked independence in their work. For example, G. Stanley Hall (1844–1924) and James McKeen Cattell (1860–1944) both studied with Wundt at Leipzig. Yet Hall is best known for his influence upon psychological theory in American education. Hall introduced the child study movement into America and wrote extensively on child psychology, adolescence, and senescence. He founded the first psychological journal in America, *The American Journal of Psychology* (1887), and was the first president of the American Psychological Association (1892). Cattell supplied the impetus to the mental testing movement and the study of differential psychology in America.

William James (1842–1910) studied memory and the transfer of training experimentally, devised a stimulating theory of emotions, and by his textbook, *Principles of Psychology* (1890), influenced American psychology and education for many years.

THE SCHOOLS OF PSYCHOLOGY

As the science of psychology emerged from the background of philosophy, physiology, and physics, with many other important contributions from biology, astronomy, and mathematics, marked differences of opinion arose as to the subject matter of psychology, the methods of observation or experimentation which were valid, and even the purpose of psychology.

Some men continued to work on what interested them without particular reference to theoretical frameworks. Thus, Ebbinghaus (1850–1909), in Germany, largely ignored both Wundt and Brentano and spent his life studying memory. He devised the first completion test; gave us the ubiquitous nonsense syllable; studied part vs. whole learning; studied relearning as a method of noting retention of material which could not be recalled; and developed many other concepts regarding memory which survive today. Edward L. Thorndike (1874–1949) studied the learning of animals without particular reference to the typical psychology of his day. Many other names will be mentioned as we deal with specific topics in later chapters of this book.

However, four main schools of psychology may be noted as flourishing between 1890 and 1930. During the height of each, a large number of psychologists "followed the creed" faithfully and devoted their efforts to securing evidence for their particular method of explaining behavior.

Introspective Psychology (Structuralism). For the introspectionists the subject matter of psychology was consciousness and the method of study was introspection. This was an extremely formalized method by which an individual analyzed the content of his experience when he was stimulated by appropriate objects or events. The recognized leader of the group was Edward Bradford Titchener (1867–1927), an Englishman who was trained under Wundt and was thoroughly indoctrinated by him. Titchener came to Cornell University in 1892 and remained until his death in 1927. The introspectionist school reached its height about 1910 and declined steadily thereafter. It failed to meet American needs and desires for study of individual differences, animal learning, mental testing, and all applied psychology. In fact, to the avowed introspectionist, such things might be interesting but they were not psychology.

Functional Psychology. Functional psychology was a definite revolt against the structures of introspectionism (or structuralism as it was called by the functionalists). James Rowland Angell (1907) wrote, "We have to consider functionalism conceived as the psychology of mental operations in contrast to the psychology of mental elements; or, expressed otherwise, the psychology of the how and why of consciousness as distinguished from the psychology of the what of consciousness." John Dewey (1859–1952), Angell (1869–1949), and later Harvey A. Carr (1873–1954), all of the University of Chicago, were the recognized leaders of the functionalist movement. Since the school was avowedly interested in functions of the individual, it welcomed all research and experimentation which led to applications of psychology. Thus, the influence of Chicago on the educational system in this country is rooted in this movement.

Behaviorism. The next important movement was a revolt against both structuralism and functionalism (about 1913). It began as a virtual one-man affair with John B. Watson (1878–   ), and in Watson found its most extreme expression. The course of behaviorism as a school was short and violent, but the effects were tremendous. Watson was a student of Angell at the University of Chicago, but he studied rats, to which he was unwilling to attribute consciousness. Since the Darwinian scale represented generally a continuum, and since one could study the abilities, capacities, etc. of animals without recourse to their consciousness, Watson argued that it should be obvious that consciousness was an unneeded concept for psychology. The thing which should be studied was behavior. Watson's psychology was purely mechanistic. His early concept was "habit," but he soon discovered Pavlov's studies of the conditioned response and made these procedures the keystone of his structure. Behaviorism welcomed the study of any aspect of psychology except consciousness. Explanations of "why" were considered unnecessary; "how" was the all-important factor.

Gestalt Psychology. In Germany a revolt against the introspectionists and the analysis of consciousness into elements was spearheaded by Max Wertheimer (1880–1943). This revolt was based on the difficulty, if not the impossibility, of analyzing a consciousness into its component parts when the perception was demonstrably different from the known nature of the stimulus situation. For example, in the phi phenomenon (apparent visual movement), which served as the point of departure, movement appears to exist where there is no real movement. Such kinds of discrepancy have led the Gestaltists to the formulation, "The whole is different from the sum of its parts" (Lewin, 1939). In the 1930's the leaders of the German group came to America to avoid Nazi domination of education. Wertheimer, Koffka, Köhler, and Lewin have become familiar names around American universities. Gestalt psychology did not restore the study of consciousness to the fore as subject matter of psychology. It has generally resulted in greater attention to interrelationships and the study of larger units of behavior.

Other Movements. It would be possible to extend the list of schools almost indefinitely. Wherever a well-known and respected teacher exists, adherents will be found who strive to further his explanations and who perform experiments aimed at amplifying the work. Many of these will be covered in later chapters where motivation, learning, emotion, etc. are discussed. Further, today's psychology is more nearly characterized by a willingness to take anyone's research data as long as proper scientific controls are used in performing the experiments. Similarly, the results of the past are not ignored because they grew out of the work of a particular school.

There are two other movements which will be mentioned here because of their impact on psychology, particularly as psychology is understood by the layman. These are: (1) McDougall and the purposivists, and (2) Freud and the psychoanalysts.

McDougall. In 1908 William McDougall (1871–1938), an Englishman who taught in America, published an *Introduction to Social Psychology*. The important point of the book was the emphasis on instincts as the primary motivating factors in man —not instincts which appear as traits, abilities, or complex reflexes, but instincts recognized in everyday conversation. There were said to be seven of these: flight, pugnacity, curiosity, disgust, parental behavior, self-assertion, and self-abasement. These instincts were paired with emotions as—flight with fear, pugnacity with anger, and so on.

FREUD. The work of Sigmund Freud (1856–1939) and the psychoanalysts has little relationship to traditional psychology, though the layman is likely to know much more of the work of the psychoanalyst than he does of psychology in general.

For Freud, the sexual desires (a very broad usage, not to be confused with everyday terminology) comprise the drive for action in the individual. These desires exist in the unconscious (id) but are repressed by conscious activity (knowledge of results represented by the *ego,* and a "censor" property represented by the *superego*). Repression results in conflict, and relief is obtained through *catharsis,* i.e., getting rid of the repression. Since these drives exist in the unconscious, and since the results are almost always in disguise, it is necessary to use a trained analyst to discover the repressed material. Adler (1870–1937) and Jung (1875–   ), two of Freud's contemporaries, held somewhat similar views but with different basic motivations.

The psychoanalyst's contributions have been mainly to clinical psychology, but Freud also made a great contribution to general psychology through his emphasis on the need for the study of human motivation.

WHAT PSYCHOLOGISTS STUDY AND DO

Specialization has become the rule in psychology, and psychologists devote their lives to study or application, or both, of findings organized about a particular area or field of psychology.

Fields of Psychology. An approach to the problem is found in college course organization and typical textbook specialization.

GENERAL PSYCHOLOGY. This field of general psychology includes the fundamental principles of all psychology. It deals particularly with the operations of the normal individual in his environment.

EXPERIMENTAL OR THEORETICAL PSYCHOLOGY. Experimental or

theoretical psychology deals particularly with sensation, perception, and behavior as studied in the psychological laboratory.

PSYCHOLOGY OF LEARNING. The study of learning, both human and animal, attempts to segregate principles of learning and formulate theoretical accounts of relationships between motivation and learning, learning and retention, and so on.

PHYSIOLOGICAL PSYCHOLOGY. The physiological aspect of psychology deals particularly with the functions of the nervous system and other bodily structures in the behavior of organisms.

COMPARATIVE PSYCHOLOGY. Comparative psychology is the name given to the study of animal behavior. It is likely to overlap greatly with both experimental and physiological psychology.

PSYCHOLOGY OF INDIVIDUAL DIFFERENCES. The field of individual differences is the study of similarities and differences among individuals, particularly with respect to race, sex, nationality, environmental conditions, etc. It relies heavily on mental testing.

ABNORMAL PSYCHOLOGY. Abnormal psychology deals with mental aberrations and affords much of the basis for the practice of clinical psychology.

CHILD PSYCHOLOGY. The processes and stages of development are the particular concern of child psychology. In recent years the idea of continuous development and change has grown so that a *developmental* or *genetic* psychology which includes infancy, childhood, adolescence, maturity, and senescence is sometimes taught.

DYNAMIC PSYCHOLOGY. Dynamic psychology is sometimes called *psychology of personality,* and deals particularly with adjustment of the individual. It is closely related to abnormal, clinical, and social psychology; the motivations and emotions of individuals are the principal subject matter.

PERSONNEL AND INDUSTRIAL PSYCHOLOGY. Personnel or industrial psychology is the study of behavior in problems of personnel selection and personnel training, and includes various on-the-job studies of perception, fatigue, motivation, etc. Laboratory psychology may afford useful cues.

EDUCATIONAL PSYCHOLOGY. Educational psychology deals with learning, motivation, and other subjects in the actual educational process.

CLINICAL PSYCHOLOGY. Clinical psychology applies findings from motivation, abnormal, dynamic, and other kinds of psychology to the diagnosis of difficulties and to the practice of therapy aimed at relief of these difficulties. It also develops its own specialized knowledge.

SOCIAL PSYCHOLOGY. Social psychology deals particularly with the study of individuals within groups and the relationship of groups, one with another.

STATISTICS AND TESTS AND MEASUREMENTS. Statistics is the portion of psychology which deals with tools of psychological measurement and research.

Divisions of the American Psychological Association. The American Psychological Association listed 16,644 members in 1958. It has eighteen divisions, established by the members themselves in terms of interests and occupations in psychology. The following distribution of division membership is shown in the 1958 Directory. Some members do not belong to any division and some belong to more than one.

NUMBER OF MEMBERS IN EACH DIVISION OF THE AMERICAN
PSYCHOLOGICAL ASSOCIATION; 1958

APA Division	Membership
1. General	482
2. Teaching Psychology	300
3. Experimental	689
5. Evaluation and Measurement	579
7. Developmental	552
8. Personality and Social	1040
9. Society for Psychological Study of Social Issues	743
10. Esthetics	104
12. Clinical	2027
13. Consulting	226
14. Industrial and Business	659
15. Educational	492
16. School Psychologists	606
17. Counseling	855
18. Public Service	194
19. Military	264
20. Maturity and Old Age	215
21. Engineering Psychologists	184
Total	10,210 *

* Includes members of two or more divisions.

Employment of American Psychologists. A given field of study in psychology may lead to more than one of the above interests or occupations. Similarly, a psychologist may bring varied interests or training to the same general type of occupation. From a sample of APA membership as listed in the 1948 Directory, Black (1949) derives the following classification of employment of members of the association:

FIELD OF EMPLOYMENT OF MEMBERS OF THE AMERICAN
PSYCHOLOGICAL ASSOCIATION

Position or Field	Per Cent
Academic	46.44
Clinical	23.34
Vocational-Educational Guidance	17.57
Business, Industry, General Government, and Defense	12.65
Total	100.00

The American Board of Examiners in Professional Psychology, holds examinations and awards diplomas to successful candidates who qualify as outstanding specialists in the fields of Clinical, Counseling, and Industrial Psychology. By the end of 1957 the Board had awarded 872 diplomas in Clinical Psychology, 249 diplomas in Counseling Psychology, and 163 diplomas in Industrial Psychology.

THE SCIENCE OF PSYCHOLOGY

Psychology has been called "the study of the mind," "the study of human nature," "the study of behavior," and many other things. In the foregoing discussion of schools of psychology, the effect of such a restriction became evident. The only definition of psychology which seems entirely satisfactory (and it could be adapted to define any other science) might be stated as follows: "Psychology is the assembled verifiable facts of investigations from the psychological point of view." This point of view may differ from psychologist to psychologist, but in its over-all aspects it is concerned with the activities of living organisms. These may be studied in part or as wholes; in consciousness or in behavior.

Psychology and Common Sense. Science and common sense deal with the same material. Everyone is a common sense psychologist, just as he is a common sense physicist, chemist, or biologist. We make judgments concerning the behavior of people before we study psychology as a science, just as we did of physical objects before we studied physics or chemistry. But because our daily life is so closely related to the behavior of other people, we are less inclined in the psychological field to recognize the distinction between scientific observations and those which are made in the haphazard fashion of daily intercourse. We accept common sense opinions immediately when they concern other people.

It must always be kept in mind that common sense psychology is based upon casual observations, which may or may not be accurate. It teaches us, through experience and through reflection upon the way others act in certain situations, how people are likely to act in the future. However, it is still common sense psychology, and its conclusions are often inaccurate. Ruch (1941) reported that 60 per cent of 103 students in a course in elementary psychology at Northwestern University marked the following statement as true: "Especially intelligent children are likely to be weak and retarded physically." The evidence is *all* in the opposite direction, but the case that comes to the attention of the common sense psychologist is the one which is the exception to the trend.

The chief distinction between common sense psychology and scientific psychology lies in the method of arriving at generalizations. The scientific method increases the reliability of observation.

Scientific Method. Psychology, like all other sciences, employs the method of observation. Observation under highly controlled techniques is called an *experiment.* In any psychological investigation numerous observations are made.

A scientific investigation involves: (1) *observation*—the collection of a large body of facts; (2) *classification*—the grouping and averaging of these facts; (3) *verification*—duplication of the conditions of the investigation until there is no doubt of the uniformity of results; and (4) *generalization*—the formulation of this uniformity into law or principle.

The ways in which psychologists adapt these steps to their specific subject matter are discussed in detail in Chapter 9.

Scientific Viewpoint. The scientist's viewpoint is fundamentally objective. The following points hold true for psychology as much as for any other science.

THE SCIENTIST IS ALWAYS A DOUBTER. The point of view of

doubting everything not proved is characteristic of all science. The scientific psychologist is the doubter and the tester of all opinions concerning the relationships of living organisms with their environment.

ONLY OBSERVABLE PHENOMENA ARE INVESTIGATED. The psychologist believes, along with other scientists, that only such matters, or phenomena, as can actually be observed to exist can be investigated. This workable scientific theory takes for granted the reality of time and space and the quality and quantity of matter, or phenomena, as they exist in time and space. Psychology does not deal with mystical forces, spiritual entities, and so on.

ALL EVENTS HAVE A CAUSE. This statement may be made for all sciences. It is called *universal determinism*. The laws of psychology are a proof of it. Each event has a cause and this event in turn was caused, and so on. Every thought has a cause; every act, a cause. There are no isolated situations in mental or behavioral life.

SCIENCE IS NOT CONCERNED WITH ETHICAL VALUES. Lack of concern with ethical values is characteristic of all sciences. Psychology investigates activity without praise or blame. There is no good or bad, no useful or useless, no vulgar or refined, no right or wrong, no moral or immoral, in science. The knowledge uncovered by the scientist may be of tremendous social importance, but to the scientist it remains merely plain fact.

SCIENCE ACCEPTS HYPOTHESES OR THEORIES. Although science aims at generalization into laws from the classification of observations, it is often necessary to accept a hypothesis or theory which explains most of the known facts, or one which has the widest application. This is then used as the point of attack for future investigation. However, science favors the simplest explanation. This is the *law of parsimony*, best stated in psychological terms in what is known as Lloyd Morgan's Canon (1894) : "In no case may we interpret an action as the outcome of the exercise of a higher physical faculty, if it can be interpreted as the outcome of the exercise of one which stands lower in the psychological scale."

THE STUDY OF PSYCHOLOGY

No person can come to grips with the facts and principles of a science through reading a general textbook on the subject. It is desirable for one to read widely, even though he reviews much that he has read before. There are numerous excellent textbooks in general psychology which are written to summarize the facts and principles of the science. These vary widely in style and content but are similar in that they are highly generalized.

After general familiarity with the science has been attained, it is not desirable to read only textbooks in general psychology. Books in the specialized fields, such as physiological psychology, learning, abnormal psychology, and the like, offer more intensive reading in facts and principles.

The basic data of psychology are not found in books. Research reports, published in articles and monographs of scientific journals, comprise the findings of psychology and are the source materials from which textbooks are written. In 1955 the *Psychological Abstracts,* a publication of the American Psychological Association which lists and describes or summarizes all reports bearing on the field of psychology, dealt with 535 journals, both American and foreign. A large number of these are not primarily psychological, but all students should be familiar with such journals as the *Psychological Bulletin, Psychological Review, American Journal of Psychology, Journal of Applied Psychology, Psychological Monographs,* and the like.

References in This Book. At the end of this text are references to books discussing the topics of each chapter. The lists, although not including all books with relevant material, are representative of recent textbooks and include references to older or specialized books where there are discussions of important facts or theories which may be of interest to the readers. No references to journals are included. Such references may be found in the *Psychological Abstracts.*

Aids to Study. The student should be aware of the intensive work done on "how-to-study." All students are urged to apply the principles which have been developed. A special volume of the College Outline Series, *Best Methods of Study* (Smith-Brittain-Shores), presents these principles in condensed form.

2

Stimulation, Integration, and Reaction

All psychological processes are responses of organisms to stimulation. The study of stimulation (S), integration (I), and reaction (R) comprises scientific psychology. This psychological activity (S–I–R) is studied as it appears in its various manifestations in all forms of life.

THE S–I–R FORMULA

Human beings and animals, which are referred to in psychology as "organisms," are reacting mechanisms. The *stimulus* is the causative factor. *Integration,* or co-ordination, of the reaction is provided by the organism. The *reaction* of the organism is an event resulting from stimulation and integration. These three related factors make up the *S–I–R formula* of psychological activity.

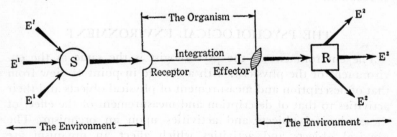

FIG. 1. Action of environmental energy changes (E1) upon the organism through receptors is called the stimulus (S). Action of the organism in producing environmental changes (E2) through effectors is called the reaction (R). The organism's contribution to the total activity is called integration (I). The environmental changes (E2) may in turn become stimuli which act upon other receptors in the same organism or in different organisms.

17

The integration provided by the organism is directly related to its *sensitivity*. In all but the lowest organisms this sensitivity is determined by *receptors,* specialized sense organs. Similarly, the differentiation and elaboration of *effectors* extend the range of responses which the organism can make.

A BIOLOGICAL CONSIDERATION OF THE ORGANISM

The organism is formed of protoplasm. Protoplasm is living substance. It makes or forms all bodily structures.

Specific Functions of Protoplasm. Besides the various vegetative functions of protoplasm, the following specific functions are essential to psychological activity: (1) irritability, (2) contractility, (3) conductivity, and (4) plasticity. These biological functions are studied on the psychological level as: (1) receptivity or sensitivity, (2) reaction, (3) integration, (4) development or learning.

The Cell Theory. Cells are living units of protoplasm. They are anatomical, metabolic, and often reproductive units. The organs and units of the body are formed by cells.

Specialized Functions of Cells. Cells are frequently specialized for the better performance of one function. This characteristic is accompanied by a low degree of specialization of other functions. Particularly in the higher forms of living organisms, cells are specialized to a high degree for sensitivity, integration, or reaction.

THE PSYCHOLOGICAL ENVIRONMENT

The environment of the psychologist is the same as the environment of the physicist, with a change in point of view from that of description and measurement of physical objects and their activities to that of description and measurement of the effect of these physical objects and activities upon an organism. The physical objects and activities which affect an organism are termed the *psychological environment,* and any unit of this environment is termed the *stimulus.* The psychological environment is divided into an explicit environment and an implicit environment.

Explicit Environment. "Explicit" refers to action external to the body, and the organism's explicit environment is made up of physical objects and activities which stimulate the body from without.

Implicit Environment. "Implicit" refers to action within the body, and the organism's implicit environment is formed of the organs, muscles, objects, and activities within the cavities of the body which stimulate the body from within.

STIMULATION

Physical and chemical energy changes in the environment, explicit or implicit, furnish the *stimulation* of the organism. Protoplasm, in all its forms, is sensitive to mechanical and chemical stimulation. However, the reception of stimulation is frequently accomplished by means of cells specialized in some one form of *sensitivity*. These cells are organized into receptor organs. Receptors perform the psychological activity of receiving stimulation. A receptor is an organ composed of specialized protoplasm highly sensitive to some particular complex of environmental changes but relatively insensitive to others.

The Stimulus. A stimulus of environmental origin consists of physical or chemical changes which are capable of producing a physiological change in receptor organs. These environmental changes may be external or internal, as related to the body, and they affect both external and internal receptors, such as the retina of the eye, the organs of equilibrium in the internal ear, and the taste buds of the tongue. There are environmental changes for which there are no receptors, and changes outside the range of receptivity of existing receptors. Examples of these are X rays, infrared waves, and air vibrations above 20,000 double vibrations per second. Even these may affect the organisms; e.g., X rays and sounds of certain frequencies and intensities may kill living tissues, but they do not stimulate receptors.

Structural Organization of Receptors. Each receptor is composed of two parts: sensitive cells and accessory apparatus.

SENSITIVE CELLS. Sensitive cells are cells which are specialized for the reception of a particular kind of stimulation. For example, rod cells and cone cells in the retina of the eye are specialized for the reception of light.

ACCESSORY APPARATUS. The accessory apparatus is formed of

cells organized into structures which focus the stimuli upon the sensitive cells. For example, in the anatomical organization of the eye, the choroid coat, the lens, the pupil, and the supporting ligaments and muscles all combine to focus light on the rods and cones.

Classification of Receptors. Receptors are frequently classified into groups according to their explicit or implicit location in the body. The classification is after Sherrington.

EXTEROCEPTORS. Exteroceptors are located in the outer surfaces of the body, and are stimulated by energy changes external to the organism.

PROPRIOCEPTORS. Proprioceptors are located in the linings of the muscles, tendons, and joints, and are stimulated by energy changes resulting from movement of these structures.

INTEROCEPTORS. Interoceptors are located in the linings of the viscera—the digestive, respiratory, and circulatory systems. They are stimulated by energy changes affecting these parts.

According to their action in relation to environmental stimulation, exteroceptors are explicit receptors; proprioceptors and interoceptors are implicit receptors.

Differences in Sensitivity among Organisms. There are marked differences in sensitivity among various organisms. These are due to different kinds of receptors and to different development of the same receptors. The differences are correlated with changes in receptor organs and with neural organization.

Range of Human Sensitivity. Compared to the range of environmental changes of any one sort, the range of sensitivity of receptors is quite limited. They have thresholds, below or above which the energy changes of the environment are ineffective as stimuli.

PHYSICAL, PHYSIOLOGICAL, AND PSYCHOLOGICAL STIMULATION

Stimulation may be measured in terms of the physical or chemical energy emitted, in terms of the physiological changes occurring in the receptor organs, or in terms of the psychological resultants. The various attempts to develop equations among the three have resulted in some of the most bitter arguments among psychologists. Entire schools of psychology have been developed around theoretical systems which attempt to explain these interrelationships.

Physical Stimulation. Physical stimuli can be measured directly. The illumination of a surface, the wave length of a filtered light, the intensity and pitch of a tone, the concentration of a chemical substance in liquid or gaseous form, the weight or pressure of an object, all these can be controlled within relatively fixed limits. They can be held constant.

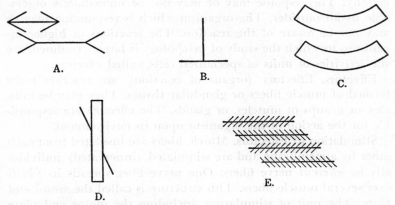

FIG. 2. Some visual illusions. A. Müller-Lyer illusion. The lines between the arrows are equal. B. Vertical-horizontal illusion. Both lines are equal in length. C. Jastrow illusion. The figures are identical. D. Poggendorff illusion. The diagonal line is continuous. E. Zollner illusion. The horizontal lines are parallel.

Physiological Stimulation. Excitation of neurons (nerve cells) ending on specialized receptor cells is physiological stimulation. Each neuron is known to act on an all-or-none principle; it is either excited to its full strength or it is not excited at all. How then are different signals given to indicate differences in size, intensity, duration, etc.? Any theory developed to explain sensitivity must take account of the limitations imposed by the physiology of the organism.

Psychological Stimulation. The psychological stimulus is what we perceive. Though it is related to physical and physiological stimulation, it is quite likely to be different from either. The most dramatic illustrations are visual illusions such as those shown in Fig. 2. Other examples are the apparent movement found in motion pictures, the tendency to make groupings or patterns of objects and events, and the effect of relationships upon judgments of brightness, loudness, and so on.

We react to the psychological stimulus. Learning may enable differentiation and correction, but the perception is unchanged.

REACTION

Any stimulation of the organism results in a response (or reaction). The response may or may not be immediately observable by an outsider. The organism which is responding may or may not be aware of the reaction. The reactions of higher organisms, to which the study of psychology is largely confined, are the activities of units of specialized cells, called effectors.

Effectors. Effectors (organs of reaction) are reaction units formed of muscle fibers or glandular tissues. They may be muscles, or groups of muscles, or glands. The effectors are responsible for the action of the organism upon its environment.

Stimulation of Effectors. Muscle fibers are insulated from each other by a membrane and are stimulated (innervated) individually by *efferent* nerve fibers. One nerve fiber spreads its *fibrils* over several muscle fibers. This structure is called the *motor end plate*. The unit of stimulation, including the motor end plate and the muscle fibers stimulated by it, is called the *neuromuscular unit*. Many neuromuscular units function together in the action of an effector.

Classification of Effectors. Effectors are classified upon the basis of both structure and function. The two main classes are muscles and glands.

Muscles. On the basis of structure, the muscles are subdivided into two groups: striped (striated) muscles and smooth (unstriated) muscles. Functional differences are related to the differences in structure.

Striped Muscles. The striped or striated muscles are so named because of their striped appearance. Each muscle is made of hundreds of tiny threadlike fibers, each of which is enclosed in a *sarcolemma* sheath and is innervated separately. The striped muscles move the bones of the skeleton and are responsible for bodily movements. They are located peripherally in the organism, and they are so placed that their action is upon the explicit environment. Striped-muscle reactions are initiated and terminated more quickly than smooth-muscle reactions. Striped muscles are also called *somatic* effectors.

Smooth Muscles. The smooth-muscle (or unstriated-muscle) effectors are muscular membranes situated throughout the viscera and in a few other organs such as the iris of the eye. They function in the pulmonary, circulatory, and metabolic activities of the organism, and their action is upon the implicit environment. Smooth muscles function more slowly than striped muscles, and their action is said to be involuntary; i.e., they are relatively uninfluenced by the conscious activities of the organism except as they play an important part in readying the organism for action or repairing the organism after action has been initiated.

GLANDS. Glands are aggregates of cells specialized for the secretion of certain chemical substances. On the basis of structure they are classified either as duct glands or as endocrine (ductless) glands.

Duct Glands. Duct glands secrete their products through small ducts opening into some cavity or onto the surface of the skin. The tear glands and the salivary glands are examples of duct glands. The action of the duct glands is involuntary. However, organisms can learn the activities which initiate this action and thus cry, salivate, perspire, etc., almost at will.

Endocrine Glands. The endocrine glands have no ducts but secrete their products directly into the blood stream or lymphatic system. Much significance is attributed to the endocrine secretions in the theoretical explanations of behavior. The more important endocrines are the adrenal, thyroid, thymus, parathyroid, pituitary, pineal, pancreatic, and gonadal glands. The secretions of the endocrines are called *hormones* or *autacoids*. Endocrine secretion is involuntary. Conscious activity has little or no effect.

Explicit and Implicit Effectors. Explicit effectors are the somatic striped effectors acting upon the environment surrounding the body. This group also includes a few other effectors, such as the sebaceous (sweat) glands which discharge their secretions on the skin. The implicit effectors are the smooth-muscle effectors and the glands, which act upon the environment within the body.

Pattern Reaction. The action of many effectors is organized or integrated into a pattern reaction, which is the behavior unit of psychological activity. Any reaction involves almost all the effectors of the body to some degree, but the essential part of the reaction is the pattern of a few effectors. For example, in throwing the arm over the head, effectors are extended and contracted throughout the body in maintaining posture, but the reaction is defined by the contraction and extension of the muscles of the arm.

Successive and Simultaneous Reaction. There are few simultaneous pattern reactions, where a single co-ordinated pattern completes the activity. Most reactions are co-ordinated in sequential order. That is to say, one pattern leads to another, and that to another. One reaction is the successor of the one preceding it, and so on. The successive pattern reaction is the unit of study in most psychological investigations of behavior.

INTEGRATION

Integration is central activity involving receptor and effector. It is performed essentially by a nervous system which affords different connections between receptors and effectors. The structure of the nervous system and the structure of the receptor and effector mechanisms occasion large differences in reaction patterns among species. The differences in neural, skeletal, and muscular structure and function of individuals of the same species result in different reaction patterns. Integration is studied from two major points of view: (1) the physiological integration of the body systems, and (2) the behavioral integration observed in the reactions of the organism to stimulation.

Physiological Integration. Physiological integration is studied in the activity of the nervous system, in the chemical action of the glands, and to a lesser degree in activities of the digestive, pulmonary, and circulatory systems.

Nervous Integration. In higher organisms, the structures of the nervous system are divided into: (1) the *cerebrospinal system* and (2) the *sympathetic (autonomic) system*. The first controls the explicit action of the striped-muscle effectors, and the second controls most of the action of the smooth-muscle and gland effectors. Stimulation of receptors affects the cerebrospinal system primarily and the sympathetic system only indirectly. The *neuron* is the structural unit of nervous integration. Many neurons are active in the conduction of stimulation from the receptors to the effectors.

CHEMICAL INTEGRATION. Chemical action is an essential part of neural excitability. In addition, chemical action in the pulmonary, alimentary, and circulatory systems facilitates or inhibits psychological activity. Metabolic processes slow or speed integration through the interrelationships between blood supply and the organs of the body. The whole physiology of the organism determines integration.

Behavioral Integration. Except for the simplest reflex actions, there is awareness of reaction (consciousness). Sensitivity is the simplest awareness of our environment. Perception, comprehension, thinking, goal-directed behavior, these are complex integrations involving a high degree of awareness. The study of such complex integrative activity comprises much of the subject matter of psychology.

Homeostasis. Physiologists, biologists, and psychologists all subscribe to the basic principle of *homeostasis*. This principle, best formulated by Cannon (1932), postulates that the distribution of activities is such as to restore the organism to a point of equilibrium. Since a vast number of systems are involved in both the physiological and behavioral integrations of the organism, this equilibrium is of necessity *dynamic*. That is, the return of one system to equilibrium is almost certain to throw another into disequilibrium.

SUMMARY

Organisms are reacting mechanisms. The stimulations which affect the organism, the reactions which are made by the organism, and the integrations performed by the organism in mediating responses to stimuli represent life as the psychologist views it. Study of these factors may be carried on from the physiological point of view, involving the study of receptor and effector mechanisms and the nervous system which integrates them. Or, study may be carried on from the behavioral point of view, involving the observed external relations and the inferred internal relations of the organism with its environment. Or, study may be carried on from the introspective point of view, in which a subject reports what he senses and feels under stimulation of the environment.

Regardless of the point of view chosen, the study must be dynamic in nature. Any stimulus operates within the framework of a number of existing tension systems. Any response is a function of the interaction of many systems.

3

Nervous Integration

The nervous system integrates and co-ordinates the activities of organisms possessing such a system. Reaction in the higher organisms probably never takes place without involving nervous integration.

THE NERVOUS SYSTEM

Nervous integration is accomplished through the action of *nerve cells (neurons)* which are in functional relation. In the organisms studied by psychologists, the nervous system appears to consist of large and small nerves which are branches of a main trunk nerve called the *central axis* (the spinal cord and the brain). In reality, these nerve units are bundles of individual nerve fibers.

The Nerve Fiber. Many nerve fibers are insulated by a covering which prevents contact with the other fibers forming the nerve. The essential covering is called the *medullary* or *myelin sheath.* Thus, the nerve fiber consists of a core of nerve protoplasm surrounded by a covering or sheath. A second covering (the *primitive sheath of Schwann,* or *neurilemma*) is often found outside the central axis. Certain fibers—for example, those in the olfactory nerve—have only the sheath of Schwann. The core of the nerve fiber is formed of nerve protoplasm specialized for the conduction of energy changes in the nervous system. The sheath, however, is formed of nonconducting protoplasm.

The Structural Unit. The structural unit of the nervous system is the *neuron* or *nerve cell.* The nervous system is formed of neurons in structural and functional relationships. It has been estimated that the number of neurons in the human organism is about 12 billion (Donaldson).

The neuron is microscopic in size and is composed of the following major parts and processes:

CELL BODY. The cell body is a microscopic speck of nerve protoplasm from which the processes of the neuron extend. The cell body is responsible for the nutrition of the whole neuron.

NUCLEUS. Located in the cell body, the nucleus carries the specific germinal characteristics of the nerve cell.

AXON. Each neuron has an axon. Axons often attain great length, reaching as far as from the brain to the sacral region of the spinal cord. The axons serve to transmit nerve impulses from the cell body to other neurons or to effectors.

DENDRITES. Dendrites are processes of the neurons which receive nerve impulses from the receptors or the axons of other neurons and transmit them toward the cell body.

COLLATERALS. Some axons have branches which provide duplicate pathways. These are called collaterals.

OTHER PROCESSES. The outreaching fibrils of the axons and dendrites comprise the *end brush*. End brushes interlace in several characteristic patterns.

GENERAL PLAN OF THE NERVOUS SYSTEM

All nervous tissue (nerve cells) can be separated into two divisions according to the functions performed: (1) the *cerebrospinal system*, and (2) the *sympathetic nervous system* (called the *autonomic nervous system* by some authors).

The Cerebrospinal System. The cerebrospinal system may be divided into two smaller systems: (1) a *central system* formed of the central axis, and (2) a *peripheral system* formed of all nerve protoplasm outside the central axis (exclusive of the sympathetic system).

THE CENTRAL SYSTEM. The central system is composed of all nerve protoplasm which is encased in the cranium and vertebral column (the central axis). The back and front of the central system in the human being are spoken of as *dorsal* and *ventral*, respectively, and the sides as *lateral*. Toward the brain is spoken of as *superior* and toward the cord as *inferior*.

Brain and Cord. The central system is divided at the *foramen magnum* into the brain and cord. Besides the continuation of the cord superior to the *foramen magnum,* which is called the *brain stem,* there are several enlargements of the brain stem. These are called the *medulla oblongata, pons Varolii, cerebellum, thalamus,* and *cerebrum.* These enlargements are masses of the cell bodies of neurons (with their dendrites), which are called *nuclei* or *ganglia.* (The term "ganglia" often refers to masses of cell bodies outside the central axis which are part of the sympathetic system.)

Medial Division of Central System. A great fissure (called the longitudinal fissure at the level of the cerebrum) divides the central axis on the dorsal side, and to a degree on the ventral side, into two parts. This fissure cuts deep into the nervous tissue almost to the central canal. It forms the two *hemispheres of the cerebellum.* All structures, generally speaking, are duplicated laterally to this medial dividing line. All *ascending fibers* and all *descending fibers* decussate (cross) either at the level of activity or at the level of the brain stem, so that impulses starting at the receptors on the right side of the body, and finding their way to the higher centers, terminate in the left hemisphere of the brain, and those starting on the left side of the body terminate in the right hemisphere.

THE PERIPHERAL SYSTEM. The peripheral system is composed of (1) the *cranial nerves,* which leave the central axis above the *foramen magnum,* and (2) the *spinal nerves,* which leave the central axis below the *foramen magnum.* The sympathetic system is often regarded as a part of the peripheral system. It is outside the central axis, and its action is controlled to a degree by the central axis. However, it has distinctive functions of its own.

The Sympathetic System. The sympathetic system has three divisions: (1) the *bulbar,* composed of four pairs of ganglia located in the cranium, (2) the *sacral,* composed of ganglia scattered throughout the viscera, and (3) the *parasympathetic,* composed of ganglia situated ventrally to the spinal column, one pair for each pair of vertebrae, and connected as a chain. The ganglia of the bulbar-sacral system are situated far from the central axis, and the ganglia of the parasympathetic system are close to the central axis.

The nerve cells of the sympathetic system pass primarily to glands and viscera, and operate smooth rather than striped muscles. Most organs receive fibers from both the bulbar and parasympathetic systems.

STRUCTURES OF THE CEREBROSPINAL
CENTRAL SYSTEM

The central system is composed of several relatively well-defined structures.

The Cord and the Brain Stem. The cord and the brain stem are composed of *projection tracts* (ascending and descending fibers) and *nuclei.* In general, the nuclei, which are formed of cell bodies and dendrites of neurons, are centrally located in the cord and brain stem. The projection tracts, which are formed of the axons and their insulating coverings (nerve fibers), are peripherally located. Below the *foramen magnum,* the peripheral nerves enter the central axis by way of the *intervertebral foramina,* two of which are situated laterally in each spinal vertebra. Nuclei, which consist of the cell bodies of afferent (sensory) neurons composing these peripheral nerves, are situated inside each lateral half of the spinal vertebra, but just outside the cord proper and in the area of the cerebrospinal fluid. These nuclei are called the *spinal ganglia.* The cell bodies of the efferent (motor) neurons in the peripheral nerves are found in the central gray matter of the cord. The nerve fibers leading from the central nuclei of the cord and brain stem go to other levels of the central axis, to striped effectors in the periphery of the body, and to the sympathetic ganglia lying outside the vertebral column of the cord or outside the brain stem in the cranium.

Coverings of the Central System. Covering the central axis (inward from the cranial and vertebral structures) are: (1) *dura mater,* (2) *arachnoid,* (3) *cerebrospinal fluid,* and (4) *pia mater.*

The Medulla. The *medulla oblongata* is an enlargement of the ventral part of the brain which is just superior to the *foramen magnum.* Besides the projection fibers of the brain stem at this point, two important nuclei are contained in each half of the medulla; the *nucleus gracilis,* immediately lateral to the medial fissure, and the *nucleus cuneatus,* lateral to the *nucleus gracilis.*

The Pons. The *Pons Varolii* is an enlargement of the ventral part of the brain stem just superior to the medulla. Besides the projection fibers of the brain stem at this point, there are masses of *commissural fibers,* circling these projection fibers to connect the two hemispheres of the cerebellum. The pons also includes various nuclei, some acting particularly as relays for the cranial nerves.

The Cerebellum. The cerebellum, the second largest enlarge-ment of the brain stem, is dorsal to the pons. The cerebellum is composed of masses of cell bodies (with dendrites) from which axons descend to lower levels of the central axis. Various fissures indent the surface of the cerebellum. See Figs. 3-A and 3-B.

The Thalamus. Often referred to as the *basal ganglion,* the thalamus is much older, genetically, than the cerebellum and cerebrum, and in some of the lower forms of life it is the largest structure of the brain. It is located centrally, superior to the pons, and is composed of two hemispheres. The thalamus in-cludes a great number of nuclei which act as organization relays to inferior and superior structures.

The Cerebrum. The cerebrum is the crowning structure of the central axis. In the human brain it includes more neurons than all the rest of the nervous system.

HEMISPHERES. The cerebrum is divided by the medial fissure into two hemispheres. At this point the fissure is called the *great longitudinal fissure.* The dorsal part of the cerebrum is separated from the cerebellum by the *transverse fissure.*

INTERLOBULAR FISSURES. The lateral surfaces of the cerebrum are divided into five lobes by three interlobular fissures: *Sylvius* (the lateral fissure), *Rolando* (the central fissure), and *parieto-occipital* fissure. This last-named fissure is more prominent on the medial (mesial) surfaces.

LOBES. The five lobes of the cerebrum are: *frontal, parietal, occipital, temporal,* and the fifth lobe, at the base of the fissure of Sylvius, called the *Isle of Reil.* This is a small inferior surface of the cerebrum (inferior to the temporal lobe).

CONVOLUTIONS. Each of the major lobes has many smaller fis-sures (*sulci*) which form smaller lobes called convolutions (*gyri*). The medial surfaces of the cerebral hemispheres are bro-ken by fissures and convolutions, all of which increase the sur-face, or *cortex,* of the cerebrum. The cortices of both the cere-brum and the cerebellum are composed of gray matter; the outer surface of the rest of the central axis is composed of white mat-ter. This white matter consists of the insulating coverings of the neurons. Since the gray matter only is conductive, the possibility

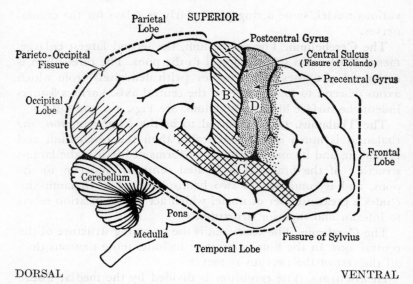

FIG. 3-A. The lateral view of the right cerebral hemisphere, showing schematically the important fissures, lobes, and projection centers of the cortex, the
medulla and pons of the brain stem, and the cerebellum. The dotted area (D)
represents roughly the origin of the main efferent tracts conducting impulses
from the cortex to the lower co-ordination centers, and cross-hatched areas
(A, B, and C) represent projection areas for vision, somesthesis, and audition,
respectively. Unidentified parts are integration areas.

of tremendously great interaction in the cerebrum and cerebellum is apparent.

STRUCTURES OF THE CEREBROSPINAL PERIPHERAL SYSTEM

The peripheral system is composed of afferent (sensory) and
efferent (motor) nerves reaching from the periphery of the body
to the central axis. These nerves are classified into the *spinal
nerves* and the *cranial nerves*.

The Spinal Nerves. The spinal nerves leave each lateral half
of the central axis by way of the *intervertebral foramina*. There
are 31 pairs of such nerves and each nerve is composed of both
afferent and efferent fibers. There are the following divisions of
spinal nerves (in pairs): 8 cervical, 12 thoracic, 5 lumbar, 5 sacral, and 1 coccygeal, corresponding to the divisions of the verte-

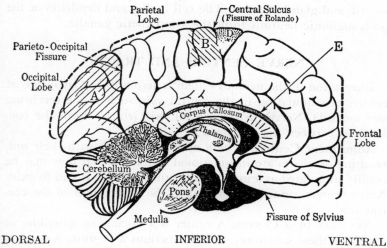

FIG. 3-B. Mesial view of the left cerebral hemisphere. This figure shows certain structures of the brain stem, the cerebellum, and the cerebral cortex. The thalamus, corpus callosum (composed of nerve fibers connecting the two hemispheres), and part of the projection area for olfaction and gustation (E) are visible. The essential area of smell and taste, which is not shown in either figure, is the uncus, situated in the hippocampal convolution on the inferior surface of the temporal lobe.

brae which compose the spinal column. The afferent neurons have their cell bodies in the spinal ganglia, and the efferent neurons in the ventral *horns* of the gray matter of the cord.

The Cranial Nerves. There are 12 pairs of cranial nerves leaving the brain stem. Some of these nerves are formed of both afferent and efferent fibers. There are the following nerves, in pairs: I–Olfactory, II–Optic, III–Oculomotor, IV–Trochlear, V–Trigeminal, VI–Abducens, VII–Facial, VIII–Auditory vestibular, IX–Glossopharyngeal, X–Vagus, XI–Spinal accessory, and XII–Hypoglossal.

STRUCTURES OF THE SYMPATHETIC SYSTEM

The sympathetic ganglia are connected with the central axis by the *preganglionic fibers.* The cell bodies and dendrites of the preganglionic neurons are in the lateral-ventral gray columns of the brain stem and cord, and the axons reach to the sympathetic ganglia. *Postganglionic fibers* make the contact with the smooth-muscle and gland effectors. The cell bodies and dendrites of the postganglionic neurons form the sympathetic ganglia.

NERVE CENTERS AND TRACTS

Integration in the nervous system is accomplished by means of *centers* of stimulation in the central axis, such as the cerebrum and medulla. Nerves in the central axis (*tracts*) form the connections between these centers.

Adjustment Centers. Where many cell bodies with their out-reaching dendrites are in functional contact so that they may be readily stimulated as a unit, an adjustment center is said to exist. Nerve centers are usually located in the gray matter of the central axis.

ANATOMY OF A CENTER. A center is a nucleus or ganglion, or a part of these structures, which functions as a unit. A nucleus or ganglion is a collection of cell bodies and their dendrites, groups of which are in functional relationship so that they can be stimulated as a unit. Axons lead from the cell bodies forming these structures to similar structures in the central axis.

KINDS OF CENTERS. Adjustments of the central axis are of two kinds: (a) *correlation* (sensory) and (b) *co-ordination* (motor).

Correlation Centers. Correlation centers are centers where afferent neurons from receptors are organized for effective distribution.

LOWER CORRELATION CENTERS. The lower correlation centers distribute the afferent stimulation by means of adjustor neurons to different levels of the central axis, either for direct stimulation of lower co-ordination centers or for the passage of stimulation to higher correlation centers.

INTERMEDIARY CORRELATION CENTERS. The intermediary correlation centers relay stimulation to higher centers. They are in the nuclei of the medulla, pons, thalamus, and so on.

HIGHER CORRELATION CENTERS. The higher correlation centers are located in the cortex of the cerebrum. Relatively well-defined areas appear to be centers for specific sensitivities.

Co-ordination Centers. Centers which have an anatomical arrangement providing for the innervation of a particular group of effectors are co-ordination or motor centers.

LOWER CO-ORDINATION CENTERS. The lower co-ordination centers are formed of efferent neurons and are usually situated in the ventral gray column of the spinal cord and brain stem. Their axons are in direct contact with the muscle fibers of the effectors through motor end plates.

HIGHER CO-ORDINATION CENTERS. The higher co-ordination centers are located in the cortex of the cerebrum. These centers are stimulated by the higher correlation centers. The higher co-ordination centers then stimulate other co-ordination centers until the conduction path to lower co-ordination centers and to eventual effector stimulation is involved.

CENTERS IN THE SYMPATHETIC SYSTEM. The sympathetic system is essentially efferent (motor) in function. The centers, situated in the ganglia, co-ordinate the reactions of smooth-muscle and gland effectors.

Descending Tracts. Conduction of efferent impulses from the higher co-ordination centers to lower centers is by means of descending tracts. The largest of these is the *pyramidal tract,* which has two branches: (1) the *crossed pyramidal tract,* which stimulates lower co-ordination centers in the lower thoracic, lumbar, sacral, and coccygeal segments of the spinal cord, and (2) the *direct pyramidal tract,* which stimulates the lower co-ordination centers in the cervical and upper thoracic segments of the spinal cord.

Ascending Tracts. Stimulation to the centers of general sensitivity is conducted by ascending tracts. There are three kinds of ascending tracts: exteroceptive tracts, proprioceptive tracts, and afferent tracts from special receptors.

EXTEROCEPTIVE TRACTS. The exteroceptive tracts conduct impulses caused by the stimulation of the cutaneous centers. They terminate in the thalamus, from which other paths lead to the cerebral cortex.

PROPRIOCEPTIVE TRACTS. The proprioceptive tracts conduct afferent impulses caused by stimulation of receptors in the muscles, tendons, and joints. Two such tracts exist, the *column of Goll* and the *column of Burdach.* These tracts terminate, respectively, in the nucleus *gracilis* and nucleus *cuneatus* of the medulla. From the medulla, impulses are transmitted upward to the thalamus, and on to the cerebral cortex.

AFFERENT TRACTS FROM SPECIAL RECEPTORS. Afferent tracts conduct impulses to intermediary correlation centers in the medulla, pons, thalamus, and other nuclei of the brain stem. The special receptors with separate tracts are: the retina of the eye, the *cristae ampullares* of the semicircular canals in the ear, the rods of Corti of the cochlea in the ear, the taste bulbs of the tongue, and the Schneiderian membranes of the nose.

Other Tracts. There are two kinds of paths of communication among the centers themselves, longitudinal and commissural.

Longitudinal Tracts. Longitudinal tracts are paths of communication from dorsal to ventral centers, and vice versa.

Commissural Tracts. Commissural tracts are paths of communication across the medial fissure of the central axis. The most prominent of these are: (a) the *corpus callosum,* at the level of the cerebrum; (b) the *middle commissure,* at the level of the thalamus, and connecting both halves of this body; (c) the *fibers of the pons,* circling the brain stem at the level of the cerebellum; and (d) the *ventral white* and *central gray commissures,* at the various levels of the cord and brain stem.

FUNCTIONS OF THE BRAIN

The whole organism—receptors, adjustors, and effectors—is involved in activity. However, from the lower animals to man there is increasing dependence upon the cerebrum for all complex psychological functions. Though the older portions of the brain, genetically speaking, retain some independent functions, conscious behavior in man is mediated chiefly by the cerebrum. Thus, most attention is devoted to functioning of its various portions and structures.

The Medulla. The medulla contains neural connections which automatically control several vital physiological processes, such as respiration and blood pressure. However, its chief function is the provision of relay centers between the spinal cord and higher centers.

The Pons. The pons contains fibers which connect the hemispheres of the cerebellum with each other; each hemisphere of the cerebellum with the opposite hemisphere of the cerebrum; and these structures with various parts of the brain stem. Equilibrium and motor co-ordination are highly dependent on functioning of the pons.

The Cerebellum. Impulses from kinesthetic and static receptors activate the cerebellum. Destruction of this part of the brain leads to disturbance of muscular co-ordination.

The Thalamus. The center for direction of all sensory impulses to the appropriate regions of the cerebral cortex is the thalamus. Sensory and motor connections between the thalamus and lower levels underlie much unconscious automatic behavior. Injury to the thalamus often results in magnification of automatic reactions.

The Cerebrum. The cerebrum is tremendously complex in organization. Out of this complexity three general functional types are usually differentiated: (1) specialized sensory areas, (2) motor control areas, and (3) association areas. (See Fig. 3.)

Sensory Areas. Specialized sensory areas are located in the parietal, occipital, and temporal lobes.

Parietal Lobe. The principal area of sensitivity for touch, pressure, and temperature (somesthetic or body feel) is a portion of the parietal lobe just posterior to the fissure of Rolando. Pain sensitivity is apparently not included. It seems to be localized in the thalamus, and the other somesthetic sensitivities may also be mediated by the thalamus if parietal tissues are destroyed.

Occipital Lobe. The area of sensitivity for vision is the tip of the occipital lobe. If this area is destroyed in both cerebral hemispheres, total blindness results.

Temporal Lobe. The area of sensitivity for hearing is in the temporal lobe. Each ear has connections with both hemispheres, so that only minor disturbances result from injury to one hemisphere. Destruction of both auditory areas results in serious loss of sensitivity. Remaining sensitivity appears to be located in subcortical centers.

Motor Areas. A portion of the frontal lobe, immediately anterior to the fissure of Rolando, contains the centers which control voluntary motor activity. Experiments suggest that retraining is at least partially successful if this area is damaged or destroyed (Lashley, 1929, 1935).

Associative Areas. In man the associative neurons, through connections both inherited and modified by training, are concentrated by function. Thus, neurons dealing with meaning for auditory sounds are found in the same general area. The associative areas are generally grouped into three classes, sensory, motor, and frontal.

Sensory Areas. The sensory associative areas contain the associative neurons for specialized stimuli such as light, sound, smell, etc. These sensory associative areas are not specifically related to sensory sensitivity.

Motor Areas. The motor associative areas contain the associative neurons for control of motor processes. Injury to these areas impairs the ability to understand the meaning of motor activities.

Frontal Areas. The frontal associative areas are apparently involved in memory, reasoning, and motivation. Injury to these areas impairs the ability to recall, and to solve problems, and also causes the individual to become passive and unexcitable.

The importance of the associative areas appears much greater with man than with the lower animals. For example, the ability 'of the rat to learn is more closely related to the total amount of brain destruction than to the portion of the brain destroyed (Lashley, 1935).

Partial, and sometimes complete, restoration of function has been demonstrated in individuals whose associative areas had been damaged or destroyed. The portion of the brain which took over the associative functions is not definitely known.

NEURAL FUNCTIONING

The highly complex and highly differentiated nervous system described in the preceding sections is completely dependent for functioning on the tiny neurons of which it is composed. These neurons are classified into three groups: (1) sensory or *afferent* neurons, which carry impulses from receptors to the spinal cord and brain; (2) motor or *efferent* neurons, which carry impulses from the brain and spinal cord to the effectors; and (3) *association* or *adjustor* neurons, found solely within the brain and spinal cord, which provide connections between sensory and motor neurons, and between association neurons.

Neuron Excitation. Neuron excitation, or stimulation, appears as a *nerve impulse.* This is an energy change, the exact nature of which is not known. It appears to be both physical and chemical. The impulse itself can be measured as a change in *electrical potential.*

THE MEMBRANE THEORY. The most widely accepted theory of neuron excitation and impulse transmission is the membrane theory (Ostwald, 1890; Lillie, 1914). The following important factors are noted with respect to the theory: (a) Each nerve fiber has a semipermeable membrane with positive ions on the outside and negative ions on the inside. (b) Stimulation of the fiber (mechanical, electrical, or chemical) renders the membrane more permeable, and positive ions pass through to unite with negative ions. (c) Local stimulation renders adjacent areas of the membrane more permeable, and the nerve impulse thus "moves" along the fiber. (d) An *absolute refractory period,* of very short duration, occurs during which the membrane remains highly permeable and no stimulus, however intense, can excite the nerve fiber. (e) The absolute is followed by a *relative refractory period* during which the membrane is not completely reorganized, and during which an unusually strong stimulus can re-excite the fiber. (f) Stronger stimuli may thus activate a neuron at shorter intervals than weaker stimuli.

INTENSITY OF THE IMPULSE. It appears that the nerve impulse is of fixed intensity for each neuron stimulated (Adrian, 1914). Appreciation of differences in the intensity of stimuli is due to (1) more impulses per second because of restimulation during the relative refractory period, and (2) excitation of more neurons receptive to the same kind of stimulation but differing among themselves with respect to threshold of excitability.

The Synapse. By far the most vexing problem of neural functioning is the determination of what happens at the synapse (the point at which nervous impulses move from one neuron to another). Each neuron is an individual cell with its own membrane. There is *no* structural continuity in neuron chains. Functional junctures with other neurons are accomplished through the synapse, from the end brush of axons to the end brush of dendrites. Most neurons have several collateral axons and several dendrites. Thus, several different neurons may be in functional relationship at the same synapse.

Numerous factors regarding synapse structure and neuron functioning have been identified or hypothesized.

FORWARD CONDUCTION. Movement of the nerve impulse is only from axon to dendrite.

THE "ALL-OR-NONE PRINCIPLE." A neuron either fires (is excited) or does not fire. An impulse will either fail to excite the neuron across the synapse or will excite in its full potential. The neuron excited across the synapse may have a higher potential than that of the neuron originally excited.

SUMMATION. An impulse coming over one or more fibers may be of insufficient intensity to cross the threshold of the synapse. However, surpluses from many fibers may operate together or *summate* to produce excitation. *Spatial summation,* joining with impulses from other summation, continuation of successive impulses in the same neuron, may also result in excitation.

THE HYPOTHESIS OF SYNAPTIC RESISTANCE. The resistance to transmission of stimulation through the nervous system is be-

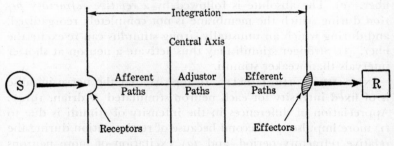

FIG. 4. The reaction-arc hypothesis. Environmental stimuli (S), acting upon specialized receptors, excite afferent neurons which lead to the central axis, where an extremely complex adjustment takes place culminating in stimulation of efferent neurons and reaction (R) by effectors.

lieved to be greater at the synapse than in the neuron itself. Support for this idea is given by the known facts that there is no direct contact between neurons and that the elapsed time required for transmission in impulses involving more than one neuron is greater than that required for simple movement of the potential along the neuron.

The Functional Unit of Nervous Integration. Neurons are organized into functional units between receptors and effectors.

THE REACTION-ARC HYPOTHESIS. The reaction, which is initiated by the environmental stimulus, is said to result from integration performed by afferent neurons, leading from receptors, through adjustor neurons in the central axis, and along efferent neurons to effectors. This is the reaction-arc hypothesis.

REACTION-ARC POSSIBILITIES. Integration possibilities vary from exceedingly simple to highly complex organizations.

The Two-Neuron Arc (Reflex Arc). The simplest reaction possibility is one in which the stimulus from a sensory fiber (originated in a receptor) is transmitted to a motor fiber (terminated in an effector). It is doubtful that such a simple reaction arc actually exists in human behavior.

Complex Organizations. It is thought that any efferent fiber may receive impulses that converge from many adjustor fibers, which may have received their impulses from one or several afferent fibers. Thus, with an estimated 12 billion neurons (Donaldson) in the nervous system, a tremendous number of connections and different reactions is possible.

SUMMARY

The mechanism of nervous integration includes receptors, afferent neurons, adjustor or associative neurons, efferent neurons, and effectors.

Peripheral System. The action of afferent and efferent neurons is observed in the contacts established in the peripheral system by the spinal and cranial nerves. These neurons conduct the nerve impulse (stimulation) to and from the central axis. Their function is clearly one of conduction, and the direction of stimulation is determined in their structure.

Central System. Integration is primarily the function of adjustor neurons, situated in the central axis (brain and spinal cord). There are insulated fibers in the central axis as well as neurons organized into nuclei or ganglia. The greater part of neural integration is performed in the enlarged structures of the brain stem with the cerebrum as the major structure for integration in the higher forms of life.

The Action of Centers. Nervous integration is effected through the action of centers and paths of conduction between these centers. The cortex of the cerebrum consists of innumerable centers which function between the higher correlation centers and the higher co-ordination centers. Theoretically, the impulses initiated in each receptor have the possibility of stimulating every effector through the action of the centers throughout the central axis.

The Reaction as a Resultant of Nervous Integration. The psychological reaction involves the following causative factors in nervous integration: (1) the reception of stimulation by means of exteroceptors, proprioceptors, and interoceptors; (2) the correlation and co-ordination of the nerve impulse by means of afferent, adjustor, and efferent systems through operation of centers and tracts; and (3) the innervation of effectors, involving striated muscles, nonstriated muscles, and glands. The psychological reaction is the objective evidence of nervous integration.

4

Development of Reaction

The study of the behavioral relationships between the organism and its environment may be carried on without specific reference to nervous integration. Investigation of the observed reactions of the organism to stimulation has revealed many principles of behavior, even though the neural functioning involved must be only hypothesized.

TYPES OF BEHAVIOR

The organism's reactions may be classified from several points of view. Reactions may be primarily *native* or primarily *learned.* Reactions may be evoked by *external* stimuli or by *internal* needs. Reactions may be *automatic* or *voluntary* and *conscious.* Reactions may be primarily *motor, ideomotor,* or *ideational.* Finally, reactions may be classified roughly by complexity, ranging from simple *tropisms* and *reflexes* to highly organized *problem-solving behavior.*

TROPISMS AND REFLEXES

The simplest forms of reaction to stimulation are tropisms and reflexes. In each tropism or reflex the stimulus is similar, and one pattern reaction completes the activity.

Tropisms. Tropisms usually involve the reaction of the whole organism, rather than some part of it. They are characteristic of lower-order organisms and are seldom found in higher organisms except in the very young of the species.

All tropisms are (1) orienting responses to stimuli, (2) responses controlled automatically by the external stimuli rather than conscious behavior, and (3) native rather than learned responses.

Examples of tropism are: *phototropism,* orientation with respect to light; *rheotropism,* orientation of water animals with respect to current; and *geotropism,* orientation with respect to gravitational field.

Reflexes. The reflex is a native, simultaneous pattern reaction of varying degrees of perfection, involving a definite kind of receptor activity. It is a prompt response of the striped or smooth muscles of the body, usually without conscious accompaniments. Explicit reflexes involve striated muscle effectors and act upon the external environment. Implicit reflexes involve the unstriated muscle and gland effectors and act upon the internal environment of the organism.

Examples of reflexes are: the *eyelid* reflex, a blinking which occurs when an object approaches the eye; the *knee jerk,* a kick resulting from a blow on the patellar tendon; and *sucking,* movements of the infant when the oral region is stimulated by any object.

The *reflex arc,* requiring a sensory neuron and a motor neuron, is the simplest form of reflex. However, this arc is more theoretical than real. In all the higher organisms, (1) several effectors are likely to be involved, (2) identical or highly similar responses may be made consciously, and (3) such reflexes may be facilitated or inhibited through stimulation of other reflexes.

The more complex reflexes of higher organisms involve receptors, afferent neurons, adjustor neurons, efferent neurons, and effectors, all in functional relation. However, reflexes are primarily unlearned acts, dependent upon maturation of appropriate receptive, integrative, and reactive mechanisms. Once established, they remain fairly stable and predictable.

Major Features of Reflexes. Certain conditions of reflex activity exist, as follows.

THRESHOLD OF STIMULATION. A certain intensity of stimulus is required to induce the reflex. The minimum amount required is spoken of as the *threshold.*

LOCALIZATION OF STIMULUS. The reflex reaction depends upon the area of stimulation.

INTENSITY OF STIMULATION. As a rule, less intense stimuli induce a weak reaction. Stimuli of greater intensity evoke a stronger reaction.

CONDITIONED RESPONSES (LEARNED REACTIONS)

Under the influence of environmental stimulation the organism reacts according to its capacities for reaction. These capacities are a joint product of maturation and learning. They are expanded in two ways: (1) a new or reorganized pattern of reactions may be connected with the original stimulus which was the adequate stimulus for a simpler reaction, or (2) a new or *conditioned stimulus* may be connected with the adequate stimulus for an existing reaction, either becoming a substitute for the original stimulus or becoming an additional adequate stimulus for the reaction.

The Conditioned Reflex. The reaction which is established as a response to the conditioned stimulus has been called the *conditioned reflex* (C.R.) because experimenters have been concerned largely with the reflex. However, conditioned reactions are formed with well-established learned reactions where new and indifferent stimuli are associated with and then substituted for the adequate stimuli to the reactions. The C.R. mechanism can operate at all levels of development of reaction.

Pavlov, a Russian physiologist, and Twitmyer, an American psychologist, were the earliest investigators of the conditioned reflex (about 1900). A typical experiment of Pavlov was as follows: (1) A hungry dog was placed in a harness and stood on a table. (2) A bell was sounded (the indifferent stimulus). (3) A piece of meat (the adequate stimulus) was presented to the dog. (4) The sight of the meat caused the dog to salivate. (5) After the stimuli were presented several times as specified, the sound of the bell alone would produce a flow of saliva.

Nature of the Conditioning Situation. There are several factors which affect conditioning situations, particularly the experimental situations from which most of our knowledge is derived.

CHARACTERISTICS OF CONDITIONING. The following are characteristics of conditioning: (1) There must be an unconditioned stimulus which elicits an unconditioned response, preferably one which is regular and measurable. (2) There must be an indifferent stimulus which does not, of itself, elicit this unconditioned response. (3) There must be repetition of the conditioned (indifferent) and the unconditioned stimuli in a controlled and specified manner.

TEMPORAL FACTORS INVOLVED. Three temporal conditions may exist with respect to sequence of the unconditioned and conditioned stimuli.

Unconditioned Stimulus First. When the adequate stimulus (unconditioned) is presented first and then followed by the indifferent (conditioned) stimulus, either no conditioning takes

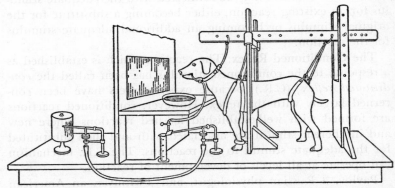

FIG. 5. A typical arrangement for one of Pavlov's experiments on conditioning. (From R. M. Yerkes and S. Margulis, "The Method of Pavlov in Animal Psychology," A. P. A. *Psychological Bulletin*, 1909.)

place or a very unstable conditioning occurs after many repetitions.

Both Stimuli Together. When the conditioned stimulus is given at the same time as the unconditioned stimulus, a conditioning usually takes place but requires many repetitions.

Conditioned Stimulus First. When the conditioned stimulus is applied first and the unconditioned stimulus is administered after it is withdrawn, a conditioning usually takes place. The reaction to the conditioned stimulus is usually delayed, with considerable exactness, by the same amount of time as that which elapsed between presentation of the conditioned and of the unconditioned stimulus. The optimal interval between presentation of the conditioned and unconditioned stimuli is about 200 milliseconds (msec.). Delays of over 5 seconds make the establishment of conditioned responses quite difficult.

CONDITIONED RESPONSE CHAINS. Once the conditioned stimulus has become effective for the desired reaction, it can be used as the unconditioned stimulus for the development of a second conditioning without recourse to the original adequate stimulus. Some experimenters have reported chains involving as many as five consecutive conditionings. Such secondary conditionings and beyond are difficult to secure and are likely to be highly unstable.

DETERIORATION OF CONDITIONED RESPONSES. The conditioned reaction is often unstable in experimental demonstrations and must frequently be reinforced through presentation of the unconditioned stimulus. However, once a conditioning has been firmly established, it is likely to persist over a long period of time if repeated elicitations are avoided. This is the phenomenon of *spontaneous recovery*.

INHIBITION OF CONDITIONED RESPONSES. A well-established conditioned response may be completely inhibited by the introduction of an additional extraneous stimulus into the situation. Similarly, the addition of more than one extraneous stimulus may neutralize this inhibitory effect.

GENERALIZATION AND DISCRIMINATION OF STIMULI. After a conditioned response to one stimulus has been established, presentation of a similar stimulus will usually elicit the response. If the two similar stimuli are differentially reinforced, discrimination of the exact stimulus will result unless the two stimuli are too nearly identical for sensory discrimination.

Instrumental Conditioning. The typical experiment of Pavlov described earlier is an example of what is called *classical conditioning*. Much more attention is currently being given to what is called *instrumental conditioning*. In general, instrumental conditioning situations are much more closely related to real life situations than are those of classical conditioning. The primary factor in the instrumental conditioning situation is this: *Reinforcement is given only after the conditioned response has been made.*

The typical instrumental conditioning experiment is as follows: (1) The organism is placed in a controlled situation, such as a Skinner box. (2) An inadequate stimulus (such as a buzzer) is presented. (3) The organism is meanwhile reacting with various responses already in its repertory. (4) The organism eventually hits upon the response previously selected by the experimenter as the desired response. (5) When the response has been

made, the reward, shock, escape, or other reinforcement is presented. (6) This procedure is continued until the organism
reacts with the desired response (which has become the conditioned response) upon presentation of the originally inadequate
or undifferentiated stimulus (which has now become the conditioned stimulus).

Four major types of instrumental conditioning are noted: reward, escape, avoidance, and secondary reward.

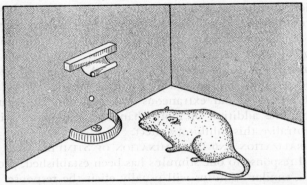

FIG. 6. Cutaway of Skinner box showing release bar which permits a pellet
of food to drop into the pan below.

REWARD CONDITIONING. In reward conditioning, the conditioned response is followed by presentation of a reward of positive nature such as food or water.

ESCAPE CONDITIONING. In escape conditioning, the conditioned
response is followed by termination of some noxious situation
such as an electric shock or confinement.

AVOIDANCE CONDITIONING. In avoidance conditioning, the conditioned response prevents the occurrence of a noxious situation
such as an electric shock.

SECONDARY REWARD CONDITIONING. In secondary reward conditioning, the conditioned response is followed by a stimulus which
has acquired reward value in previous conditioning.

Universality of Conditioning. Conditioned responses have been
established among a wide variety of organisms, involving widely
differing stimuli and the use of many different receptors and
effectors.

ORGANISMS. Conditioned responses have been formed by protozoa, worms, snails, crabs, fish, reptiles, pigeons, chickens, rats, sheep, dogs, monkeys, and infants, children, and adults of the human species. Some evidence of conditioning in fetal states has been reported.

STIMULI. Among the unconditioned stimuli used are electric shock, acid, morphine injection, thermal stimuli, patellar blows, air puff, rotation, food, change in illumination, and increased water intake.

Stimuli to be conditioned have included lights, bells, tones, buzzers, clicks, colors, odors, and patterns involving both temporal and spatial relations.

RESPONSES. Among the unconditioned responses which have been tied to new stimuli are such diverse reactions as salivation, change in galvanic skin resistance, vasomotor reactions, pupillary reflexes, eyelid reflexes, knee jerk, change in respiration, change in pitch of voice, withdrawal movements, locomotion, diuresis, and previously conditioned responses.

TIME OF REACTION

Human nerve conduction is at a rate of about 12 centimeters per millisecond. Reflex reactions are completed in about twice this time. For example, the eyelid reflex requires about 30 msec. and the knee jerk reflex requires about 50 msec. This difference is said to be due to the slower functioning of receptors, effectors, and synaptic contacts in the nervous system rather than that of the neurons themselves. The time interval between presentation of a prescribed stimulus and the intended reaction is called the *reaction time* and is interpreted as the time of integration between stimulus and response.

Simple Reaction Time. Simple reaction time is the time required to react where there is only one possible stimulus to a prescribed reaction. The average times vary for individuals and for different sensitivities. Sensitivity variation has been established as follows: vision, 150–255 msec.; audition, 120–180 msec.; warmth, 180 msec.; cold, 150 msec.; and pain, 400 msec. These reaction times would not exceed 20 msec. if the only factor involved were nerve conduction.

Complex Reaction Time. Complex reactions involve discrimination and choice. The observer makes one prescribed reaction to one of several stimuli which may be presented, or makes one of several possible reactions according to the appropriateness of the stimulus presented. The reaction time is lengthened in accordance with the complexity of the situation. For example, in word association experiments where the observer is required to form a verbal reaction to a stimulus word, the average reaction time is about 2000 msec.

ORGANIZATION OF REACTION

Any reaction involves numerous effectors, perhaps all of the explicit effectors. It is the sum total of stimulation and inhibition of all effectors, happenings which take place simultaneously. But a reaction is focused in the activity of a relatively limited number of effectors, particularly as efficiency of response is developed. The reaction is then defined according to the pattern of these few effectors.

Origin of Reaction. Certain behavior is apparently fixed, or nearly so, by innate patterns of neural connections and merely awaits maturation and appropriate stimulation. However, most of the relatively complicated behavior of the higher organisms is learned. Such learning grows out of *general activity* or *general exploratory behavior*. Most such behavior is apparently aimless, random, and subject to change with each new stimulus situation.

Relation of Activity to Needs of the Organism. Most exploratory behavior results from needs or tensions within the organism. These may be innate, such as those derived from a condition of hunger, thirst, sex deprivation, uncomfortable thermal stimuli, etc. They may also be acquired or socially imposed, such as a desire for attention, entertainment, companionship, or particular kinds of food, drink, air, etc. Most psychologists conclude that these acquired *motives* are based upon original *drives*. However, the student who attempts to trace some of the most important motives of human beings will have an exceedingly difficult if not impossible task.

Certainly the random movements of the young of the species are almost completely dominated by the degree to which essential needs are satisfied. Cannon (1933) proposes that the organism seems to maintain a condition of *homeostatic equilibrium* and is designed to react to change in such a way as to restore disturbed equilibrium. Since the implicit and explicit environment of the organism is constantly changing, some form of activity is almost certain to be taking place.

Development of Reaction Patterns. When the random activity results in satisfaction of need, the activity is likely to be repeated when the need again arises, particularly if other elements of the stimulus situation are similar. Thus a combination of reactions, leading to a final or consummatory reaction, is eventually effected.

This subject will be discussed more thoroughly in the chapter on learning.

INSTINCTIVE BEHAVIOR

Behavior is usually termed *instinctive,* particularly by the layman, if it occurs without apparent opportunity to learn, if it seems to appear regularly at some stage in maturation, or if it appears to be virtually universal to the species. The type of behavior involved is usually a chain of reflexes or a sequence of activities, much of which is determined by the structure of the organism. Earlier contemporary psychologists had much to say about instinct, and laymen still attribute many of the common activities of organisms to instinct. Present-day research, particularly in the field of learning, has been gradually reducing the list of activities considered to be instinctive. For example, Kuo (1930) studied the origin of the cat's responses toward rats and mice. He showed that kittens reared with rodents and not permitted to observe other cats killing rats during the early part of their life were very unlikely ever to kill a rat. This held, even though special attempts were made to train these kittens to kill rodents after the kittens had reached maturity.

Migration, pecking in various birds, suckling of the child, cocoon-building by insects, nest-building, etc. have all been studied extensively. Though all the explanations are not worked out, it appears clear that there is no instinctive behavior in man and probably not in animals. What is commonly regarded as instinctive behavior is due either to structure of the organism or to environmental factors. Most research shows that the supposed instinct changes if the environment is changed.

Two things to note particularly are: (1) So-called instinctive behavior depends upon maturation of inherited neural patterns-

(2) Behavior which is apparently instinctive in nature improves with practice, and the finished act is usually a product of both maturation and learning.

HABITUAL BEHAVIOR

Habitual reactions are successive reactions which have been organized primarily because of relatively regularized stimulations of the environment. Some of these reactions are the later forms of the more inexact instinctive type of reactions, developed and modified by learning. Others are the result of organization of random behavior.

A habit is a complex system of reactions, functioning successively, in which the integration of the separate elements has been thoroughly learned.

There are three forms of habitual behavior: (1) motor habits, including all bodily movements, (2) language habits, and (3) emotional habits. The language habits are based upon random vocalizations, and the motor habits are based in a large degree upon random bodily movements. The emotional habits are somewhat unoriented expressions of either or both. These forms of habitual behavior may be implicit or explicit.

SYMBOLIC BEHAVIOR

In higher organisms, and particularly in man, symbols are substituted for a great number of direct environmental stimulations, and symbolic processes, including determination of possible effector action, take the place of overt actions.

Symbols as Substitute Stimuli. The conditioned response represents one of the simplest cases of substitute stimuli based on symbols. The previously indifferent stimulus becomes capable of eliciting the response which originally was evoked only by some reflexly adequate stimulus.

Verbal symbols, both oral and written, develop meaning only through the process of being associated with reactions to objects, events, or relationships, or to other symbols for which meaning has previously been acquired.

Symbols as Substitute Responses. Verbal symbols are an example of the use of symbols as substitute responses. Most of our preparatory acts are symbolic responses rather than direct. A hungry individual sits at a table and orders food from a menu instead of going to the restaurant kitchen for direct satisfaction. The infant's cries which express hunger, pain, or displeasure become meaningful symbolic responses to need states long before the child is able to use what are commonly thought of as verbal symbols.

Redintegration. The symbolic processes are tremendously enhanced by the phenomenon of redintegration. In redintegration a *part* of the antecedent stimulus situation is sufficient to provoke the complete response. Redintegration operates for verbal, muscular, glandular, or visceral responses. Thus, hearing a tune may arouse emotional states, approaching or withdrawing reactions, verbalizations, etc., connected with the tune in prior experiences.

COMPLEX BEHAVIOR

Natural behavior, particularly in human beings, involves highly complex activities in which simple reactions are mingled with ideational behavior and emotional states, and all this within a social framework which requires the continual adjustment of the individual for survival. Yet, the basic phenomena of differentiation of stimuli and elaboration of response remain constant as the determiners of reaction.

SUMMARY

The behavior of organisms, as demonstrated by their responses to stimulation, comprises a large part of the subject of psychology. Reactions range from simple reflexes to complicated ideational behavior. The propensities for all behavior are inherited, though maturation is necessary before many behavior patterns can emerge or be learned. Some behavior patterns are relatively fixed and occur, under appropriate stimulation, with little possible variation. This type of behavior decreases in the more complex organisms. Greater variability of neural connections is possible, and learned reactions take precedence over much behavior which would satisfy the needs of the body in simpler fashion.

5

Sensation and Perception

Sensitivity to stimulation is a necessary condition to living. Stimulation comes from energy changes of the environment which are capable of setting off a response in the organism. In higher organisms this energy change excites specialized receptor cells. These specialized receptor cells have become particularly sensitive to certain kinds of energy changes and are relatively insensitive to other energy changes.

The special sensitivities are commonly grouped into five categories—*visual* (sight), *auditory* (hearing), *olfactory* (smell), *gustatory* (taste), and *cutaneous* (touch). These five classes have several clearly defined subclasses, and we should add as general categories *kinesthetic, equilibrium,* and *organic* sensitivities.

The sensitivity of the receptors and the subsequent reactivity of the organism involve many paradoxes. The relations between the physical intensity of the stimulation and the awareness and interpretation afforded by the organism seem to depend upon many factors.

CONSCIOUSNESS, SENSATION, AND PERCEPTION

Consciousness, or conscious activity, consists of all psychological activities that involve *awareness.* The simplest awareness is sensitivity to stimulation. Excitation of a receptor results in a *sensation.* This sensation affects conscious activity as a *perception.* The perception is an *immediate sensitivity,* but there is hardly a perception which is not influenced by past experience, *recalled sensitivities.*

Many texts ignore differences between sensation and perception. The same phenomena are classified under sensation in one text and under perception in another. However, all schools of

54

thought admit that there is a *sensory core* to all effective stimulation. Illusions, figure-ground relations, transpositions, and contextual relations may make the understanding of stimulus energy changes and the resulting responses a more difficult subject. The fact remains that organisms respond in terms of their interpretation of the stimulus situation, regardless of the "true" nature of the stimulus.

The activities of organisms are based on observed relations of objects and events within a framework of space and time. The genetic study of reactivity thus proceeds from the simple sensitivity to the highly developed integrations of *reasoning* and *conceptual thinking*.

THE CONCEPT OF THRESHOLD

The smallest quantity of energy capable of exciting a receptor is called the *threshold* (also *limen*). The concept has both a neurophysiological and a psychological meaning. Attempts to equate these two through study of the relationships between physical stimuli and psychological reaction have been the basic problems of *psychophysics*.

The Neurophysiological Threshold. The threshold of a nerve or muscle fiber is defined as the minimal electrical current which will evoke detectable discharge along the nerve or muscle fiber when such minimal current is acting for an indefinite period. This minimal strength is called the *rheobase*, and the *excitation time* required for stimulation with an electrical current twice the value of the rheobase is called the *chronaxie* (Lapique, 1926).

THE RESULT OF DIFFERING CHRONAXIES. The typical receptor organ comprises many sensitive cells, with different chronaxies represented. Thus, one aspect of the relationship between stimulus and response is postulated as the number and identity of the cells excited.

THE PRINCIPLE OF SUMMATION. A given energy change may be insufficient to energize the neuron. However, if repeated energy changes occur before decay of the local potential aroused in the neuron, the neuron may still be energized. For the highly complex neuron chains involved in reception of a stimulus and activation of a response, this summation may be required at many points (*synapses*) before the chain is completed.

VARIABILITY OF NEUROPHYSIOLOGICAL THRESHOLDS. A neuron in a normal resting state exhibits a condition known as *oscillation;* the threshold varies about an average value. In addition, firing of the neuron changes its threshold. After the neuron has been energized there is a *relative refractory* period during which a greater stimulus intensity is required for excitation. This is followed by a brief period in which the neuron is even more excitable than is normally the case, and this, in turn, is followed by another period of subnormal excitability.

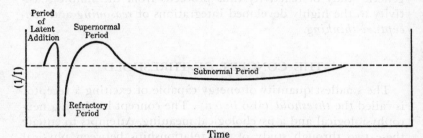

FIG. 7. Excitability cycle of a typical sensory neuron. Subthreshold stimuli may summate, reducing intensity required of any one stimulus to fire the neuron. Immediately after firing there is an absolute refractory period during which the neuron will not fire; this changes to a relative refractory period in which a stimulus more intense than normally required will fire the neuron. Then comes a period in which a stimulus less intense than normal is operative and then a more extended period in which more intense stimuli are required. (From C. T. Morgan, *Physiological Psychology,* McGraw-Hill, 1943.)

Repeated stimulation of a neuron results in a condition of *tetanus* in which the threshold of stimulation is greatly increased and neuron excitability is greatly depressed.

The *internal environment* of the organism also influences the neurophysiological threshold.

Acid-alkaline Balance of the Blood (pH). In general, lowered pH is directly related to low excitability of neurons, and conversely.

Oxygen. The initial result of oxygen deprivation is increased excitability, changing rapidly to a condition of complete nonexcitability.

Calcium. Calcium contentration is inversely related to pH. Thus a high calcium content is related to low excitability.

Potassium. Potassium concentration is inversely related to a high calcium content, directly related to a low pH and consequent low excitability.

The Psychological Threshold. The psychological threshold is usually defined as the smallest stimulus which will result in an *observed* reaction. Two types of threshold are customarily distinguished: (1) an *absolute* threshold and (2) a *differential* threshold. The psychological threshold is determined from analysis of the reactions of the organism. This analysis is most frequently based on the *introspective* reports of the subject. Thresholds have also been determined through conditioning experiments; the lowest stimulus intensity, or the smallest difference in intensity, which will serve as a substitute for the unconditioned stimulus is a threshold.

ABSOLUTE THRESHOLDS. The absolute threshold is usually defined as the smallest stimulus intensity which will be judged present on 50 per cent of the trials (75 per cent is sometimes established as the standard). Following are two frequently used methods for determination of the absolute threshold.

The Method of Minimal Changes. Also known as the *method of limits,* the method of minimal changes involves (1) introduction of a subthreshold stimulus which is gradually increased in intensity until the subject reports his awareness of the stimulus, and (2) introduction of a suprathreshold stimulus which is gradually decreased in intensity until the subject fails to report awareness. Numerous trials are given, and an ascending and a descending threshold are obtained. Frequently, a single threshold is obtained by averaging the results for all the individual trial thresholds.

The Method of Constant Stimuli. The method of constant stimuli involves introduction of a number of fixed (constant) stimuli which bracket the probable threshold. The subject identifies as present those stimulations of which he is aware, obviously indicating by omission those of which he is unaware. The stimulus value reacted to 50 per cent (sometimes 75 per cent) of the time is the absolute threshold. Since the fixed stimuli represent a limited number of values, the observed data must frequently be treated mathematically in order to estimate the threshold.

DIFFERENTIAL THRESHOLDS. In everyday life the organism is much more concerned with differential thresholds than with ab-

solute thresholds. The subthreshold stimulus does not obtrude
upon awareness, though it has been shown through conditioning
experiments and through situations which required guessing that
the threshold may be considerably lower than that which is
found under conditions such as those described in the preceding
paragraphs. Suprathreshold stimuli may appear equal or different along one or more dimensions of sensitivity. But the differential threshold is the stimulus difference, along whatever dimension or dimensions, which will be detected on 50 per cent
(sometimes 75 per cent) of the trials.

The Method of Minimal Changes. The presentation of a stimulus with two values constitutes the only difference between the
use of this method in determining the differential threshold and
its use in determining absolute thresholds. The difference between these two values is increased and decreased until the subject arrives at a point of change in judgment. The average of
several such determinations defines the differential threshold for
the subject. It is the amount of change in stimulus which represents a *just noticeable difference* (j.n.d.).

The Method of Constant Stimulus Differences. The method of
constant stimulus differences involves introduction of a number
of fixed stimulus differences which bracket the probable differential threshold. The differences may involve use of one standard
stimulus and one variable stimulus. The subject is presented
with both stimuli and asked to make judgments of greater, lesser,
or (in some instances) equal.

The Method of Average Error. The method of average error
involves introduction of a fixed standard stimulus and a variable
stimulus *which the subject controls.* The subject adjusts the variable stimulus until it appears to coincide with the standard. The
average error made in a number of settings indicates the approximation of equality which the subject is capable of making. The
standard deviation of the distribution of the subject's judgments
affords an indication of his precision.

JUDGMENT OF INTERVALS. A variant of differential threshold determination, but still related to the problem of judging stimulus
values, is the judgment of intervals. The subject may be given
two fixed stimuli and one variable stimulus, and then asked to
adjust the variable stimulus until it is midway between the two
fixed stimuli. He may be given one fixed and one variable stimu-

lus, and asked to adjust the variable stimulus until it is twice the value of the fixed stimulus. Or, he may be given a large number of stimuli and asked to grade them into equal-appearing intervals.

The Weber-Fechner Function. There is a positive correlation between the physical magnitude of the stimulus situation and the psychological interpretation of the magnitude. Weber (1834) and Fechner (1860) believed that this relationship could be expressed as a constant, relatively unvarying within the limits imposed by individual differences and varying environmental situations. In general, as psychological judgment of magnitude increased arithmetically, the stimulus intensity was increased geometrically. The equation is as follows: $S = K \log R$.

This equation is now known to hold only for the middle range of intensities. For intensities near the absolute threshold, sensitivity is lessened, possibly because of oscillation in the relatively small number of neurons excited.

The Weber-Fechner function has been used to compare the relative sensitivity of the various senses. Though some difficulties are encountered in selecting representative values, and specific environmental conditions exert marked effects, it still seems evident that there are large differences in the sensitivity of the various senses. Deep pressure and visual sensitivity have much lower Weber ratios than do light pressure, hearing, taste, and smell.

ATTRIBUTES OF SENSATION

A stimulus, and the resulting sensation, may vary along one or more of several *dimensions*. These possible dimensions constitute the *attributes of sensation*. Four such attributes are generally considered common to all sense modalities— (1) *quality*, (2) *intensity* (3) *extensity*, and (4) *duration*. Additional attributes are frequently found associated with particular sense modalities. The original conception of these attributes postulated that each was an independent entity which could vary while other attributes of the sensation remained constant. This theory is only partially upheld.

Quality. Quality is the name given to what is sensed. It is the hue of a visual sensitivity; the pitch of an auditory sensitivity; the bitter, salt, etc. of a gustatory sensitivity; the fragrant,

burned, etc. of an olfactory sensitivity, or the pressure, temperature, etc. of a cutaneous sensitivity.

Intensity. The magnitude of the sensation is its intensity. As
pointed out in the previous discussion of thresholds, the magnitude of the sensation is related to the energy of the stimulus. Intensity is loudness, brightness, weight, sharpness, concentration,
and so on.

Extensity. Extensity is a spatial characteristic. Changes in size,
distance, and location are extensity cues. Spatial awareness is
primarily visual, auditory, and tactual.

Duration. Duration is a temporal characteristic. It is a function
of the time that a given quality exists. A succession of stimulations with very short temporal separations (less than 750 milliseconds as a maximum) results in fusion and awareness of one
continuous stimulation. If the succession is separated by somewhat longer intervals, both the stimulus interval and the unfilled time take on the characteristic of duration.

ATTENTION TO STIMULATION

Determination of thresholds and attributes of sensations is usually carried out under conditions of rigid environmental control
in which distracting or confounding stimuli are held to a minimum. This is virtually opposed to normal everyday activity. A
multitude of stimuli, well above threshold level if taken individually, are constantly present. Yet, many of these seem to be
ignored completely and to affect our conscious activities only
when they "gain attention." The difference between the focus of
attention and the surrounding background is so omnipresent that
a dimension of *clearness* is sometimes included in discussions of
the attributes of sensation.

Reaction is a selective process. Attention is the set, or attitude,
which is the most important aspect of the selective process.

Adjustments toward Attention. Attention is characterized by
several adjustments of the organism itself.

RECEPTOR ADJUSTMENTS. The organism when set to receive a
stimulus exhibits a posture which represents the receptors in
the most favorable position. The eyes are directed toward the
source, or probable source, of a visual stimulus. The head is
turned to get the most direct auditory stimulus. Substances are

moved about over the tongue to stimulate more taste buds. The receptor organs themselves adjust. The pupil of the eye dilates under conditions of low illumination or contracts with high illumination. The curvature of the lens changes as the distance between the viewed object and the eye is changed.

MUSCLE TENSION ADJUSTMENTS. General neuromuscular activity is involved in all attending. Under conditions of heightened attention, such as that required when distractions are present, this muscular tension may become quite marked. Measurements of muscular tension made under such conditions indicate that the heightened attention is frequently associated with an increase in muscle tension (Morgan, 1916; Freeman, 1931; Katzell, 1942).

CENTRAL NERVOUS SYSTEM ADJUSTMENTS. Experiments involving an identical response to either of two different sensations, e.g., vision and hearing, suggest that a set may be retained which will facilitate or inhibit attention. Sets established during hypnosis may completely inhibit, exaggerate, or displace attention.

Varieties of Attention. Attention is sometimes classified as (1) *involuntary,* (2) *voluntary,* and (3) *habitual.*

Extremely intense stimuli, or quite unexpected stimuli, are likely to receive involuntary attention despite the completeness of the previously existing set of the organism.

On the other hand, a large portion of attention is voluntary or habitual. The dividing line is often difficult to ascertain. In familiar situations most of our sets are habitual. This merely means that our sets are continuing rather than abruptly assumed. They are clearly related to drives, interests, attitudes, and other factors which control behavior. Voluntary attention is a set related to a less frequently recurring need. This departure from the habitual may be due to the "distance" of the immediate situation from the goals of the individual. An example of the voluntary type is attention to advertisements for watches because of impending Christmas gift problems. An example of the habitual type is attendance at, and attention to, a lecture in chemistry because it contributes to a goal of becoming an erudite person, rather than because of a highly developed interest in chemistry.

The relationship of attention and motivation should be obvious. In Chapter 13 additional aspects are discussed.

Determiners of Attention. Within the framework discussed above there are numerous rather specific determiners of attention. Objects and events emerge from their surroundings because of certain characteristics.

CHANGE. Any change in the stimulus situation is likely to gain attention—loud to soft, red to green, hot to cold, going to stopped, stopped to going, and so on.

SIZE, MAGNITUDE, INTENSITY. Other things being equal, stimuli of greater magnitude are more likely to gain attention than are stimuli of lesser magnitude.

DIFFERENCE OR NOVELTY. The unexpected is very effective in gaining attention. The white cow stands out in a herd of otherwise black ones.

REPETITION. A recurring stimulus has more attention-getting value than a constant stimulus of the same magnitude. However, if the repetition continues over a long period of time it may develop a continuity of its own and lose effectiveness.

BASIC DRIVES. The stimulus most closely related to an organic need is likely to be highly potent. Hungry individuals are extremely sensitive to restaurants, cooking odors, and things of this type.

SOCIAL SUGGESTION. The influence of other persons on attention ranges from specific comments to "Look there!" (with perhaps the added stimulus of a pointing finger) or to such a very general stimulus as staring toward the sky or running for a bus.

INTERESTS. As indicated earlier, what is attended to is greatly influenced by interests. As will be shown in greater detail later, the factor of interest is of paramount importance in determining the meaning which will be attached to the stimulus.

Fluctuations of Attention. There are two aspects of fluctuation: (1) changes in the efficiency of response, and (2) shifts from one response to another. A stimulus which is barely perceptible is found to oscillate in attention, being present at one instant and not present the next. Experimental evidence suggests that the efficiency of the whole organism plays a very important part in this phenomenon.

Shifts of attention are strikingly illustrated in the oscillations of ambiguous figures. Steady attention to such a figure results in appearance of one figure, then the other. The oscillation occurs without volition of the observer though there is some evidence that control in the direction of bringing about the shift is possible.

There seems to be little relation between the special type of shifting referred to above and the "ordinary shifting of attention" observed in everyday life. Ordinary shifting of attention seems merely to be the change in focus from the peripheral to central sensitivity, from unclearness to clearness, or, as the Gestaltists would put it, from ground to figure. These alternations

 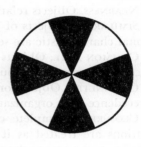

FIG. 8. Ambiguous figures. One moment you see a white figure on a black ground and then with no apparent effort on your part it shifts to a black figure on a white ground.

may be accomplished at extremely rapid rates. Apparent simultaneous performance of two quite different activities is often accomplished by such alternation. However, such performances involve the integration of several elements into a single co-ordinated task.

Adaptation. The experience of adaptation is common to all senses, with the probable exception of hearing. Under conditions of continued constant stimulation, sensitivity grows less and less until the stimulus does not seem to exist. There are wide differences among the various senses in the rate of adaptation.

THE CONSTRUCTS OF PERCEPTION

The individual *perceives* stimulations as meaningful objects and events, not as energy changes. The stimulation is perceived as a locomotive whistle, a pot of brewing coffee, a wall, or whatever is appropriate from the individual's experience. If the stimulation is outside his experience, it is treated as nearly as possible like similar situations within the range of his experience.

Primary Organizational Tendencies. Individuals can respond to large constellations of stimuli as if only one stimulus existed, if these can be organized into a meaningful whole. Though most organizational tendencies are the outgrowth of experience, some basic principles seem to operate independently of learning or set. These were first summarized by Wertheimer (1923), particularly with respect to visual stimulation. The most important of these follow.

NEARNESS. Objects relatively close together are seen as a group.

SIMILARITY. Objects of the same color, shape, or other dimensional characteristic are seen as a group.

COMMON FATE. Objects moving simultaneously in the same direction are seen as a group.

CONTINUITY. Objects organized for continuity of pattern take precedence over organizations which change direction.

CLOSURE. Incomplete objects which suggest complete organizations are treated as if they were actually complete, less the missing parts, rather than as partial groupings sufficient in themselves.

All these factors can be combined or contrasted to secure stronger or weaker organizations.

Grouping occurs in senses other than vision. Auditory stimuli are grouped into rhythms. Successive stimulation of relatively contiguous points on the skin is interpreted as movement.

The Influence of Habit and Learning. Perceptions are in terms of expectancies. These expectancies develop throughout life and most of them operate without recognition of them by the individual.

FIGURE AND GROUND. The objects of perception are primarily figures, in the sense that they are separated from the ground by having a different quality, intensity, extensity, or duration, or a specific combination of all of these.

CO-OPERATION OF THE SENSES. Different sensitivities are integrated, particularly from past experience. A steel ball is perceived as heavy, whereas a rubber one is "seen" as relatively light. Velvet is "seen" as soft and smooth, and perhaps even sensual, though the only immediate stimulus is the energy change involved in the reflected light stimulating the receptor cells in the retina.

CONSTANCY PHENOMENA. An object is correctly perceived as to size or intensity within a wide range of actual stimulus variation. An automobile seen at a distance of 100 yards does not appear smaller than one seen at 20 yards, even though there is a great disparity in the size of the retinal image. A shout heard from afar is still recognized as a shout instead of a whisper, even though the actual stimulus intensity may be quite low by the time the auditory mechanism is stimulated. A lawn is seen as the same shade of green, even though part of it lies in bright sunshine and part in shadow.

SET AND SUGGESTION. The momentary set of the individual may greatly influence the perception. This situation is furthered by the great use of symbols in describing perceptions. An ambiguous figure described as resembling some familiar object is later reproduced in imagery to resemble the object much more nearly than did the original ambiguous figure (Carmichael, Hogan, and Walter, 1932).

REDINTEGRATION. A portion of the originally effective stimulus pattern may come to be quite as effective as the total. Sight of a man's hand means that the whole man is present. The barking of a dog in the next room is quite sufficient for identification of the whole dog.

SYMBOLIC FACTORS. Perception may become a matter of reacting appropriately to some recognized relationship of sign-and-thing-signified. In man, the use of symbols, primarily words, has become the highest order of perception.

Memories, Images, and Ideas. Recalled perceptions are not correlated with environmental stimulation (when checked with introspective reports of others). There may be environmental changes which are causative of the recalled sensitivity, but the recalled sensitivity itself is largely the conscious trace (memory, image, or idea) left by previous experience.

Ideation is awareness in which recalled sensitivity predominates to the general exclusion of the here-and-now perceptions. However, the ideation is generally related to the problems of the immediate environmental situation.

Imagination refers to recalled sensitivities with little exact relation of configuration or organization to the immediate environmental situation.

Recalled sensitivities may be classified in the same ways as immediate sensitivities. They do not exist independently of immediate sensitivities. Even the hallucination, which is far removed from correlation with environmental stimulation, consists of some immediate sensitivities. The controlling factor is the amount of integration of the recalled and the immediate sensitivities.

INDIVIDUAL DIFFERENCES. There are wider differences among individuals in recalled sensitivities than there are in immediate sensitivities. Individuals also vary widely in the senses through which they can express recalled sensitivities.

DIMENSIONS OF RECALLED SENSITIVITIES. The dimensions (attributes) of recalled sensitivities are exactly the same as those of the immediate sensitivities. The difference between the immediate and the recalled is purely one of degree of clearness of the dimensions. Extensity and intensity are the ones to be noted particularly in this connection. Of special interest is the *eidetic image,* a recalled sensitivity of exceptional clearness. Eidetic images are reported more frequently in young people but occasionally are reported in adults.

FORMS OF RECALLED SENSITIVITIES. Recalled sensitivities exist in two forms: (1) *concrete,* in which the sensitivity is of the object, and (2) *verbal,* in which the sensitivity takes the form of the word or symbol which represents the object. Recalled sensitivities tend to become more and more verbal with increasing age, and the form that these recalls take is a product of experience.

COMBINATIONS OF RECALLED SENSITIVITIES. Observation and report of recalled sensitivities indicate that a variety of combinations are used by different individuals. This is particularly true of adults. Outstanding combinations are the following: visual, auditory, and verbal-motor; visual and verbal-motor; verbal-auditory and verbal-motor; verbal-motor.

INTEGRATION IN AWARENESS

Awareness integrates into patterns, configurations, or units (called "wholes" by some authors). Both immediate sensitivities and recalled sensitivities are awarenesses of relationships. These relationships exist in two dimensions: (1) *space* and (2) *time*. All the senses contribute to orientation in space and time, but to highly differing degrees with respect to particular kinds of energy changes in the environment. The contributions of the various senses will be discussed in the chapters relating to those senses.

The differences in integration among individuals exist in all aspects of adjustment—motivation, learning, emotional behavior. The development and breakdown of sequences of immediate and recalled sensitivities will be the principal subject matter of chapters covering these aspects of behavior.

SUMMARY

Specialized receptor cells are sensitive to certain kinds of energy changes in the environment. Each cell has a threshold, and energy changes less than this threshold value are not capable of exciting the neuron. There is a difference between the neurophysical threshold and the psychological threshold. The proper functioning of higher organisms is much more dependent upon differential thresholds, the ability to detect differences in stimuli of the same kind, than upon absolute thresholds, the ability to detect existence of a stimulus.

A stimulus, and the resulting sensation, may vary in quality, intensity, extensity, and duration. Whether we attend to a stimulus or not depends upon its clearness, a function of the amount of separation of figure and ground. Most distinguishing characteristics are a product of the individual's experience, but there are a number of rather specific determiners which seem to operate without learning.

The basic difference between the recalled sensitivities (such as memories, images, and ideas) is the clearness which accompanies these sensitivities as reported.

6

Vision and Visual Phenomena

Man's orientation to his environment is generally considered to be most highly dependent on the sense of vision. A wide variety of experiments suggests that when there is a conflict between the senses, the perceptions afforded through use of the visual apparatus are most likely to be trusted.

The principal visual functions are: (1) determination of *visual brightness*, (2) determination of *color*, and (3) perception of *form and space*.

THE VISUAL STIMULUS

The sensitive receptor cells of the eye are stimulated by *radiant energy*. Only a very small portion of existing radiant energy is effective for visual stimulation. It is conventional to speak of this energy as wavelike in motion, though modern physicists postulate the added existence of a corpuscular structure, embodied in the minute bundle of energy called the *quantum*.

Composition of Light. The various kinds of light may be characterized as to *wave length* (a factor of the frequency of vibrations), and as to *intensity* (a factor of the amplitude of the vibrations). Most visual stimuli consist of many different wave lengths of light, *heterogeneous* light. Light composed of energy with the same wave length, *homogeneous* light, may be obtained by passing a beam of heterogeneous light through a prism or by use of carefully constructed filters (usually Wratten filters) which stop passage of all but the desired wave length.

The wave lengths to which the human eye is sensitive range from about 760–390 mμ (millimicrons, millionths of a millimeter from crest to crest of the wave).

Within the visible range, different wave lengths give rise to different color perceptions in the vision of the normal human being. The relation of color quality and wave lengths is shown below. (After Warren, *Dictionary*, p. 316.)

COLOR QUALITY	WAVE LENGTH $(m\mu)$
Red	760–647
Orange	647–588
Yellow	588–550
Green	550–492
Blue	492–433
Violet	433–390

There is no clearly definable point of separation between these color qualities. They shade imperceptibly from one into another.

Measurement of Light Intensity. Several different measures of light intensity are employed.

INTENSITY OF THE LIGHT SOURCE. The most commonly used measure of intensity of the light source is the *international candle*. This is defined as the total light emitted by a standard candle of carefully prescribed composition and dimensions.

ILLUMINATION OF AN OBJECT. The *foot-candle* (sometimes the *meter-candle*) is used to measure illumination. A foot-candle is the amount of light falling on one square foot of area placed at a distance of one foot from an international candle.

BRIGHTNESS OF AN OBJECT. The *millilambert* is used as a measure of light reflected from an object, i.e., brightness. A millilambert is the light reflected by a perfectly diffusing and reflecting surface one foot square and illuminated by 0.93 foot-candle.

BRIGHTNESS OF THE RETINAL IMAGE. The *photon* is the unit of measure of the intensity of light on the retina. Since the size of the pupil varies with intensity of the external stimulation, a correction is necessary for determination of retinal stimulation. A photon is a stimulus intensity with a brightness of one tenth of a millilambert acting on a pupillary area of one square millimeter.

THE VISUAL APPARATUS

The specialized sensitive structure for vision is the *retina* of the eye, one of the inner tissues of the eyeball. Reception in the retina is considered to be a chemical process involving breakdown and regeneration of photosensitive substances in the sensitive cells, both rods and cones. The substance of the rods, *rhodopsin* (sometimes referred to in earlier texts as *visual purple*), has been isolated and studied in considerable detail. Much less is known about *iodopsin,* the substance of the cones.

Accessory Apparatus. Extensive accessory apparatus assists in focalizing light waves upon the most sensitive, central part of the retina. Light waves travel inward through (1) the *cornea,* (2) the *aqueous humor* (a transparent liquid holding the outer

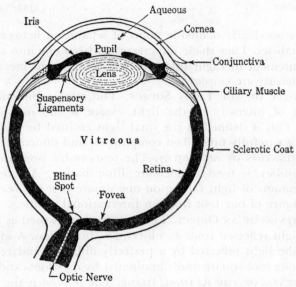

FIG. 9. Cross-section of the eye showing major structures.

part of the eye in place), (3) the *lens* (which is accommodated by the action of *ciliary muscles* to focus light from different distances on the retina), and (4) the *vitreous humor* (a transparent supporting liquid), to reach the *retina* (an inner layer of nerve cells surrounded by the *choroid* and *sclerotic* coats). The choroid is opaque and is differentiated ventrally as the *iris.* The iris is a muscle which contracts and expands under different intensities of light stimulation to form the pupillary opening. Six muscles operate to move the eyeballs in their sockets so that there is convergence of the two eyes upon environmental stimuli.

The Retina. The details of retinal organization are necessary to understanding of the visual process. The retina of the eye is differentiated by histologists into ten layers. Three of these are of particular importance: (1) the sensitive cells called *rods* and *cones*, (2) *bipolar neurons*, and (3) the *ganglion cells*.

RODS AND CONES. There are about 137,000,000 rods and cones in the retina of each eye (Krause), and they vary in diameter from 0.002 to 0.006 mm. There are many more rods than cones. The cones are concentrated toward the center of the retina (the *fovea centralis*), and fewer cones and more rods are found as the periphery of the retina is approached. Cones are most sensitive to color and to light of normal intensity. Rods are sensitive only to light, and they are most sensitive to light stimuli of low intensities. The rods and cones constitute two distinct types of receptor cells, but the interconnections of the rods and cones with bipolar and other cells suggest that they do not form two distinct visual systems.

BIPOLAR CELLS. The bipolar neurons collect impulses from one or a number of rods and cones, and a given rod or cone may be connected with several bipolar neurons. In the *fovea centralis* there is one-to-one correspondence between cones and bipolar cells. In the periphery there may be as many as 200 rods connected with one bipolar cell.

GANGLION CELLS. The ganglion cells collect from the bipolar neurons, though several intermediate processes such as the *horizontal* and *amacrine* cells may serve to spread excitation still further from point-to-point correspondence with the rods and cones stimulated.

FOVEA CENTRALIS. Located approximately in the center of the retinal area is a small depression in which receptor cells, cones only, are crowded very closely together. This area is known as the *fovea centralis*. Under normal conditions fixation of an object to obtain maximum visibility results in localization of the retinal image on the *fovea centralis*.

THE BLIND SPOT. The axons of the ganglion cells run along the ventral layer of the retina and finally leave the retina as the *optic nerve*. At this point on the retina, the blind spot (discovered by Mariotte in 1668), there are no rods or cones.

A point frequently overlooked in consideration of the light energy reaching the sensitive rods and cones is the fact that these rods and cones comprise the innermost layer of the retina. Thus, the bipolar neurons, the ganglion cells, and all the other processes are *between the light source and the sensitive cells.*

The Central Visual System. The two optic nerves meet in the *optic chiasma* at the base of the brain, just anterior to the stalk of the pituitary body. In mammals the fibers from the lateral side of the retinas do not cross and are represented in the same hemisphere of the brain. The fibers from the medial side of the retinas do cross and so are represented on opposite sides of the brain. This differentiation of representation furnishes protection against injuries. It also occasions anomalies of vision called *hemianopsias,* in which only a portion of the visual field is represented. The optic nerve fibers end in subcortical centers—the *lateral geniculate bodies,* the *superior colliculi,* and the *pretectal nuclei.* Elementary aspects of vision may be controlled by these subcortical centers but, in man and the other higher mammals, the more complex visual functions depend upon cortical bodies. The *striate area* of the occipital lobe is the most important in this connection.

VISUAL PHENOMENA

Everyday visual experience is always in terms of complex perceptual organizations, i.e., the individual sees objects, events, and interrelationships. It is a difficult task for the average individual to resolve these phenomena into such elementary sensations as color and brightness and into considerations of simple spatial and temporal relations. The attributes of vision are inferred from laboratory studies. They are frequently called quality, intensity, extensity, and duration. In 1672 Newton presented the evidence that a beam of white light could be refracted into the component light waves of the visible spectrum. Yet, as late as 1810, Goethe argued that such a finding was patently absurd.

Normal human beings experience the different qualitative visual attributes of *hue, brightness,* and *saturation.* The *hues* are the reds, greens, blues, and other colors. *Brightness* is related to the intensity of the stimulus, generally the amount of illumination, but it is also dependent upon other characteristics. It is described as both a qualitative and a quantitative attribute of intensity. Psychologically, it is the amount of black and white sensed. *Saturation* refers to the purity of the hue, its freedom from other hues and from black and white. The interrelations of these three characteristics give rise to a vast number of color sensitivities, variously estimated as being from 35,000 to 300,000.

Visual stimuli are usually dichotomized into *chromatic* (colored) and *achromatic* (uncolored). Both may vary in brightness. These differences in brightness are sufficient for most visual discriminations; witness the ability of the color-blind to behave normally with respect to most environmental stimuli, or the ability to interpret black and white photographs.

Hue, brightness, and saturation factors also contribute markedly to estimates of distance, size, and movement, though in relatively complex combination with many other cues.

COLOR

Color is a psychological function based on some form of differential reception of the various wave lengths of the visible spectrum. The exact nature of this function is not known, but the relationships between stimulus manipulation and visual perception have been thoroughly studied. Almost all these relationships have been determined introspectively, since no one else can observe the stimulus-response pattern.

The Color Pyramid. The interrelationships of hue, brightness, and saturation are frequently shown schematically by a color solid in which hues are arranged around the horizontal axis in a parallelogram (some authors object to these breaks in an apparent continuum and use a circle), brightness is organized on the vertical axis, and saturation is represented on the radii from the vertical axis. Red, yellow, green, and blue are placed on what amounts to four corners. These four, along with black, white, and sometimes gray, are frequently called unique or unitary colors since they do not resemble any other color and all other colors appear to be mixtures of these.

On the surfaces and within this pyramid can be represented all color sensitivities. The pyramid is not equilateral since different wave lengths do not evoke equal subjective brightnesses at the same objective intensities of illumination. See Fig. 10.

Color Mixture. Homogeneous light results in a specific hue if the intensity is sufficient to stimulate the color receptors. However, the identical hue can also be secured from mixture of other

wave lengths (Newton, 1704). (It must be noted that this is mixture of lights, quite different from the mixture of pigments such
as those used by a painter.)

Three principal laws of color mixture exist: (1) For every
color there is a *complementary* (*antagonistic* or *opposite*) color
which produces a sensitivity of gray if the two are mixed in the
proper proportions, or produces a color sensitivity of lowered
degree of saturation and of the hue of the stronger component if
mixed in any other proportions. (2) The mixture of any two

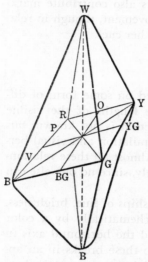

FIG. 10. Titchener's color pyramid (after
Titchener, *Textbook*, 1910) representing
graphically the qualitative relationships of
visual hues, saturations, and brightnesses.
The double pyramid shows two mutually
related systems of sensitivities: a system of
light sensitivities and one of color sensitivities. Hue is color-tone. Black and white are
hues, as are all the colors. Saturation is the
variable representing the degree of the hue.
The light system introduces the variable of
brightness into the color series. The variables of saturation and brightness are reduced to one variable in the consideration of
the light series. The R–Y–G–B parallelogram
can be represented with varying degrees of
brightness at any point between black and
white. Neutral gray (brain gray) is represented at the midpoint, and black has many
undistinguishable hues.

colors which are not complementary produces a color sensitivity
of intermediate hue. This hue varies with the relative amounts
of the two component colors, and the saturation varies with their
nearness or remoteness to gray. (3) If two color mixtures arouse
the same visual sensitivity, a mixture of these mixtures will also
arouse the same color sensitivity.

Appearance of Color. Most colors noted in everyday life are
due to reflected light waves from objects which have absorbed all
the light waves except those required to produce the particular
color sensitivity. This mode of appearance is called *surface color*
(Katz, 1911; Martin, 1922). Color also appears in other ways:
(1) *expanse*, *free*, or *film* color, such as the blue of the open sky
when seen without contrasting horizon effects, or a color seen
through a peephole or reduction screen; (2) a *bulky* color, such

as that of a transparent colored object or a colored object viewed through fog or mist; (3) a *luminous* or *glowing* color, such as that given by a flame or a neon sign; and (4) a *lustrous* color, such as that of silk or metallic objects whose reflecting surfaces are highly regular.

Afterimages. The perception of the visual stimulus does not disappear immediately upon removal of the stimulus. Instead, afterimages of two sorts appear: (1) *positive afterimages* in which the color resembles the original color, and (2) *negative afterimages* in which the color is the complementary of the original.

In everyday visual experience afterimages go unnoticed because their persistence is related to the intensity and duration of the original stimulation, neither of which is normally sufficient to excite pronounced afterimages.

Positive afterimages are most noticeable when a bright stimulus is followed by a relatively dark afterfield. The trail of light following the "falling star" is mostly afterimage.

Most persons have experienced the spots before the eyes which come after looking directly at the sun or other source of bright light. These are negative afterimages. They are the direct result of adaptation. The area stimulated has become less sensitive to the wave lengths of light involved in the original stimulus and is relatively more sensitive to other wave lengths in the succeeding stimulus situation.

Contrast Effects. The color stimulus appears to change hue if it is contrasted with another color. The change in hue is always in the direction of the complement of the surrounding color. Thus, a red stimulus surrounded by blue will take on a yellowish tinge. A red stimulus surrounded by green will appear redder. The contrast effect is maximal when the brightness of the stimulus and its surrounding is equal. The contrast effect is directly related to the saturation of the two colors when the brightnesses are equal.

Binocular Rivalry and Fusion. When the two eyes are individually stimulated by different colors, such as are afforded by placing different-colored patches on the two sides of a stereoscope, a binocular rivalry usually results. First one color is seen and then the other. Conscious effort has no effect; the shift occurs without warning. Differential brightness of the two colors, pres-

ence of figures, and movement all contribute to the differences
in the amount of time each field is dominant, but the shift still
occurs.

Under certain rather restricted conditions, and in some individuals, presentation of different colors to the two eyes results in
fusion (Hecht, 1928). Where this fusion is reported, it is of the
nature demanded by the laws of color mixture.

Retinal Color Zones. All colors tend to become gray as the
point of stimulation is moved from the *fovea centralis* toward
the periphery of the eye. Many investigators have reported centrally located zones as follows: (1) a restricted area where all
colors are seen, (2) a less restricted area in which blue and yellow may be seen, but in which red and green appear as blue or
yellow, or in some instances gray, and (3) the remainder of the
visual field in which only gray is seen, with this gray often appearing as movement rather than as color. It should be noted
that the pairs of colors involved in the color zones are complementary colors.

The boundaries of the color zones are not fixed. With increased intensity of stimulus, greater areas of the retina appear
to be responsive to each color. Ferree and Rand (1919) even
found changes in the relative positions of the four color zones
with changes in the energy level of the stimulus.

Color Blindness. Though color blindness as a phenomenon
is commonly recognized today, largely because of the publicity
given by the requirements of the armed forces, it was not until
1794 that a case was described in detail (Dalton).

Color blindness is almost exclusively a male disfunction, following approximately a sex-linked form of inheritance.

Most color deficiencies involve only red and green. A few cases
have been reported in which the only colors seen were black,
gray, and white.

Persons with partial color blindness are called *dichromats*
(König and Dieterici, 1886) as they can match the entire spectrum with combinations of a proper two colors, whereas normal
individuals (*trichromats*) require three. The dichromats are further divisible into *deuteranopes* and *protanopes* (von Kries,
1896). Deuteranopes see reds as poor yellows and greens as grays,
but the relative brightness of the spectral colors is unchanged.
Protanopes have the reds missing or see them as black, and the

greens appear as whitish grays. The relative brightness of the spectral colors is shifted toward the short wave lengths. (This shift in brightness appears to be related to *photopic* and *scotopic* vision, a point to be discussed in the next section.)

Color weakness, rather than color blindness, is also quite in evidence. This weakness may involve diminished sensitivity to green *or* to red (Rayleigh, 1881; Hayes, 1911; Terman, 1929).

Theories of Color Vision. Three principal theories of color vision have been advanced. Chronologically, these are: Young-Helmholtz (1852), Hering (1874), and Ladd-Franklin (1892). None of the three satisfactorily explains all the phenomena of color vision. The Young-Helmholtz theory has the widest acceptance today. The Hering theory best satisfies the laws of color mixture.

Young-Helmholtz Theory. In 1801 Thomas Young postulated a three-fiber hypothesis of retinal action, utilizing Newton's principles of color mixture to explain color perception. However, it was not until Helmholtz virtually rediscovered the theory in 1852 that the hypothesis was given much credence.

The Young-Helmholtz theory postulates three different photoreceptor processes, one maximally sensitive to the wave lengths commonly known as red, one to green, and one to blue (sometimes violet). Proper mixture of these three can be shown to give the entire spectrum. One of the most often used arguments against the theory is the lack of adequate explanation of the psychologically unitary yellow in negative afterimages and the position of yellow in retinal color zones. Hecht (1928) reported consistent results in securing binocular yellow from stimulation of one eye with green and one with red, but the conditions involved were highly restricting.

Hering Theory. Taking as a point of departure the seemingly natural transitions from red to yellow to green to blue, with the impossibility of securing a reddish green or a yellowish blue, Hering proposed three visual substances in the retina. Each of these three was held to be capable of both *anabolic* and *catabolic* processes. Thus a white-black substance would result in a perception of white while breaking down and of black while building up, a yellow-blue substance would result in yellow while breaking down and in blue while building up, and a red-green substance would result in red while breaking down and in green while building up. All other colors result from mixtures of these processes. The phenomena of color blindness, negative afterimages, and retinal color zones are all easily explained with the Hering theory. The appearance of neutral gray is very difficult to explain by this theory, as is the central fusion of red and green into yellow.

LADD-FRANKLIN THEORY. In 1892 Christine Ladd-Franklin postulated an evolutionary, or genetic, development of color sensitivity. According to this theory, the primitive visual sensitivity is the black-white of achromatic vision. White sensitivity became differentiated into yellow-blue vision. The yellow, in turn, became differentiated into red-green vision. The basis of color sensation was postulated as a retinal color molecule whose product of decomposition stimulated the nerves selectively. Color blindness, retinal color zones, and chromatic afterimages are easily explained by this theory. But, as in the Hering theory, the summation of red and green presented binocularly and fused as yellow is difficult to explain in terms of dual processes in the retina.

VISUAL BRIGHTNESS

Differences in illumination are sufficient stimuli for determination of a great many visual phenomena.

Visual brightness is related to stimulus intensity, but it also depends upon other aspects of the stimulus situation such as the wave length, time of presentation, size or shape of the stimulus, and previous conditions of illumination of the eye. Two principal theories are put forth for explanation of visual brightness phenomena. The *photochemical theory* (Hecht) postulates changes of photosensitive materials in the retina as the principal basis of explanation. The *statistical theory* (Crozier), while not denying chemical changes, postulates changes in number and frequency of neural impulses as the primary determiner of visual experience.

Adaptation Effects and Perceived Brightness. The threshold for stimulation of the visual receptors varies according to the intensity of the stimulus light to which the organism is subjected, though this is not a linear relationship. This threshold is greatly affected by a process of adaptation. Two kinds of adaptation occur in the retina: (1) light adaptation and (2) dark adaptation.

LIGHT ADAPTATION. When one leaves a dimly lit place or turns on a light in the middle of the night, a dazzle effect is produced. In a very short time the dazzle disappears. The eye has become light-adapted. The dazzle effect is accompanied by a sensation of pain if the change in light intensity is too great.

Light adaptation is a rapid process. The rods are rendered inactive by the bleaching of the photochemical substance rhodopsin (visual purple). The threshold of the cones is also raised by breakdown of the photochemical substance more rapidly than it can be replenished. As the cone threshold is raised, a point of equilibrium is reached and further light adaptation does not occur. This point of equilibrium is reached in about 90 seconds (Troland).

DARK ADAPTATION. The light-adapted eye recovers its sensitivity to low intensities of illumination in a very characteristic manner (Aubert, 1865). The increased sensitivity begins to appear rapidly and tapers off after about 10 minutes. This is the period of cone adaptation. Adaptation again increases in rate, tapers off, and is virtually complete after 30–45 minutes. This latter phase of adaptation is attributed to regeneration of rhodopsin in the rods.

At levels of illumination below the threshold of the cones, the ordinary line of regard which fixates objects on the *fovea centralis* must be shifted toward the periphery of the eye.

Effect of Wave Length. Visibility varies with the wave length of the light stimulus. Two curves are noted: (1) a *photopic* curve obtained under conditions of high illumination, and (2) a *scotopic* curve obtained under conditions of low illumination. The maximally effective wave length for photopic vision is 554 mμ; that for scotopic vision is 511 mμ (Hecht and Williams, 1922). The general nature of the phenomena was first mentioned by Purkinje (1825) as a shift in the relative brightness of colors with changes in the intensity of illumination.

Summation and Fusion Effects. Several summation effects are noted, both spatial and temporal.

EFFECT OF AREA. The larger the area of the retina stimulated, the lower the intensity for the light to be seen by the observer

(Pieron, 1920; Wald, 1938). The threshold for the same stimulus presented to both eyes simultaneously is lower than that for one eye (Crozier and Holloway, 1939).

FLICKER AND FUSION EFFECTS. An alternation of dark and light flashes is seen as a continuous light with a steady brightness at, and above, a certain frequency of alternation. The point of change is the *critical flicker frequency* (c.f.f.). In general, the brilliance of the apparently continuous light bears the same pro-

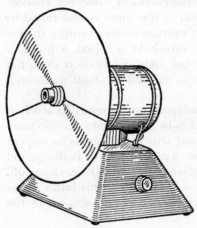

FIG. 11. Color wheel used to study c.f.f. and also to study color mixing. Discs slotted so they can be fitted together to present different proportions of black and white, or any two colors, are placed on the wheel. As rotation becomes rapid the two colors mix and only the color which represents the mixture of the two is seen.

portion to the actual brilliance of the light flash as the proportion of stimulus time is to total time (Talbot, 1834; Plateau, 1835).

The critical flicker frequency has no single value. Where light and dark periods of the cycle are held constant, c.f.f. varies as a function of the logarithm of the intensity (Ferry-Porter law). C.f.f. also increases with an increase in the area of the flickering field (Granit and Harper, 1930).

THE DUPLICITY THEORY

In 1894 von Kries brought together the known physiological and psychological data into the duplicity (duplexity) theory, stating that the rods and cones comprise two different functional types of receptors in the retina. Almost no other theory on sensitivity has so much clearly established factual data to support it, as follows.

Histological studies differentiate rods and cones by structure. Rods contain rhodopsin (visual purple) whereas the cones contain iodopsin and one or more unidentified substances. Rods function only under conditions of very low illumination, and cones are inactive under these same conditions. Stimulation of cones by appropriate light results in perception of color whereas rods give no such perception of color. Curves of brightness sensitivity have different maxima for rod and cone vision (scotopic and photopic curves).

THE PERCEPTION OF FORM AND SPACE

The world about us is filled with patterns, objects, and events, all in some relation, one with another. These visual stimuli are perceived as reasonably correct representations of the actual objects or events. These perceptions are dependent on both physiological and psychological cues.

Physical and Physiological Factors. The field of vision normally consists of a somewhat circular field in which a great many differences of brightness may be represented. This field is projected on the retina (through the cornea, lens, and supporting humors), forming a two-dimensional, cup-shaped image.

VISUAL ACUITY. In order for a stimulus to be visually effective within this field, resolution must be present. This is normally some form of two-point threshold, the minimal separation necessary for distinguishing disparate stimulation. The threshold varies with conditions of brightness. Under best conditions the average two-point threshold at the fovea subtends an angle of 60 seconds of arc. With this threshold separation taken as the normal, ratios in relation to distance are used as measures of near- and far-sightedness (myopia and hyperopia).

THE RETINAL IMAGE. In 1637 Descartes, using the eye of a bull, produced an image on a piece of thin paper placed in the position of the retina. It is doubtful that the image itself is so important as believed by the early experimenters and theorizers. However, the fact that numerous lawful relationships exist among the factors of retinal image is of paramount importance.

Clarity of the Retinal Image. The clearest image is cast on the center of the retina (the *fovea centralis*). This area is tightly packed with cones, each with its own bipolar cell. Contrastingly, in the periphery, many rods are likely to be connected with one bipolar cell.

Size of the Retinal Image. The linear size of the retinal image is inversely proportional to the distance from the object. Obviously, perception does not follow this law, and a tendency toward perceptual size constancy is evident.

Inversion of the Retinal Image. The retinal image is inverted with respect to the field represented by the image. This inversion occasions no difficulty in perception, as all relationships within the field are maintained. In fact, complete inversion of the visual field (making the retinal image "upright") is followed by a relatively rapid adjustment toward normal perception (Stratton, 1897; Ewert, 1930).

ACCOMMODATION. When the normal eye is focused on objects within a distance of 9 feet the lens must be accommodated, becoming bulged. When relaxed, the lens is nearly flat and is accommodated for distance vision. As the lens is accommodated to focus objects within the 9-foot distance, proprioceptive cues from the lens itself and from the ciliary muscles controlling accommodation may add to judgment of depth and distance. Experimentation is inconclusive at the present time.

BINOCULAR FACTORS. In human beings the two eyes are situated about $2\frac{1}{2}$ inches apart. The two eyes normally focus with a high degree of accuracy, providing three consistent cues of space sensitivity—*double stimulation, double images,* and *convergence.* However, beyond about 60 feet the lines of regard for both eyes are so nearly parallel that these cues are of little importance.

Double Stimulation. When the two eyes are fixated on the same object, two slightly different retinal images are formed (*retinal disparity*). The importance of the cues thus given is illustrated by use of the *stereoscope,* an instrument which presents to each eye independently the view which it would normally see in a three-dimensional scene (stereoscope invented by Wheatstone, 1838). An interesting corollary is provided by the *pseudoscope* (also Wheatstone, 1852), which reverses the images normally given each eye. Under these conditions objects appear in reversed relief so that nearer objects appear farther away and vice versa. However, familiar objects are not easily reversed by the perceiver.

Double Images. On both sides of the point of regard, relative to the position of the eye, double images are present in the visual field. These are normally disregarded in vision, but it is highly probable that they contribute to the perception of space. The existence of these double images can easily be demonstrated. If a finger is held vertically between some object and the eyes, the finger will be seen as double while the eyes are fixed on the more distant object, and the more distant object will be seen as double while the eyes are fixed on the finger. Closing one eye will indicate the image associated with each eye. It will also be noted that nearer objects are crossed and farther objects are uncrossed, while fixated objects do not appear to change position. The fixated object image falls on corresponding points of each retina; nonfixated objects fall on noncorresponding points. The *horopter* (Aguilonius, 1613) represents the locus of all points seen as single in the binocular field of vision. In the horizontal plane this is a circle.

Convergence. In order to fixate, the eyes must converge or diverge according to the distance of the object from the eye. The proprioceptive impulses from the six extrinsic muscles which control eye movements afford a cue for space perception. Since it is virtually impossible to eliminate other cues, the relative contribution of muscular torsion is difficult to ascertain.

Psychological Factors. A great number of the cues of form and space result from the retinal patterns themselves. Interpretation of form and space from these is largely learned and is likely to be quite persistent.

INTERPOSITION. If one object partially covers another, it is perceived as nearer.

LIGHT AND SHADE. Patterns of highlights and shadows suggest the character of the object. If the shadow is cast on the lower portion of the image, the object is considered as convex; if the shadow is on the upper portion, the object is considered as concave. In addition, shadows falling laterally to the object viewed frontally give further indications of form and depth.

APPARENT SIZE. Objects of known size appear nearer with larger retinal images. This is one of the most important cues since there are very few everyday visual scenes which do not include one or more very common objects.

CLEARNESS. Objects with texture appear nearer when the texture is clearer. Objects with sharp outlines appear nearer than objects with hazy outlines. Color plays an important part in this connection. The brightness of colors dissipates with increasing distance.

MOVEMENT. As the individual moves, faraway objects appear to move in the same direction; near objects move in the opposite direction.

Illusions. A special group of perceptual situations, usually studied in the psychological laboratory, are called *illusions*. These are situations in which the perception does not conform to established knowledge of the environment. The following are the most prominent of these.

SIZE ILLUSIONS. The size of the sensitivity is a function of the part of the retina stimulated, particularly as regards the fovea and the periphery. Objects stimulating the periphery appear larger than those stimulating the fovea.

AMBIGUOUS PERSPECTIVE ILLUSIONS. Where there are relatively few secondary cues of space or distance in a figure, the stimulus becomes equivocal, as in the reversible staircase illusion or in Titchener's water tank illusion where shadows are seen either as dents or protrusions according to the position of the picture.

AMBIGUOUS MEANING ILLUSIONS. Where spatial cues are present in a figure, but where there has been little or no past experience, the stimulus is equivocal. For example, Rubin's vase may be seen as a vase or as the faces of two persons.

VERTICAL-HORIZONTAL ILLUSIONS. Vertical lines appear longer than horizontal lines of the same length.

LINEAR ILLUSIONS. Linear surfaces are illusionary when angles are included in parallel lines, such as in the Müller-Lyer illusion and Poggendorf illusion.

FILLED AND UNFILLED SPACE ILLUSIONS. Filled areas appear greater in size than unfilled areas of equal size.

The appearance of the illusions has been one of the principal phenomenological studies of Gestalt psychology in the emphasis on "wholes" and "fields" as the basic characteristics of perceptions. Regardless of the point of view to which the conclusion is attached, ". . . it can be shown that many of the characteristic features of perception are added by the central nervous system, some of them determined, not by the stimulus, but by the organism, its attitudes and its past experience" (Boring, *Sensation and Perception in the History of Psychology,* 1942, p. 246).

Laws of Form. The various Gestalt experiments and phenomenological observations have been the foundation of a vast number of laws of *Gestalten* (forms). Helson (1933) listed 114 such laws, most of them pertaining to visual form. The following are the most important ones (after Boring, *op. cit.*).

NATURALNESS OF FORM. A field tends to become organized and to take on form. Groups tend to form structures, and disconnected units tend to become connected.

FIGURE AND GROUND. A form tends to be a figure set upon a ground, and a figure-ground dichotomy is fundamental to all perception.

ARTICULATION. Forms vary from simple to complex in the degree of articulation or differentiation that they possess.

GOOD AND POOR FORMS. A good form is well articulated and as such tends to impress itself upon the observer, to persist and recur. A circle is a good form.

STRONG AND WEAK FORMS. A strong form hangs together and resists attempts to analyze it into parts or fuse it with another form.

OPEN AND CLOSED FORMS. An open form tends to change toward a certain good form. When a form has assumed stable equilibrium, it has achieved closure. Thus a series of dots which almost make a circle are perceived as a circle with a part missing, rather than as a part-circle.

DYNAMIC BASIS OF FORM. A form is a dynamic system or is based upon a dynamic system. Since the dynamic principles operate within the organism, a strong form is one which depends more upon the dynamic properties of the organism than upon the properties of the stimulus.

PERSISTENCE OF FORM. A form once perceived tends to persist, and to recur when the stimulus situation recurs. The recurrence of part of a previously perceived form tends to reinstate the whole.

CONSTANCY OF FORM. A form tends to preserve its proper shape, size, and color.

SYMMETRY OF FORM. A form tends toward symmetry, balance, and proportion.

INTEGRATION OF SIMILARS AND ADJACENTS. Units similar in size, shape, and color tend to combine to make better articulated forms.

MEANINGFULNESS OF FORMS. A form tends to be meaningful and to have objectivity.

FUSION OF FORMS. Two forms can fuse, giving rise to a new form; or, in combination, the stronger one may persist, eliminating the weaker.

TRANSPOSITION OF FORM. A form exists independently of its constituent elements and may thus be transposed without change to other elements. For example, the principle of "greater than" can be maintained in a wide number of pairings, despite variation in the absolute size of the two objects being compared.

PERCEPTION OF MOVEMENT

The attribute of duration of stimulation is the basis for the perception of movement. Two types of perceived movement must be noted: (1) perception of a moving stimulus and (2) apparent movement of a stationary stimulus.

Perception of a Moving Stimulus. An object must move at a certain minimum speed and over a minimum distance to be perceived as moving. (At a distance of 2 meters, the lower temporal threshold is 0.2 cm. per sec.) Conversely, there is a maximum velocity above which a blur or flicker, rather than a moving object, is the only perception. (At 2 meters the upper temporal threshold is about 150 cm. per sec.) Movement may also be perceived in objects which do not cross the field of vision. An increase in brightness, distinctness, or size denotes an approaching object in the absence of cues to the contrary.

IMPORTANCE OF REFERENCE POINTS. Movement is seen with respect to a fixed frame of reference. The basis of the frame of reference is not always readily determinable. *Size* may be an important aspect, as when the moon is seen to move over the expanse of a partly clouded sky. *Experience* may be the determiner, as when a car moves past the window and the window is known to be stationary. *Set* may be a factor, as when the train next to yours moves and you perceive your train as moving until some obviously fixed point of reference intervenes.

HEAD AND EYE MOVEMENTS. The eyes see objects only when they are fixated. Only blurs and streaks of light are perceived while the eyes are in motion. Thus following a moving object entails a series of fixes and movements of the eyes, a gradual turning of the head, or both. The proprioceptive cues derived contribute to the perception of movement. Perception of what is moving depends upon the frame of reference. This perception also operates in reverse. If the head and eyes remain fixed, an object traversing the visual field is seen as a blur and is perceived only as something in motion.

AFTERIMAGES OF MOVEMENT. Continued attention to a moving stimulus produces an afterimage of movement. Objects which have been receding will appear to be approaching; objects which have been moving in one direction will appear to reverse direction.

Apparent Movement. The most familiar form of apparent movement is that afforded by the motion picture or animated cartoon. If a series of pictures or drawings representing the different positions involved in an actual movement are presented chronologically at a slow rate of speed, the pictures appear discrete. At slightly greater speeds, movement appears but flickering and jerkiness are noted. Finally, an optimum point is reached (about 25 per sec.). If speed is further increased, movement again becomes jerky and blurs appear.

Apparent movement has generally been studied with simpler stimuli than motion pictures and cartoons. Flashing lights, simple lines, and simple ground-figure relationships permit isolation of important factors with less disturbance brought about by the set of the subject.

PHI PHENOMENA. The appearance of movement for which there is no obvious physical stimulus is frequently termed the *phi phenomenon* (Wertheimer, 1912). Wertheimer's phi was restricted to "pure movement," with reference to or identification of an object. However, the other types of apparent movement are also usually identified as phi. The principal types follow.

Beta Movement. Two discrete stimuli (lights, lines) spatially separated in varying degrees, and further varied with changes in intensity of illumination and interval of presentation, will appear as one object in motion under optimum conditions. The relationships among the three variables (time, intensity, and distance) have been worked out in some detail (Korte's laws, 1915). The laws are now known to hold with any exactitude only through a limited range of values, but the general nature of the relationship is as follows: (1) If the intensity is held constant, the time interval varies directly with the distance between stimuli. (2) If the time interval is held constant, the distance varies directly with the intensity. (3) If the distance is held constant, the intensity varies inversely with the time interval.

Delta Movement. The type of presentation which would normally secure beta movement sometimes results in a curious reversal. If the brighter of two stimuli is presented second in the sequence, movement may appear in reverse, from the later to the earlier stimulus position.

Gamma Movement. If the illumination of a figure in a stable field appears suddenly, or is suddenly increased, the figure appears to increase in size. Conversely, cessation of the stimulus or sudden lowering of illumination results in apparent contraction and diminution of size.

AUTOKINETIC MOVEMENT. One special type of apparent movement is that which occurs when a spatial framework is lacking. A point of light fixated in an otherwise dark room will appear to drift. The phenomenon is frequently experienced by aviators flying at night in a relatively unstructured field of stars and scattered (as opposed to patterned) lights.

SOCIAL FACTORS AND VISUAL PERCEPTION

The fact that the organism functions as a whole, in a dynamic situation, is nowhere brought out better than in discussions of perception. That "Perception is of definite and probable things" (James, 1890) is a principle which has not changed with all the additional physiological and psychological evidence that has been accumulated since the statement was made.

A striking example of the influence of social factors is found in an experiment by Bruner and Goodman (1947). When ten-year-old children adjusted a visible patch cast on a ground glass screen to make it look equal in size to various coins, the coins themselves were associated with a greater patch area than were cardboard discs identical in size with the coins. Further, the experimenters found that a group of children from poorer families estimated the size of the coins to be considerably greater than a group of children from wealthier families. Other experiments of this type are needed and will undoubtedly add to the knowledge of perception.

SUMMARY

The stimulus for vision is radiant energy. The small portion of existing radiant energy to which visual receptors are sensitive is discriminated as to brightness and to color by the human organism.

Rod and cone cells located in the retina are the sensitive receptors for light. An extensive accessory apparatus, commonly called the eye, serves to focus and otherwise control the light stimulus.

The rod and cone cells appear to have somewhat different functions, though numerous interrelationships are in evidence. The differences between rod and cone functions give rise to the duplicity theory of vision.

Perception of form and space is accomplished through both physiological and psychological cues. The physiological cues are sometimes called primary since they are due to the construction of the visual apparatus. The psychological cues are sometimes called secondary since they are learned. In case of conflict the learned cues are likely to take precedence.

Perception is greatly influenced by the dynamics of the organism. Attitudes, expectations, experience, all mold the stimulus into a meaningful perception.

7

Audition and Auditory Phenomena

Audition is a distance awareness. Sensitivity to sounds extends the range of potential stimulation in all directions. The focus of attention may be directed towards some specific object or event, but the sounds of the environment still permit awareness of the many things happening about us. It has often been said that hearing lets us know that the world is "alive." Certainly loss of hearing usually results in loss of social adjustment. Deaf persons nearly always become less responsive to personal contacts.

The principal auditory functions are: (1) recognition of *tones* and *noises,* and (2) perception of *distance* and *direction.*

THE AUDITORY STIMULUS

Stimulation of hearing is provided by vibrations of the air or of other physical media, which are called *sound waves.*

Composition of Sound Waves. Sound waves may be either (1) periodic or (2) nonperiodic; and the periodic may be either (1) pendulum or (2) nonpendulum in composition. Nonperiodic sound waves stimulate *noise* sensitivities. Periodic nonpendulum vibrations stimulate compound *tones.* Pendulum vibrations (sine waves) stimulate pure tones. These are the usual correlations between stimuli and sensitivities, but there are many exceptions.

Frequency of Vibrations. All sound waves travel at a uniform rate in the same medium. In dry air of 32° F. this rate is about 1087 feet per second. Sound waves are like ripples in water, and the length of the waves (from one crest to the next) determines the number of vibrations which arrive at a given point in a certain time. One vibration includes both the crest and the valley of a wave and is called a *double vibration* (d.v.). Different fre-

90

quencies of these vibrations are the major determiners of the pitches of sounds. The amplitude of the vibrations, i.e., the height of the crest and the depth of the valley, is the major determiner of the intensity, or loudness, of the auditory sensitivity.

Complexity of Sound Waves. The simplest wave is a sine wave in which only one frequency is represented. Such waves are rarely

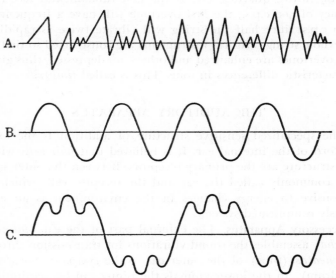

Fig. 12. Sound waves. A. Nonperiodic, characteristic of noise. B. Periodic-pendulum, characteristic of a pure tone. C. Periodic-nonpendulum, characteristic of a compound tone.

produced outside the laboratory. The result of such a wave is a *pure tone*.

Complex waves result from combination of two or more sine waves. In fact, any complex wave can be reduced to its sine-wave components by means of the *Fourier analysis* (1822). The total complexity of the wave is affected by: (1) the *frequency* of its component waves, (2) the *amplitude* of the components, and (3) the *phase* of each component.

These complex waves are the result of *summation*. For example, if two pure tones of the same amplitude but differing in frequency as 100 and 101 cycles per second (c.p.s.) are sounded simultaneously (in phase), there will be periodic reinforcement when the peaks of the two frequencies coincide and periodic cancellation when the peak of one frequency coincides with the valley of the other.

Some tones attain their complexity by virtue of *overtones* or *harmonics*. A plucked string vibrates with a frequency which establishes the *fundamental*. At the same time it also vibrates in halves, thirds, quarters, etc. If the first fundamental has a frequency of 500 c.p.s., the first overtone will have a frequency of 1000 c.p.s. since half the string will vibrate twice as rapidly as the whole string. Musical instruments are constructed so that certain overtones are enhanced and others are depressed, thus giving characteristic differences in tone. This is called *timbre*.

THE AUDITORY APPARATUS

The specialized sensitive structure of audition is the *organ of Corti* of the internal ear. It is believed that *hair cells* within this structure are the primary receptors. Between the outer structure commonly called the ear and the receptor cells which are responsive to energy changes in the environment is an enormously complicated system.

Accessory Apparatus. The external part of the ear (*pinna* or *concha*) assembles the sound vibrations for transmission through the *meatus* (tube) of the outer ear to the *tympanic membrane* (eardrum). In the lower animals the pinna can be manipulated toward the source of the sound, but this ability is lacking in man.

Attached to the tympanic membrane is a small ossicle (bone), the *malleus* (hammer), which moves when the tympanic membrane vibrates. Joined to the malleus is a second ossicle, the *incus* (anvil), which articulates with still a third ossicle, the *stapes* (stirrup). The stapes is attached to the membrane of the *oval window* of the *cochlea* (spiral cavity) of the inner ear. The cavity in which these ossicles are located is usually referred to as the *middle ear*. The air pressure in this cavity is kept constant relative to outside pressure by means of the *Eustachian tube* which connects it with the mouth cavity. Near the entrance of the Eustachian tube into the middle ear is the *round window*, a second membrane separating the cochlea from the middle ear.

The inner ear has two labyrinths, the *semicircular canals,* which serve as organs of equilibrium, and the cochlea of audition. The cochlea is a spiral structure resembling a snail's shell. The cochlear cavity is divided into three parts: (1) an ascending canal (*scala vestibuli*), which begins at the oval window and continues toward the apex, (2) a descending canal (*scala tympani*), which begins at the apex and terminates at the round window, and (3) the cochlear canal, which lies toward the outside of the cochlear cavity and between the tympanic and ves-

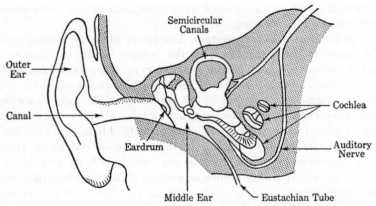

FIG. 13. Cross-section of the ear showing major structures.

tibular canals. The tympanic and vestibular canals are filled with *perilymph* (a liquid) and the cochlear canal is filled with *endolymph* (also a liquid). The vestibular and tympanic canals are connected at the apex of the cochlea by a very small opening, the *helicotrema*. The vestibular canal is separated from the cochlear canal by a thin membrane, *Reissner's membrane,* which apparently has nothing to do with hearing but allows movement in one canal to react upon the other. The separation between the cochlear canal and the tympanic canal is accomplished by a membrane. This is the *basilar membrane,* the most important structure of the ear for understanding the mechanism of hearing.

The Basilar Membrane. The membrane itself is comprised of tendinous fibers and extends from the base of the cochlea to the apex. The organ of Corti rests on the basilar membrane. On the upper surface of the organ of Corti are four rows of hair cells, so called because of hairlike projections at the top of each cell. These are embedded in a gelatinous structure called the *tectorial* *membrane* and are separated by rodlike structures into an inner row and three outer rows. Beneath the hair cells are the well-arborized endings of the auditory nerve fibers.

Sound waves collected in the outer ear are transmitted through the middle ear by the ossicles and into the vestibular canal through action of the stapes on the oval window. As they progress through the fluid of the canal, they cause the basilar membrane to vibrate and the hair cells to change shape. This vibration is in some way associated with excitation of the nerve fibers and the sense of hearing.

The Central Auditory System. The nerve fibers associated with the organ of Corti emerge from the bottom of the cochlear coil as the auditory branch of the VIIIth nerve. This soon joins with the vestibular branch from the semicircular canals, utricule, and saccule (see *equilibrium,* in Chapter 8). The two branches later divide again, and the auditory portion divides still further into a *dorsal* branch and a *ventral* branch. These branches end in the nuclei of the medulla. In man some of the axons from each auditory nerve cross over in the *trapezoid body* and the *superior olivary complex* before ascending through subcortical nuclei of the *lateral lemniscus,* the *inferior colliculi,* and the *medial geniculate bodies,* to the *superior temporal convolution* of the cerebral cortex, the auditory area. This double representation serves as a protection against deafness resulting from brain damage, by permitting impulses received in either ear to be mediated in both halves of the brain. Brogden (1936) has shown that the same situation exists in animals other than man. Removal of one cerebral cortex resulted in a very small decrement of performance.

AUDITORY PHENOMENA

What we hear is *sound*. Identification and discrimination of different sounds are dependent upon differences along several psychological dimensions, or attributes. Sounds are frequently classified into (1) *tones* and (2) *noises*. Tones are smooth and organized. Noises are rough and disorganized. However, differences in other attributes are of greater importance to the understanding of sounds.

Separation and identification of the attributes of auditory

phenomena have been difficult. Boring (1942) presents seven possible psychological attributes of sound: (1) pitch, (2) loudness, (3) brightness, (4) volume, (5) vocality, (6) tonality, and (7) density. Of these, the two most important are pitch and loudness.

Pitch. The pitch of a sound is primarily dependent upon the frequency of the sound waves reaching the ear. High pitches are associated with high frequency and low pitches with low frequency of vibration, though pitch is also affected by the intensity of the stimulus.

PITCH THRESHOLDS. A frequency of about 20 cycles per second produces the lowest pitch which can be heard, and the intensity of the stimulus must be quite high (about 10 dynes per square centimeter) before this pitch is audible. In man, a frequency of about 20,000 c.p.s. produces the highest pitch which can be heard (Wegel, 1922). Many animals and birds appear able to hear pitches associated with higher frequencies (Galton and others).

There are about 1500 psychological pitch steps distinguishable between 20 and 20,000 c.p.s. Above 1000 c.p.s. the differential threshold approximates the requirements of Weber's law very well. The fractional difference is about 0.3 per cent per second. Below 1000 c.p.s. the differential threshold is roughly 3 c.p.s.

SCALES OF PITCH. The most familiar pitch scale is the ordinary musical scale, a diatonic scale. The seven familiar notes within the octave of this scale are unequally spaced in frequencies, but each note of the octave has been established in frequency as one-half or double that of the same note in the octave above or below it. Pitch discrimination does not proceed according to any such ratios of frequency. Two notes in the treble portion of the scale are farther apart psychologically than are two notes in the bass portion, but not in proportion to the actual differences in frequencies involved. Scales have recently been constructed so that the notes used sound equally far apart in pitch. The distance between any pair of notes in the series is a *mel* (Stevens and Volkman, 1940). This new scale probably has little musical importance, particularly since part of the music we like is based upon the dissonances which occur with our present scale.

Loudness. Loudness is the intensity attribute or dimension of the heard sound. It is primarily dependent upon the amplitude of the sound wave, and thus upon the pressure of the vibrating stimulus on the hearing apparatus.

LOUDNESS THRESHOLDS. The lowest absolute intensity which will produce an audible sound is less than .001 dyne per square centimeter applied to a tone of 3600 c.p.s. (Wilska, 1935). In contrast, an intensity of about 1 dyne per sq. cm. must be applied to a tone of 32 c.p.s. before the threshold of audibility is reached.

THRESHOLDS OF FEELING. The opposite of bare audibility in terms of intensity of stimulation is called the threshold of feeling. As the sound is increased in intensity it is perceived as a tickle in addition to its tonal character, and with a still greater increase in intensity of stimulus it grows painful. Exact determination of these thresholds of feeling has not been made extensively, largely because of fear of producing deafness. In ordinary experience it has been observed that persons exposed to even a moderately loud noise for a long time show a measurable deafness, concentrated in the area of the particular pitch or pitches involved.

LOUDNESS DISCRIMINATION. The physical scale used to measure the amplitude of sound is the *decibel* scale. This is a logarithmic scale in which equal steps stand for equal ratios (1:1.13). This relationship does not correspond exactly to judged loudness throughout the audible range. Stevens and his associates have developed a psychological scale in which steps of equal psychological loudness are called *sones*.

Other Auditory Phenomena. The reinforcement and cancellation effects which occur when tones of different frequency exist simultaneously result in some curious auditory phenomena.

BEATS. When two tones with fundamentals of slightly different vibration frequencies are sounded together, a pulsation known as a *beat* occurs. The number of beats per second is the vibration difference between the two frequencies.

COMBINATION TONES. Two combined tones may produce many other tones. Among those reported are the *intertone,* which has a pitch belonging to the frequency intermediate between the frequencies of the fundamentals of the original tones; the *difference tone,* which has a pitch belonging to the frequency equal to the difference in frequencies of the original tones; and the *summation tone,* which has a pitch belonging to the frequency equal to the sum of the frequencies of the original tones. If the primary tones contain strong overtones, still other combination tones from these overtones may be detected. Observation of such tones is possible under strict laboratory conditions and by skilled observers.

MASKING. One tone or noise may make another inaudible. Masking effects are determined by first establishing the audible threshold of a tone, introducing a second or masking tone, and then measuring the increase in intensity necessary to bring the first tone to audibility again. Masking is greatest when the primary and secondary tones are close together in frequency, with the exception that beats may be heard while the masked tone itself is still inaudible. Low tones have a greater masking effect than high tones.

THEORIES OF HEARING

There are a great number of theories of hearing. Boring (1942) reviews twenty-one. Wever (1949) discusses sixteen. No one of these theories adequately accounts for all the known auditory phenomena within the scope of present knowlege of the physiology of the auditory apparatus and the principles of neural functioning. The theories may be generally classified into three types: (1) *place,* (2) *frequency,* and (3) *volley.*

Place Theories. The primary hypothesis is that every tone has a specific location within the cochlea which responds whenever that tone is sounded. There are two principal classes of place theory—resonance, and nonresonance or wave.

RESONANCE THEORIES. The basilar membrane and its subsidiary structures are regarded as a series of resonators. Those which vibrate in response to a particular tone stimulate corresponding hair cells and thus produce impulses in the auditory nerve fibers. Helmholtz (1863) was the originator of the theory, and important modifications have been made by Ranke (1931) and Raboul (1937).

WAVE THEORIES. Traveling bulges are said to displace the basilar membrane. With a spatial arrangement of the frequency scale along the membrane, the area stimulated by the bulge determines the pitch. The first of such theories was advanced by Hurst (1895), but Watt (1914) and Bekesy (1928) made important modifications.

Frequency Theories. The ear serves as a relay mechanism for the stimulus, and the stimulus frequency is conveyed more or less faithfully by the auditory nerve. Rutherford (1886) likened the ear to a telephone in which the basilar membrane and the hair cells performed the same functions as a microphone. Max Meyer (1896) proposed that the basilar membrane itself would be moved up and down at the rate of the stimulus displacement, with the particular point of membrane movement determined through the action of the fluid up and down the cochlear canals and the degree of membrane vibration determined by the amplitude of the initial stimulus. Under this theory the cochlea would serve as a tone analyzer.

Volley Theory. Frequency theories have been hampered by the knowledge that the frequency of neural impulse in a single fiber cannot exceed 1000 per second and more probably reaches about 600–700. Boring (1926) suggested the possibility of summatory action within the auditory nerve. Wever and Bray (1930) suggested that for frequencies above 1000 c.p.s. the nerve fibers fire in volleys or squads. Thus pitch is dependent on the frequency of volleys, not the frequency carried by the individual fibers.

The theoretical formulation of Wever and Bray was preceded by research which demonstrated that the auditory nerve actually conducts frequencies above the 1000 maximum previously believed possible. They tapped the auditory nerve of a cat with shielded electrodes, led amplified potentials to a telephone receiver in a soundproofed room, and showed that frequencies from 100 to 5000 c.p.s. played into the cat's ear were faithfully reproduced in the receiver. Adrian in 1931 discovered that this microphonic effect might be picked up in the cochlea rather than in the auditory nerve. However, Davis shortly proved that both types of conduction were possible but that the action potentials from the nerve did not duplicate the stimulus as faithfully as Wever and Bray had reported.

AUDITORY SPACE PERCEPTION

Our ears do give some cues for distance and direction, but judgments based on these cues are poor when compared with judgments based on visual cues.

Distance. The most obvious cue for determination of distance is loudness. As distance increases, loudness decreases.

At greater distances sounds are less complex. Overtones and small incidental sounds disappear before the stronger fundamental tone dies out. Thus the pureness of a tone becomes a distance cue.

Direction. Localization of sounds common to everyday experience is greatly dependent upon familiarity. We look overhead for the airplane and to the road for the automobile horn. Or, having seen a likely source for the sound, we associate the heard sound with that source. Such expectations are of great help to the ventriloquist and to the movie industry.

Where cues of familiarity and vision are not available, sound location is possible only when auditory cues stimulate each ear differently. Three factors are involved: (1) difference in original time of arrival of the sound wave at the ears, (2) difference in phase of the stimulus upon arrival at the two ears, and (3) difference in intensity at the time of arrival. An interaction among these three factors occurs, and they vary in importance with the type of stimuli involved.

TIME. A discrete stimulus such as a click is probably localized best by means of time differences. The maximum time difference involved is about .03 millisecond, based on the knowledge that sound waves bend around obstacles and that the maximum difference in distance traveled to reach the two ears is about 11 inches.

PHASE. The sound wave may arrive in different phase at each ear. That is, the crest of the wave may arrive at one ear while the trough of the wave is arriving at the other.

INTENSITY. If the stimulus is of high frequency, the differences in intensity at the two ears may be very significant since the short waves associated with high frequency lose amplitude much more readily than long waves traveling the same distance. In addition, when complex sounds are involved, the higher overtones are the first to drop out.

Right and left discriminations of sound are quite accurate. Up and down, front and back discriminations are very inaccurate. In everyday life we change position, move the head, and change the time, phase, and intensity relations in other ways, in order to accomplish accurate localization. The sound locators of the military services employ the same principles, detecting the direction of the sound source by turning mechanical "ears" until the stimuli picked up appear to be equal to the human observer's ears.

Where both visual and auditory cues are possible, the visual cues take precedence. Young (1928) devised a *pseudophone* which reversed the stimuli coming to the two ears. When the eyes were closed, sounds coming from the right were actually heard as coming from the left and vice versa. When the eyes were open the sounds were properly localized in spite of the reversed auditory stimuli.

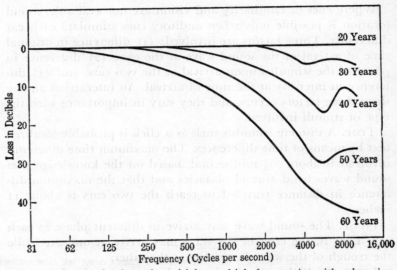

FIG. 14. Progressive loss of sensitivity to high frequencies with advancing age. The audiogram taken at 20 years of age is used as the standard of comparison. (From C. T. Morgan, *Physiological Psychology*, McGraw-Hill, 1943, after C. C. Bunch, A. M. A., *Arch. Otolaryngol.*, 1929, IX, 625–636.)

LOSS OF HEARING

A few persons are born deaf, but most cases of loss of hearing occur as a result of infection or injury. Losses may be in conduction, where the stimulus is prevented from reaching the nerve because of poor operation of the eardrum or the ossicles. Losses may also be in perception, due to some injury or malfunctioning of the nerve fibers in the basilar membrane or, of course, in the cerebral centers. Numerous investigators have shown that animals exposed to loud sounds incur histological damage to the organ of Corti (Guild, 1919; Davis, *et al.*, 1935).

Hearing loss is commonly shown by an *audiogram*. The loss is measured in terms of the number of decibels a tone must be increased in intensity before audibility is established. In conduction deafness, there is generally a loss at all frequencies. In perceptive deafness, there is frequently a "notch" in which a relatively narrow range of frequencies shows a marked loss with other frequencies remaining relatively normal. Another very common audiogram is one in which sensitivity to low frequencies remains relatively unimpaired while sensitivity to high frequencies decreases rapidly. This type is frequently found with advancing age (Bunch, 1929).

SPEECH

The perception of speech involves much more than mere interpretation of differences in pitch, loudness, volume, and so on. For example, certain so-called speech sounds are hardly sounds at all but are really ways of starting or stopping other sounds.

The frequencies found in ordinary speech range from about 125 c.p.s. to about 5000 c.p.s. Interference by other noises, masking tones, etc. affect different sounds in different ways. The problem is one of particular importance for telephone and radio engineers, and a vast amount of research on audibility under different conditions is now in progress.

SUMMARY

The stimulus for hearing is sound waves produced by vibration of the air.

Sound waves are collected in the outer and middle ear and are transmitted to the cochlea of the inner ear. Structures of the basilar membrane are stimulated through action of the cochlear fluid, and nerve fibers of the auditory branch of the VIIIth nerve are there innervated. The auditory nerve impulses pass through several subcortical nuclei and are finally represented in the temporal lobe of both cerebral cortexes.

A simple sine wave will produce a pure tone. Combination of

two or more such waves produces complex sounds. Frequency, amplitude, and phase contribute to complexity.

Pitch and loudness are the principal attributes of sounds. Pitch is primarily dependent on frequency of the sound waves. Loudness is primarily dependent on amplitude. Pitch and loudness interact to modify pitches of tones.

Three principal types of theories have been advanced as explanations of hearing: (1) place, (2) frequency, and (3) volley.

The ears alone do not function efficiently as indicators of the distance and direction of sound stimuli. Distance cues are loudness and complexity. Directional cues are familiarity, time, phase, and intensity. The last-named three depend upon binaural hearing.

Deafness may result from damage to the accessory apparatus or to the receptor organs. Understanding of speech involves both reception of sound and perception.

8

Our Other Senses

Traditionally there are three senses other than those already discussed—smell, taste, and touch. Actually, touch has been separated into four distinct cutaneous sensitivities (warmth, cold, pressure, pain), and kinesthesis and equilibrium have been established as independent sensitivities.

OLFACTION

Compared with vision and audition, there has been little research in olfaction (smell). This is largely due to the insignificant role of smell in the adjustment of man to his environment.

Smell is a distance awareness. In the absence of seeing and hearing, it is the only sensitivity which will inform us of the presence of objects before we are in actual contact with them. There are three attributes or dimensions of smell: quality, intensity, and duration. From interrelations of these three, judgments of extensity are made in much the manner described for audition.

Olfactory Stimulus. Olfactory stimuli are gaseous particles carried to the sensitive receptor cells located in the upper cavity of the nose. No classification similar to wave length has been found for olfactory stimuli. Several investigators have shown that mixtures of certain basic stimuli give rise to other odors, much as mixtures of certain wave lengths of light give rise to colors which may be attained independently of the particular mixture employed. This suggests that there may be some central stimulus with several dimensions, but as yet it has not been identified.

CLASSIFICATION OF OLFACTORY STIMULI. The best-known classification is that of Henning (1915). He lists six primary odors: (1) fragrant, (2) fruity, (3) spicy, (4) putrid, (5) resinous, and (6) burned.

103

OLFACTORY THRESHOLDS. Absolute intensity thresholds are usually determined as the minimum concentration which can be detected. Absolute thresholds for olfactory sensitivity are very low when compared with the other senses. For example, vanillin can be detected when the concentration is 0.0000002 milligram per cubic meter of air.

Differential thresholds are determined as *olfacties*, the increase in concentration necessary before the subject can discriminate an added amount of the odor (Zwaardemaker, 1895).

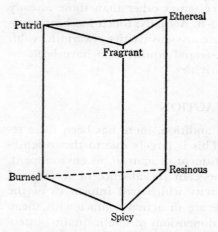

FIG. 15. Henning's odor prism (after Henning, *Der Geruch*, 1916) representing the different olfactory qualities, which are said to grade off into each other. The prism is hollow, and all odor qualities can be represented upon its surface.

ADAPTATION. As in other sensitivities, continued exposure to stimulation results in adaptation. In olfaction, the rate of adaptation is more rapid than in any other sense department.

MIXTURES. Stimulation of the olfactory sense organ by more than one odor may result in *fusion* and a somewhat new odor. This may change by adaptation, particularly if the fused odors have different rates of adaptation. The mixture may also result in *compensation* in which the resulting smell is less intense than either of the contributing stimuli. There may be *masking* of one odor by another, even though the masked odor would be above threshold level if presented singly.

Olfactory Receptors. The receptors of olfaction are in the two *Schneiderian membranes* situated at the uppermost part of each nostril. Nerve cells form the sensitive tissue, called *olfactory bulbs*. Only eddy currents reach these receptors.

Impairment of olfactory sensitivity is called *anosmia*. A partial anosmia occurs whenever we have colds or catarrhal conditions. Some individuals are reported as having anosmia for some odors but not for others, a situation somewhat analogous to partial color blindness.

GUSTATION

Much of the sensitivity customarily attributed to gustation (taste) is actually due to the odor of the stimulus. When olfactory reception is eliminated, recognition of many common substances is diminished or even eliminated. The reader may recall how "flat" many things taste when he has a cold in the head.

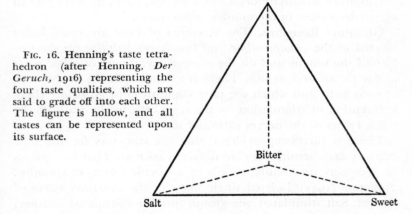

FIG. 16. Henning's taste tetrahedron (after Henning, *Der Geruch,* 1916) representing the four taste qualities, which are said to grade off into each other. The figure is hollow, and all tastes can be represented upon its surface.

Gustatory Stimulus. The effective stimuli for taste are substances soluble in saliva. They must be introduced into the mouth. Taste is not a distance sensitivity.

CLASSIFICATION OF GUSTATORY STIMULI AND TASTES. There are four kinds of gustatory stimuli which give rise to the four elementary tastes: (1) sweet, (2) salt, (3) sour, and (4) bitter. Henning (1916) proposed that other taste sensitivities are all mixtures of these four. In everyday life, identification of substances taken into the mouth involves not only taste but also pressure, warmth, cold, pain, and the different odors.

GUSTATORY THRESHOLDS. Various reports of gustatory absolute thresholds have been given, one of which (Postman and Egan, 1949) is as follows:

Stimulus	Sensitivity	Threshold Concentration (per cent)
sugar *	sweet	0.5
table salt	salt	0.25
hydrochloric acid	sour	0.007
quinine	bitter	0.00005

* Saccharin is reported as detected in a solution of 0.0001%.

ADAPTATION. With continuing stimulation the threshold of gustatory sensitivity rises rapidly. The amount of adaptation is directly related to the concentration of the stimulus. Successive contrast effects are noted. A sour stimulus tastes more so after adaptation to sweet. It has been suggested that adaptation to one quality lowers the threshold for other qualities.

Gustatory sensitivity decreases with age, partially owing to an actual decrement in the number of receptors.

Gustatory Receptors. The receptors of taste are small bulbs located in the *circumvallate* and *fungiform papillae* on the surface of the tongue and on the mucous membrane of other parts of the throat and mouth. There is a small opening in the neck of each bulb into which the taste stimulus must go before there is reception of stimulation by the taste cells in the walls of the bulb. Fibers of the nerves surround these cells.

There is increasing evidence that the receptors for the four primary taste sensitivities are different systems. That is, particular receptors are stimulated only by a specific variety of stimulus. Pfaffman (1941) isolated single fibers of the gustatory nerve of the cat. Salt stimulated one group; quinine stimulated another; acid stimulated the first two plus additional fibers; and sugar gave very few potentials. Allen and Weinberg (1925) used electrical stimulation in rapid succession to accomplish fusion (c.f.f., critical flicker frequency), the point at which the subject reported continuous stimulation of the gustatory receptors. They were able to construct four separate curves of c.f.f. They then drugged the tongue to eliminate the taste for sweet, repeated the electrical stimulation, and found that one of the four curves disappeared.

COMMON CHEMICAL SENSITIVITY

Closely related to taste and smell, but sufficiently different to merit independent discussion, is the *common chemical sense*.

Scattered throughout the body, but particularly in parts covered with a mucous membrane, are a number of free nerve endings which are sensitive to chemical stimuli. The resulting sensitivity is reported as sharp or prickling. Spices, acids, alcohol, pepper, and numerous other substances serve as stimuli for the common chemical sense. Pain may be included as part of this sensitivity.

CUTANEOUS SENSITIVITIES

In popular parlance the cutaneous sensitivities are referred to as touch. They are contiguous sensitivities; i.e., surface contact is required for stimulation.

Cutaneous Receptors. It is found that the surface of the skin is not uniformly sensitive to stimulation, that there are insensitive areas, and that the sensitive areas have a degree of specialization (Blix, 1882; Goldscheider, 1884; Donaldson, 1885). Specialized spots are found for pressure, pain, warmth, and cold, but combination of these sensitivities can also be found at some of these spots. Research suggests that the receptors for each of these specialized sensitivities can be segregated, though the sensitivity can be more accurately related to the stimulus spot than to any particular receptor. The reported relations are generally as follows:

SENSITIVITY	RECEPTORS REPORTED TO BE CORRELATED WITH SENSITIVITY
Pressure . . .	Hair bulbs, Meissner and Merkel corpuscles
Pain	Free nerve endings
Warmth . . .	Ruffini cylinders, free nerve endings
Cold	Krause end bulbs, free nerve endings

The hair bulbs for pressure and the free nerve endings for pain are most conclusively established as cutaneous receptors.

Dendrites of afferent neurons of the spinal nerves either are in functional contact with the receptors or form them. The cell bodies of these neurons form the spinal ganglia, and the axons form the exteroceptive tracts leading to the *nucleus gracilis* and *cuneatus* of the medulla. Several relay centers are involved in transmitting impulses from these exterocepters to the somesthetic area of the cerebrum.

Cutaneous Qualities. Exploration of the various areas of the skin may be accomplished by stamping a fine grid on the skin and systematically stimulating each small area. The reported sensitivity is relatively stable for the spot stimulated.

PRESSURE. Pressure spots vary widely in density for various areas of the body, with an average of about 25 per sq. cm. There are differences in intensity of stimulus required for various spots. Density tends to increase and the absolute threshold tends to decrease with areas toward the periphery of the body.

The pressure sense receptors also mediate the sensations known as *vibration* and *tickle*. These sensations are usually the result of intermittent stimulation and have sometimes been referred to as *pressure in movement*.

PAIN. Pain spots have a greater density than pressure spots. Areas of the body vary widely in density, with an estimated average between 100 and 175 per sq. cm. The absolute threshold for pain is lower for areas with greatest density of spots. Unpleasantness, often associated with pain, is not necessarily a part of pain sensitivity.

COLD. Cold spots also vary in density for various areas of the body, with an estimated average from 7 to 13 per sq. cm. The temperature range for cold stimulation is usually from $-10°$ to $30°$ C. with varying *physiological zeros* (no sensitivity reported at that point, though a change in temperature will secure a report) according to adaptation conditions. A paradoxical cold is frequently stimulated at $45°$ to $50°$ C. (von Frey, 1895).

WARMTH. Warm spots appear somewhat less frequently than cold spots and there is no close relationship between the distribution of the two. The temperature range for warmth is usually from $35°$ to $70°$ C. with varying physiological zeros according to adaptation conditions. A paradoxical warmth is sometimes stimulated at $25°$ to $31°$ C., though it is much rarer than paradoxical cold.

Heat is not excessive warmth. It is apparently a fusion of warmth and cold and is an unanalyzable quality correlated with simultaneous warmth and cold stimulation. Pain is also usually reported as part of the sensitivity. The best condition for securing reports of heat is warmth stimulation at about $45°$ C. where paradoxical cold is a part of the sensitivity. Similarly, heat may be experienced at about $25°$ to $28°$ C. where paradoxical warmth occurs. *Synthetic heat* is frequently reported when a combination of two stimuli, one at about 38° and one at about 20° C., are presented together.

COMPLEX CUTANEOUS SENSITIVITIES. Numerous complex sensitivities (touch blends) are reported to be combinations of the four sensitivities mentioned above. Among them are:

> Sharp and blunt—pain and pressure.
> Clamminess—cold and pressure.
> Wetness—pressure and warmth or cold.
> Intense cold—cold and pain.
> Intense heat—cold (paradoxical), warmth, and pain.

Adaptation Phenomena. Adaptation differs somewhat among the various cutaneous sensitivities.

PRESSURE ADAPTATION. It is suggested that the sensitivity of pressure is experienced only while the stimulus intensity is increasing. Certainly, adaptation to pressure is a rapid phenomenon.

PAIN ADAPTATION. Adaptation to pain is slow and difficult to demonstrate, particularly since it is almost impossible to keep the subject from moving and thereby changing the stimulus. Even when the stimulus is kept rather constant, such as heat sufficient to produce pain sensitivity, adaptation is very slow as compared with other sensitivities.

TEMPERATURE ADAPTATION. Adaptation to warmth or cold results in a shift of the physiological zero. Thus, if the hand is immersed in water at 20° C. the water first feels cold, but the experience of coldness gradually disappears. Then, if the hand is changed to water at a temperature between 20° and 32° C. (32° is the normal physiological zero), there is a sensation of warmth though these same temperatures would have given sensations of cold before adaptation. There are limits to the shifting of physiological zero, though some adaptation occurs within the limits of about 5° and about 47° C., the temperatures of painful cold and burning heat, respectively.

Adaptation also affects the threshold requirements for detecting the presence of cold or warmth. When the physiological zero is near normal, a difference of from 0.033° to 0.050° C. is sufficient for sensations of warmth or cold. Under adaptation conditions this may be raised to as much as 0.5° C.

Tactual Localization of Stimuli. The accuracy of localization of stimuli which affect the cutaneous sensitivities varies according to the density of receptor spots. Kinesthetic sensitivities of deep pressure and pain integrate with these cutaneous sensitivities in bodily space localizations, direction of movement, size, and weight.

TWO-POINT THRESHOLDS. The tactual two-point threshold is a measure of acuity of tactual space sensitivity. The extreme differences with respect to the portions of the body involved are shown in the following representative thresholds:

Tongue tip	1.1 mm. (.04 inch)
Palm side of last phalanx of finger .	2.2 mm. (.08 inch)
Red part of lips	4.4 mm. (.16 inch)
Tip of nose	6.6 mm. (.24 inch)
Back of second phalanx of finger .	11.0 mm. (.44 inch)
Heel	22.0 mm. (.88 inch)
Back of hand	30.8 mm. (1.23 inches)
Forearm	39.6 mm. (1.58 inches)
Sternum	44.0 mm. (1.76 inches)
Back of neck	52.8 mm. (2.11 inches)
Middle of back	66.0 mm. (2.64 inches)

TACTUAL ILLUSIONS. Spatial accuracy, in terms of the comparison of the judgment with the known physical stimulus, is better for tactual sensitivity than for other sense departments. One important tactual illusion (Aristotle's illusion) is observed when the index and middle fingers are crossed and the stimulus is applied (by an experimenter when the subject is blindfolded) between the two fingers. The illusion is of two objects.

KINESTHESIS

Sensitivities arising from the structures involved in bodily movements are referred to as kinesthetic sensitivities. They differ in intensity and duration. Also they make it possible to judge accurately the position of the limbs and to make complicated muscular adjustments, thus adding the attribute of extensity.

Kinesthetic Receptors. The kinesthetic receptors are usually referred to as *proprioceptors* (Sherrington, 1906). *Pacinian corpuscles* and *free nerve endings* are found in the ligaments of the joints and in the bone coverings near these joints. *Golgi spindles* are found in the tendons, and sensitive structures known as *mus-*

cle spindles occur in the muscles themselves. These are thought of as the receptors of kinesthesis. The neural mechanism is analogous to that of the cutaneous senses.

Kinesthetic Phenomena. Any movement of muscles, tendons, or joints affects many kinesthetic receptors. However, exact knowledge is limited. Pathological conditions have provided most information on the specific contribution of each kind of receptor to our kinesthetic awarenesses. Kinesthetic sensitivities from the joints are primarily responsible for awareness of posture and movement. Those from tendons are the source of the strains or aches of extreme exertion.

The thresholds of joint movement vary from about 0.2 to 0.7 degree. The shoulder joint gives the smaller of these two values.

EQUILIBRIUM

The ability to detect body position and movement in the absence of visual cues is effected through special structures located in the inner ear, normally aided greatly by kinesthetic sensitivity. Movement of the head is particularly important in awareness of position or movement.

Equilibrium Receptors. The receptors of equilibrium, or static sensitivity, are located in the internal ear, in the *semicircular canals,* and in the *vestibule* with its two membranous *sacs,* the *utricle* and *saccule.*

The three semicircular canals on each side of the head lie at approximately right angles with each other, thus affording a three-dimensional system. They are filled with fluid (*endolymph*) which flows in one or more of the canals when the head moves, either with the body or independently. This flow affects the shape of the *cupula* (the bony apex of the cochlea), which in turn distorts the *cristae,* specialized nerve endings which are hairlike in nature.

The contribution of the sacs is through the nerve endings in the *maculae*. These are hairlike projections which have tiny particles of calcium carbonate (*otoliths*) at their ends. These particles, embedded in a gelatinous mass, are thought to make the hair cells more susceptible to gravitational pull and acceleration effects.

Equilibrium Phenomena. Our organs of equilibrium might be considered out of date. In this day of speed of movement their sensitivities are frequently interpreted wrongly. They function only during acceleration or deceleration. Thus, in the absence of other cues, after the initial change has been recorded the organs of equilibrium will not record continuous movement. The typical experiment (first performed by Mach, 1873) gives results as follows: A blindfolded subject is seated in a chair which can be rotated with a minimum of auditory or kinesthetic cues. As the chair is started, the subject can report the correct direction of rotation. As a constant speed is reached and maintained, the subject reports no perceived motion. Finally, if the chair is braked silently, the subject reports that he is rotating in the opposite direction.

ORGANIC SENSITIVITY

Organic sensitivities are diffused feelings, seldom localized with any great degree of exactness. The areas involved are the mucous membranous surfaces of the respiratory, alimentary, genital, and urinary systems, and the surface linings of organs and tissues of the thoracic and abdominal cavities. No special receptors have been localized for these organic sensitivities. The basic sensitivity seems to be pressure, though pain may be felt if the stimulation is sufficiently intense. The stomach and the esophagus are also sensitive to both warmth and cold.

Interpretation of organic sensitivities involves interpretation of the total stimulus situation. These are normally so intimately related to maintenance of physiological homeostasis that they are referred to as the basic drives of the organism. For example, *thirst* seems to be an awareness of pressure (and pain under extreme stimulation) reported as localized on the tongue, roof of the mouth, and throat. What makes it "thirst" is the total situation, which probably even includes memory of the stimuli relieving the condition. *Hunger* is a complex of pressure and pain referred to the region of the stomach. Again, it is the total situation that makes this particular pressure-pain a hunger. *Nausea, defecation* urges, and *urination* urges are other examples of a particular pressure-pain pattern which is resolved into a perception that acts as a motive.

SUMMARY

Gaseous particles stimulating olfactory bulbs in the Schneiderian membranes of the nose give rise to perception of odors. No classification similar to wave length for vision and audition is possible, though there is the suggestion that some common chemical relation between odors is present.

Substances soluble in saliva stimulate taste buds on the tongue and other parts of the mouth and throat. Four separate sensitivities are involved— (1) sweet, (2) salt, (3) sour, and (4) bitter. Common taste experiences are frequently complicated by odorous qualities of the stimulus situation.

Certain substances stimulate receptors located in and on various parts of the body, particularly those covered with a mucous membrane. The various sharp or prickling sensations reported are referred to as the common chemical sensitivity.

The ordinary sense of touch has been broken down into four specific sensitivities— (1) pressure, (2) pain, (3) cold, and (4) warmth. A number of receptors have been identified as mediating these sensitivities, but correlation of receptor and sensitivity has been difficult to obtain.

Specialized receptors located in the muscles, tendons, joints, and the bone coverings near the joints give rise to kinesthetic sensitivities, permitting judgments of the position of the limbs and the making of complicated muscular adjustments.

The semicircular canals of the inner ear and the sacs of the vestibule contain hairlike cells which are sensitive to movement and position of the body. Thus, body equilibrium is maintained and sensitivity of acceleration and deceleration is possible.

The body organs also contain receptors which mediate sensitivity to pressure and pain. Combinations of these, interpreted in the light of the total stimulus situation, give rise to perceptions such as thirst, hunger, and nausea.

9

Collection, Analysis, and Interpretation of Data

The study of behavior is the primary activity of psychologists. This may include antecedent activity, ongoing activity, and predicted future activity. The validity of conclusions drawn concerning behavior is greatly dependent upon the sources of information used, the analysis performed, and the interpretations placed on the data.

SOURCES OF INFORMATION

Controlled observation is the foundation of scientific procedure. Simple observation may be supplemented by use of tests, questionnaires, interviews, and mechanical or electrical instruments. In the last analysis, no observation can be made which is independent of the observer.

Simple Observation. Simple observation is usually employed in situations where "natural" behavior is the desired object. Either the situations recur regularly in ordinary life or the introduction of tests or other variables would be likely to distort the situation. Several controls may be introduced into observational situations.

SYSTEMATIZATION OF OBSERVATIONS. Observers are trained to select in advance the particular responses or situations to be observed.

SYSTEMATIZATION OF RECORD-KEEPING. Check lists or rating scales are frequently used to assist the observer in recording his observations.

TIME SAMPLES. The frequency of specific occurrences during a constant time interval is recorded. Samples are systematically collected to show frequency per hour, per day, and so on.

ONE-WAY SCREENS AND SPECIAL ROOMS. Devices are set up which prevent the subjects from seeing the observer and being influenced thereby.

PHOTOGRAPHY. Pictures are used to obtain a permanent record and one which can be studied repeatedly. Motion-picture photography is opening up a whole new area for observation.

Biographies, Records, and Reports. Reference is frequently made to the past history of individuals in order to determine the antecedents of behavior. School records, parental histories, work productions, diaries, etc. are investigated. These sources are becoming of very minor importance. In addition to sampling problems and the frequent existence of bias, the process of "affirming the consequent" (finding data to confirm a previous conclusion, frequently biased) may lead to unwarranted conclusions. The Kallikak studies (Goddard, 1919) and the studies of genius (Galton, 1897) are excellent examples of use of the technique.

Interviews. The interview is usually a conversation between the observer and the subject or someone who can give information about the subject. The interview is used in a wide variety of situations—such as securing historical information, counseling and guiding individuals, polling public opinion.

Much work has been done to standardize and objectify the interview. Development of standard questions, use of specially prepared record blanks, including many with rating scales or scoring keys, and addition of electrical recording devices for tabulating interaction of individuals are the most important advances.

Projective Techniques. The study of personality and adjustment problems is frequently performed with materials which are relatively impersonal in themselves but on which the individual may *project* his behavior. Among materials used for this purpose are dolls, puppets, drawing and finger-painting materials, dramatic situations in which role-playing is observed, ink blot figures such as the Rorschach, and pictorial materials such as the Thematic Apperception Test.

There is considerable argument between experimental psychologists and clinical psychologists concerning the use of these materials. The experimental psychologists wish them quantified and subjected to standard research tests. The clinical psychologists generally say that a large portion of the value of the techniques is lost in any attempt to quantify responses.

Questionnaires, Opinionnaires, and Inventories. Question lists may be aimed at collection of facts or collection of opinions. They may be answered by the individual concerned or by an observer. They are usually used where information secured from a large number of individuals will give data which could not be secured from a more limited sample. The large numbers are also necessary because of the relative unreliability of the questionnaire or inventory as contrasted with methods in which better control of responses is possible.

FACT-FINDING. Questionnaires and inventories are used to secure information on such varied subjects as: hours spent in study by college students; food preferences of children; movements made by a workman in doing his job; tools used by a workman; items for which family income is spent; number of items of electrical equipment in the home; and frequency and variety of sexual habits.

OPINION-GETTING. The most familiar are the public-opinion polls which cover everything from attitude toward birth control to policy concerning atomic development.

The typical adjustment inventory, interest inventory, and attitude scale fall into this category, though they are often loosely treated as tests.

The difference between fact and opinion is often very small, and most persons are prone to treat their opinions as if they were facts.

Tests. The term is normally applied to all relatively formal situations in which a subject is asked to perform an operation or select certain answers which may then be graded against some norm. In a sense each test is a miniature experiment in which the individual's behavior is sampled.

ABILITY AND APTITUDE TESTS. Certain tests are designed to measure the ability of individuals independently of environmental influences or with the influences of the environment interacting in a more or less uniform manner. Included among these are the typical intelligence test, the mechanical ability or aptitude test, clerical aptitude tests, music aptitude tests, art aptitude tests, and others.

ACHIEVEMENT TESTS. Training programs are frequently followed by achievement tests which indicate progress or success in learning the materials of the course. These tests range in complexity from simple teacher-made tests to standardized examinations with norms based on large populations.

DIAGNOSTIC TESTS. In educational and clinical situations where irregularities of accomplishment or behavior are noted, certain tests may be used to ascertain areas of difficulty.

Experiments. The term *experimental psychology* generally refers to studies performed in the psychological laboratory. However, an experiment is actually a study based on a *procedure* and a *point of view* rather than a study localized in any particular situation or investigating a particular type of behavior. The basic experimental design involves: (1) determining a carefully delineated item of behavior for study, (2) introducing some experimental modification, and (3) charting the item of behavior after the experimental modification has had opportunity to affect the behavior. Thus, it is necessary to keep as many factors constant as possible while systematically varying the particular one under study.

USE OF THE CONTROL GROUP. A change in behavior following introduction of the experimental variable is not always attributable to the experimental variable. Measurement of a control group which was not subjected to the experimental variable gives indication of how much of the change in behavior may be attributable to the experimental variable. Experimental and control groups may be selected in the following ways.

Random Sampling. Two groups are selected from the available population under the assumption that chance differences will be equally distributed in the two groups.

Matching. Each member of the experimental group is paired with a control subject who is as similar as possible on the experimental variable and the related variables.

Co-twins. One twin is used as the experimental subject while the other acts as control. Identical twins are preferred.

ELIMINATION OF EXTRANEOUS VARIABLES. In many instances it is desirable, and it may be absolutely necessary, to eliminate factors which might influence the result. For example, dark-adaptation experiments require elimination of all light which would bleach the visual purple of the rod cells. Again, the tremendous activity associated with estrus (the sex cycle) in the female white rat may seriously complicate a learning experiment.

COUNTERBALANCING AND ROTATION. Where the study of sequential operations is desired, or where the same subjects are employed in various phases of an experiment, the order of presentation may have considerable effect on the results. Thus, if the efficacy of continuous versus distributed practice in memorizing lists of nonsense syllables is being studied, the order of practice should be balanced and the lists should be rotated so that practice effects or effects caused by unequal difficulty of the lists are eliminated.

STATISTICAL CONTROL. Where other controls are not possible, or would require an inordinate amount of labor, certain statistical techniques may sometimes be used to eliminate the effect of particular variables or to determine the relative effect of several variables. The most important of these are partial correlation, analysis of variance, and analysis of covariance.

DESCRIPTION AND MEASUREMENT

Private data are worthless to science. Experiments and observations must be capable of repetition with results within the limits of tolerance specified by the original experimenter or observer. This requires that the variables studied, procedures used, and results obtained be described so that understanding and duplication are possible. Both qualities and quantities must be established.

There are several levels of description and measurement.

Classification. Identification of objects or events in terms of the traits or relations which they have in common is classification (naming). Classification does not require either ordering or quantification.

Ordinal Series. Objects and classes can frequently be arranged in a regular order with respect to some attribute which they have in common. The resulting arrangement may be numbered so that a given number, e.g., 9, will represent a greater quantity of the attribute than that represented by all smaller numbers, e.g., 8, 7, 5, etc. No conclusions can be drawn concerning the amount represented by the difference between 7 and 8, 8 and 9, and so on.

Graduated Ordinal Series. Certain serial arrangements have equal intervals between the steps in the series. They are still ordinal because no zero point exists. The everyday temperature scale affords a good example. Each degree of temperature is an equal unit of a column of mercury. Under carefully controlled conditions, and within certain limits, an equal amount of energy will raise the temperature one degree at any point on the scale. The typical mental age scale is based on the same principle.

Ratio Scales. The most complete measurements have both a zero point and equal intervals. They are the only measures which can legitimately be treated mathematically. Scales of weight, length, and time are examples of ratio scales (cardinal series). The elements of these scales can be added, subtracted, divided, and multiplied with the outcome always constant within the limits of the measuring devices used.

Psychophysical Measurement. It was discovered quite early in psychological history that individuals do not react to stimuli according to their exact values. As it has been crudely but accurately put, a dollar is worth more to a poor man than to a millionaire. However, though exact magnitudes do not appear equal, some ratio does appear to hold true. Thus, serial arrangement of certain classes of data may be made in terms of what are called *equal-appearing intervals.*

Weber (1834) made the point that two sensations are just noticeably different as long as a given constant ratio obtains between the intensities of their stimuli. Thus, if a subject can discriminate between 15 and 17 pounds, he can also discriminate between 15 and 17 ounces. Similarly, if he cannot distinguish between 15 and 16 ounces, he cannot discriminate between 15 and 16 pounds. Weber proposed a fraction to be used in determining the *j.n.d.* (just noticeable difference) for various sensitivities. Fechner (1860) integrated the Weber fraction to secure what is known as Fechner's law. The law is $S = k \log I$, in which S is the sensation, I is the stimulus intensity, and k is a constant for the individual subject, sensitivity, and environmental situation.

At the present time, scales constructed by the method of equal-appearing intervals are widely used in the measurement of attitudes (Thurstone and Chave, 1929; Remmers, 1933).

STATISTICAL METHODS

The basic purpose of statistical methods is the reduction of masses of data to descriptive terms which lead to better over-all comprehension of the data and which permit the reader to interpret the results with a minimum of effort. The answers to psychological questions are nearly always given in statistical terms.

Central Tendency. The result of a series of measurements is almost invariably a number of different values. Some single value is usually used to express the over-all series. This is a measure of central tendency. There are three commonly used measures.

MEAN. The mean value is the arithmetic average of all the measurements in the distribution.

MEDIAN. The median value is that point in the distribution above which and below which 50 per cent of the observed values fall.

MODE. The modal value is that value which is observed most frequently.

Each of the above has its advantages and disadvantages. The *mean* is the only measure of central tendency which takes into account the actual size of each value. Thus, it is the only one which can be given further mathematical treatment. However, one or a very few extreme values may have a very great effect on the mean, particularly if a limited number of measurements is involved. The *median* is not affected by a few extreme values and gives better representation of the data when marked *scatter* or marked *skewness* is present in the distribution. However, the median cannot be treated mathematically. Two different sets of measurements could not be combined if only the median values were known. The *mode* is particularly valuable when the distribution of observed values is *leptokurtic* (peaked).

Variability. Wherever possible the measure of central tendency reported is amplified by some indication of the variability or spread of the measurements involved.

RANGE. The simplest measure of spread or dispersion of the measurements is the range: the simple difference between the highest and the lowest value. The range gives no indication of the possible concentration of data, and one extreme case may exaggerate the general interpretation of the findings.

QUARTILE DEVIATION OR SEMI-INTERQUARTILE RANGE. The quartiles, Q_1, Q_2, and Q_3, are points which divide the set of measurements into four equal quarters according to the number of measurements. The *quartile deviation* is one-half the difference between the values at the first and third quartile points. The quartile deviation is not influenced by a few extreme cases. Quartile deviations are usually employed with medians (the second quartile point).

STANDARD DEVIATION. The standard deviation is the square root of the mean of the squares of the individual deviations from the mean of a distribution. Thus the standard deviation, like the mean, takes into account the size of every value in the series of measurements. The mean plus the standard deviation permits reconstruction of the actual distribution with little distortion unless the original series of measurements was markedly skewed. In general, approximately 68 per cent of the cases will be found within one standard deviation (sigma unit) on each side of the mean, 95 per cent of the cases within two units, and practically all the cases within three units.

Relationship. Many of the problems of psychology involve determination of the relationship or degree of association between two sets of measurements, made either on the same variable or on different variables. The *coefficient of correlation* is the statistical term most frequently used to express this relationship or association. The existence of a correlation does not demonstrate cause and effect relationship. Several types of correlation coefficients are used, with the type selected largely dependent upon the nature of the values in the distribution.

PEARSON PRODUCT-MOMENT COEFFICIENT OF CORRELATION. The product-moment type is usually used when both variables are expressed in values having a continuous distribution. It is the most common type, and a correlation coefficient (r) referred to without specification of type is invariably the Pearson product-moment.

SPEARMAN RANK ORDER COEFFICIENT OF CORRELATION. The rank order correlation coefficient disregards the actual values of the distribution and merely indicates the degree of relationship between ranked pairs of scores.

BISERIAL COEFFICIENT OF CORRELATION. The biserial type is used when the scores on one variable form a continuous distribution and the scores on the other variable are expressed in two categories. There is an underlying assumption that the variable which is expressed in two categories (dichotomized) is really found in a continuous normal distribution. If a variable, such as sex, cannot be tenably assumed to be so distributed, the biserial r should not be used.

POINT BISERIAL COEFFICIENT OF CORRELATION. The point biserial r is used as the biserial r except that the underlying assumption is made that the variable which is distributed has only two values rather than a continuous distribution.

TETRACHORIC COEFFICIENT OF CORRELATION. If both values being studied yield only dichotomized information, the tetrachoric correlation coefficient may be used. The assumption is then made that both variables are really found in a continuous normal distribution. Numerous computing diagrams (nomographs) are available for rapid estimation of the tetrachoric r. This is likely to result in use of the tetrachoric r when product-moment r's could be computed. The practice should be avoided since the tetrachoric r is subject to much greater sampling errors than the product-moment.

FOURFOLD POINT COEFFICIENT OF CORRELATION. When both variables are dichotomized with the underlying assumption that each has but two values, the fourfold point r is used. Such situations rarely arise in psychological experimentation.

CONTINGENCY COEFFICIENT. When only categorical information is available about two variables, regardless of the number of categories, the contingency coefficient is likely to be the best measure of relationship. There are no underlying assumptions of continuously distributed variables, normal curves, etc. The contingency coefficient simply expresses the relationship between observed and expected frequencies of occurrence for each possible pair of categories or classifications under consideration. The contingency coefficient cannot be compared directly with other estimates of r, nor can contingency coefficients be compared directly with each other unless the same number of categories or classifications was used in establishing the contingency table.

THE CORRELATION RATIO (ETA). Two variables may be related or associated even though values for one variable increase continuously while those of the other increase and then decrease, or vice versa. This is called a curvilinear relationship and is determined by application of the correlation ratio. An example of this relationship is age-weight. Though age increases linearly, weight is subject to various accelerations and decelerations, even showing a decrement in old age. Yet, a correlation ratio will show a substantially higher relationship than a product-moment r.

Measuring Significance and Levels of Confidence. Each and every generalization made with respect to findings expressed in statistical terms is accompanied by limits. These limits determine the confidence which can be placed in the findings. Such factors as the sample used for determining the value, the reliability of the measuring instrument, and the interaction of variables other than the experimental one, all affect significance and levels of confidence.

Significance and levels of confidence stem from the concept of probability.

STANDARD ERROR. The probability that a given statistic derived from a sample is a true representation of the variable studied is estimated by use of the standard error. Where the mean is the statistic involved, the standard error is a function of the variability (standard deviation) of the values and the number of cases included in the sample. Where the correlation coefficient is the statistic involved, the standard error is a joint function of the degree of correlation recorded and the number of cases in the sample. The standard error is a measure of the expected variability of the statistic involved in terms of the differences which would probably be found if successive samples were drawn from the same population.

Interpretation is in terms of the normal probability curve. A mean or a correlation coefficient within the limits established by one standard error is expected approximately 68 times out of 100, one within two standard errors 95 times in 100, and one within three standard errors as a virtual certainty.

CRITICAL RATIO. The probability that the difference between means found in two samples of behavior is a "true" difference is determined by the critical ratio (C.R.). This is determined by dividing the actual difference between means by the *standard error of the difference between means*. This standard error is a joint function of the standard errors of the two independent sample means.

Where a function is measured before and after introduction of an experimental variable, there is a distinct possibility that the two sets of measures are correlated. In this instance the term to be used in testing for significance or probability of recurrence must include the correlation coefficient. Where a high correlation is observed, differences of the same absolute magnitude are more significant than when low correlations are observed.

The C.R. is interpreted in terms of the normal probability curve. A critical ratio of 1.0 indicates that the chances are about 68 in 100 that the observed difference was not due to chance.

CHI SQUARE. The chi square is used to test the *relationship of observed to expected data* in three situations: (1) where observed data are expected to fit some a priori principle, such as the transmission of color coats in mice; (2) where the relationship of one classification with another is questioned, such as the relative and associated incidence of color blindness and sex; and (3) where observed data are expected to fit some specified frequency, such as the distribution of height among college students.

Chi square distributions involve use of data in a slightly different form from that involved in testing by use of standard error formulas. Use of chi square involves the concept of *degrees of freedom,* generally determined as the number of categories into which the data are broken down less the number of operations which have restricted the number of cases which may be placed in any one category. Where the number of such degrees of freedom exceeds 30 the chi square can be treated as C.R.[2] Where the number of degrees of freedom is less than 30 a table of chi square distributions can be used to determine the probability that an observed frequency might be again encountered by chance.

VARIANCE RATIOS. Originally introduced as an improvement in the interpretation of statistics based on small samples, use of the variance ratios is becoming increasingly more common because of their applicability to several samples at the same time and to the identification of the interaction of variables, even where large samples (N greater than 30) are employed.

The variance techniques employ the same data and computations as those involved in determination of means, standard deviations, standard errors, critical ratios, etc. However, the basic datum is the *variance estimate* which is the sum of squares of the deviations.

The following example is offered for illustration: Suppose six fifth grade classes took the same arithmetic test under standard conditions. The following statistics could be computed—a mean and variance estimate for the total number of pupils involved (the *total* variance estimate) ; a mean and variance estimate for each fifth grade class (the sum of this would then constitute the *within groups* variance estimate) , and a mean and variance estimate based on the deviation of the mean of each of the six classes from the mean of the total (this would constitute the *between groups* variance estimate) .

Application of the appropriate number of degrees of freedom to correct for sampling would then give the corrected variance estimate for the between groups variance and within groups variance. Dividing the between groups estimate by the within groups estimate gives the variance ratio. Inspection of a table of F with reference to the number of degrees of freedom allotted the between and within estimates will reveal the probability that such a variance ratio could have occurred by chance, or conversely, the probability that there is a real difference between the scores of these six classes on the arithmetic test administered.

INTERPRETATION OF STATISTICAL RESULTS

It is axiomatic in psychological experimentation that nothing is ever proved. Rather, further experiment and analysis are aimed at decreasing probabilities that observed data might have occurred by chance. This is known as testing the *null hypothesis*. Students are frequently confused by this expression and think that the only possible tests are those which contrast an observed difference with the possibility that no difference exists. This is not true. The tests mentioned above can be applied to hypothetical differences and relationships which are greater than or less than the observed data. For example, let us suppose that there is ample proof that a college entrance examination can be constructed which will have a greater than zero relationship with college grades, and that two such examinations have been constructed. Testing that the relationship is probably greater than zero will afford little evidence for a choice between the two examinations. In this instance the null hypothesis established would be that there was no difference between the two examinations with respect to their relationship with college grades. If one examination were significantly better, the statistics would render the null hypothesis untenable.

For all the statistics mentioned above, standard textbooks in statistics give tables which enable ready determination of probabilities. For F, t, and X^2 these probabilities are usually given at the .001, .01, .02, .05, and .10 levels. If a report includes the statement that a given finding is significant at the .01 level, the author is indicating that there is not over one chance in one hundred that the observed difference could have occurred by chance under the conditions of his experiment.

The standard deviation, standard error, and critical ratio are all normal curve functions. By inspecting the table which shows the area of the normal curve existing on either side of the ordinate which represents the deviation score, the experimenter can construct his own probability table.

Significance of Differences. Determination of what level of P (probability) to accept as demonstrating the existence of differences is a matter of convention. The majority of experimenters accept a P of .05 (C.R. of 1.96) as the lowest level of probability allowable. With this standard an experimenter runs the risk of reporting five experiments out of one hundred as showing real differences when no actual difference existed. Some experimenters thus insist on a P of .01 (C.R. of 2.58) for the conclusion that differences have been shown. Although this certainly makes for greater assurance, it introduces another element of possible error. The conclusion may be drawn that no differences have been shown even though there may be only two chances in one hundred that the results indicated no difference.

Statistical significance is no guarantee of social significance. Statistical proof that 100 pounds of corn will put more meat on a pig than 100 pounds of barley is not likely to cause a farmer to feed corn if he has a surplus of barley, or if he can convert the corn into more cash than he can the barley.

Significance of Relationships. Where a relationship exists between two variables, it is possible to predict values of one variable from knowledge of values of the other. If the data are plotted, the line of predicted values is called a *regression line*. If the correlation is 1.00, perfect prediction is possible; *no* errors will be made. If the correlation happens to be *minus* (negative), it merely means that high scores on one variable are associated with low scores on the other, and the relative accuracy of the prediction is unhampered. A correlation coefficient of .00 indicates that there is no relationship between the two variables being considered.

The significance of a correlation coefficient does not increase linearly. For example, a correlation coefficient of .80 is four times as good as one of .40 in terms of the proportion of variance eliminated. It is almost five times as good in terms of the proportion of standard error eliminated.

CHOICE OF TESTING INSTRUMENTS

Testing instruments must obviously be applicable to the population being tested, must give some range of scores (at least *pass-fail*), and must be feasible within the limitations of available equipment and personnel. However, utility of the measures is most dependent upon *reliability* and *validity* in the testing instrument.

Reliability. The reliability of a test is the degree to which it is a *consistent* measure of whatever it is measuring. Scores must not be highly subject to chance fluctuations. The *reliability coefficient* is derived from two determinations of the scores of individuals in a group.

SPLIT-TEST METHOD. Each test paper is divided by some random method into two halves which are assumed to have equal representation of the body of knowledge tested. The correlation between the two halves is computed and the reliability for the entire test is *estimated* by the Spearman-Brown prophecy formula. (This formula indicates the increase in reliability resulting from doubling the length of a test.)

EQUIVALENT FORMS METHOD. Two or more forms of a test are constructed. Tests are administered in *counterbalanced* order to minimize practice effects and other variables. Correlation between the forms is the estimate of reliability.

TEST-RETEST METHOD. Only one test is constructed, but it is given twice with an elapsed period varying from a few hours to several weeks. Interpretation is difficult since the effect of the intervening time is unknown. Use of this method should be avoided unless the material included is known to be subject to neither practice effect nor forgetting. Even if this is known, maturation, general quotidian variability, and numerous extraneous factors may seriously affect the results.

METHOD OF RATIONAL EQUIVALENCE. The reliability is estimated as a correlation between one experimental test form and a hypothetically equivalent form. Reliability is estimated by applying one of the Kuder-Richardson formulas to determine the relationship between the variance of the test and the variance expected in terms of the elements used to construct the test.

ANALYSIS OF VARIANCE. Two or more forms of a test are compared in terms of the variability due to individual differences as contrasted with the variability due to measurement errors. The technique leaves much to be desired since significance only indicates that it is fairly certain that individual differences exist which are greater than differences which might be accounted for by test errors or measurement.

Though the term *test* has been used consistently in describing the above methods, they are applicable in varying degrees to such measures as maze learning, pursuit rotor learning, questionnaires, scored interviews, rating scales, etc. For example, in maze learning, reliability might be estimated from correlation of errors for odd and even blinds, first half and last half, alternate trials, equivalent but reversed mazes, and so on.

Validity. The validity of a test is the degree to which it measures what it is supposed to be measuring. Thus it is essential that some criterion of success or failure be found which is independent of the test itself. The scores on the test are then correlated with these external measures. No measuring instrument has validity per se. Validity is always *for what* and the *what* must be rigorously defined. Satisfactory criteria are enormously difficult to find. A brief listing of examples of criteria which have been used will give some indication of how validity is usually determined.

IN THE SCHOOL SYSTEM. Tests given in schools are usually for the purpose of predicting future success, measuring present accomplishment, or both. They have been validated against such criteria as: (1) school grades, (2) passing or failing, (3) teachers' ratings of pupils, (4) frequency and time of withdrawal from school, and (5) other tests.

IN BUSINESS AND INDUSTRY. Tests given in business and industry are usually for the purpose of predicting job success in one form or another. These have been validated against such criteria as: (1) promotion, (2) salary or wages, particularly where individual production can be measured, (3) turnover, (4) absenteeism, (5) ratings of foremen and supervisors, and (6) various production measures.

IN COUNSELING AND GUIDANCE. Tests given for counseling and guidance are usually for the purpose of predicting vocational or personal success and adjustment. These have been validated against such criteria as: (1) school success, (2) job stability, (3) success in avoiding placement in correctional institutions, mental hospitals, and the like, (4) success in avoiding generally undesirable events such as divorce, arrest, drug addiction, etc., and (5) other tests.

IN CLINICAL WORK. Tests given for clinical purposes are usually to diagnose the extent or direction of deviation from some socially acceptable pattern. These have been validated against such criteria as: (1) psychiatric diagnosis, (2) institutionalization, (3) test profiles of supposedly well-adjusted individuals, (4) occurrence of undesirable events, and (5) other tests.

IN PSYCHOLOGICAL EXPERIMENTATION. Tests given in the psychological laboratory are usually given to determine the composition of a group before the members are subjected to experimental treatment or to separate groups for varying treatment. Criteria of success are usually: (1) time required to learn or perform a given operation, (2) errors made in reaching a certain degree of proficiency, (3) maximum or minimum performance attainable, and (4) measures of physiological states which may vary concomitantly with psychological operations.

SUMMARY

Data used in the formulation of psychological principles are drawn from a wide variety of sources. The more important are: (1) simple observation; (2) biographies, records, and reports; (3) interviews; (4) projective techniques; (5) questionnaires, opinionnaires, and inventories; (6) tests; and (7) experiments.

In order to make findings communicable from one individual to another, some simplified system of classifying and reporting data must be used. Data are usually reported in terms of: (1) names or nominal numbers; (2) ordinal series; (3) graduated ordinal series; (4) cardinal series; or (5) psychophysical scales.

Statistical methods are used to reduce masses of data to more easily comprehended concepts. The principal statistics are: (1) measures of central tendency such as the mean, the median, and the mode; (2) measures of variability such as the range, quartile deviation, and standard deviation; (3) measures of relationship such as the various correlation coefficients and the contingency coefficient; and (4) indications of probability such as the standard error, critical ratio, chi square, and variance ratios.

No research finding ever results in proof. Rather, degrees of probability or certainty are established. A possibility of chance occurrence which is less than 5 in 100 is usually the lowest level acceptable in psychological studies.

Psychological study is limited by the measuring instruments available. Any measuring instrument used must satisfy two criteria; it must be consistent (reliable) and it must be related to the variable being studied (valid).

10

Birth, Growth, and Maturation

The behavior potentialities of the organism are determined by the neurological and physiological equipment with which it is provided. In higher organisms the full complement of skeletal cells, muscle cells, nerve cells, and glands is present at birth. Before the ultimate behavior of the organism becomes a reality, some growth and maturation are necessary. This period of growth and maturation may extend over several years.

REPRODUCTION

Organisms which are formed from union of male and female germ cells receive an equal contribution of factors from both parents. The gene theory of factor transmission is the most commonly accepted explanation of how this contribution takes place (Mendel, 1865; Weisman, 1886; Morgan, 1923).

Composition of Cells. Each cell is enclosed in a *membrane*. Within this membrane is the *cytoplasm,* a jelly-like substance which surrounds the *nucleus.* The nucleus contains *chromosomes.* These have internal structures called *genes.* These genes are usually invisible, even under high-powered microscopes, but they can be observed in some organisms. The genes are believed to function chemically, acting as catalysts to influence the growth of surrounding substance without themselves undergoing any change.

Each of the cells of human beings contains forty-eight chromosomes. In the female of the species these are arranged in twenty-four pairs. In the male there are twenty-three pairs of chromosomes, plus two others which are not paired. One of these two is called the Y chromosome and can come only from the male. Each of the forty-eight human chromosomes contains an unidentified number of genes.

Formation of New Cells. New cells are formed by division of existing ones. In ordinary cell division *each chromosome* splits so that the pattern of each of the two cells formed by the division is identical. In mature organisms certain cells are specialized for reproductive functions. In these cells *each pair of chromosomes* separates so that the *ovum* of the female gets only one-half of the mother's chromosomes and the *sperm* of the male gets only one-half of the father's chromosomes.

Fertilization, in which the sperm and ovum unite, re-establishes the full complement of chromosomes. The new cell then develops into the fetal organism by the process of ordinary cell division. The characteristics of the organism, except as they may be modified by environment, are established when the fertilization is accomplished.

Mechanisms of Heredity. The heredity of a particular factor in an individual is determined by a gene, a pair of genes, or a group of genes. Many factors are distributed over a wide range of quantity or quality in the organism, and study of the transmission of these factors is very difficult. For example, intelligence appears to be distributed so widely and in such a way that many genes must be involved. However, some traits are unitary in nature, or are at least transmitted on an all-or-none basis. These unitary traits furnish the subject matter for most of the research of trait transmission, and a particular relationship among genes called *dominance-recessiveness* gives the necessary clues for study (Morgan, 1923).

For example, the offspring of gray and white mice will all be gray. The gene carrying the gray color is *dominant* to that carrying the white. However, all these first-generation offspring are *hybrid.* That is, the pair of genes which determines coat color contains one gray gene (G) and one white gene (w). Inbreeding of these hybrids will result in ¾ gray mice and ¼ white mice. Further, ¼ of these mice will be pure grays and will breed true, whereas the other grays will reproduce in the 3:1 ratio. The determiners of color remain separate units in the hybrids.

The determination of which set of chromosomes will be provided by a parent for a particular sperm or ovum is a matter of chance.

Variations in Hereditary Patterns. Two major determinants appear to cause variation from the expected hereditary characteristics. These are (1) changes in the germ plasm itself and (2) marked changes in the environment in which the genes do their work.

MUTATIONS. Germinal variations occur, sometimes causing marked changes in the species. If the change is too severe and out of keeping with the environment, the mutated organism is

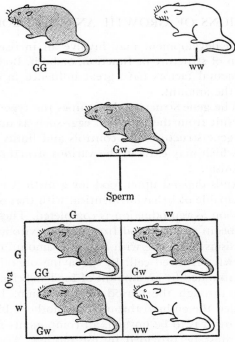

FIG. 17. Inheritance of coat color in mice.

not likely to survive. If the organism survives and can reproduce, the mutations are transmitted to its descendants. Black sheep, many albino animals, six-fingered hands and six-toed feet in man, are examples of mutations in which the organism did survive. Mutations have been produced experimentally in certain organisms through use of X rays.

ENVIRONMENTAL MODIFICATIONS. In certain animals a change in the environment in which they develop apparently modifies the controlling character of the genes. Fruit-fly experiments (Morgan) have included instances in which supernumerary legs appear if the fly is hatched and raised in a low temperature. Certain salamanders retain their gills throughout life and live in the water. Under certain changed temperature conditions the gills disappear and the same species comes out on land to remain there. Offspring kept under the same conditions become land animals for generation after generation.

CONDITIONS OF GROWTH AND DEVELOPMENT

Growth and development may involve an increase in size, a differentiation of structure or function, or both. Both hereditary and environmental factors have great influence in determining the rate and the amount.

Heredity. The gene structure determines the type of organism which will result from the fertilized egg—such as man, dog, rat, pigeon. The gene structure also controls and limits the amount of variation which may exist in the various structures of the individual organism.

Food. All cells depend upon food for growth. Unicellular organisms are capable of behavior identical with that of the parent organism as soon as reproduction is completed. These organisms immediately begin seeking food from their environment. Multicellular organisms begin life with a certain amount of food present in the newly fertilized cell. In egg-laying organisms the cell nucleus is surrounded by an amount of food sufficient to nourish the organism through the period of incubation. In mammals food is provided the embryo through the mother's blood stream. If prenatal growth is to be normal, all components necessary for such growth must be provided by the mother. After birth the organism must ingest its own food. Without food, or lacking the ability to handle food, the organism perishes. Food may be present in sufficient quantities to maintain the vital processes but may still be lacking in certain elements necessary for normal growth. Under such conditions the capacities established by the gene structure may not be realized.

Endocrine Action. *Hormones* secreted by the endocrine glands regulate many of the elements of growth. Hormones are chemical substances, emptied directly into the blood stream, which influence the distribution of chemical materials in the blood and various tissues, and influence other chemical reactions of an oxidative nature. Disturbances or imbalance of hormone secretion may result in abnormalities of growth or behavior.

PHYONE. The growth hormone secreted by the anterior lobe of the *pituitary* body is called phyone and exerts a direct influence on the size of the organism, particularly the skeleton. Deficiency of secretion results in *dwarfism* or *infantilism,* in which there is underdevelopment of bones and sexual organs. Excess results in *gigantism,* in which there is overdevelopment, particularly elongation, of the skeletal bones and of the jaw and cheek bones. If the condition should occur after adolescence, an excessive growth of the jaw, *acromegaly,* is the result.

THYROXINE. Secreted by the *thyroid* gland, thyroxine affects *metabolic rate* by influencing the oxidation of materials within the cells of the various tissues. Thyroxine also appears to affect directly certain processes of development. Deficiency results in slowing or stopping of growth, causing the kind of dwarf known as a *cretin.* Excess is related to premature maturation.

ESTROGENS AND ANDROGENS. Estrogens (female) and androgens (male), secreted by the *gonads* (sex glands), stimulate the growth of the secondary sex characteristics such as changes in hair, voice, and body build which occur in adolescence. Numerous other changes are involved such as the production of ova and sperms and the changes in the uterus which occur with the advent of pregnancy.

OTHER HORMONES. A number of other hormones are involved in the maintenance of growth potentialities, principally through their influence on cell membrane permeability and thus, generally, on the composition of the blood stream. Among the more important of these are *insulin,* the hormone of the pancreas, which is associated with the blood-sugar level; *parathormone,* the hormone of the parathyroid glands, which is associated with the amount of calcium in the blood; *adrenalin,* the hormone of the adrenal medulla, associated with the blood-sugar level and with the number of red corpuscles in the blood stream; *cortin,* from the adrenal cortex, associated with the sodium level of the blood; and *pituitin,* from the posterior lobe of the pituitary, associated with the water balance and blood pressure of the organism.

TROPIC HORMONES OF THE ANTERIOR PITUITARY. In addition to the hormones that are regularly secreted by the various endocrine glands, tropic hormones are secreted by the *anterior pituitary* (*prehypophysis*). One of these tropic hormones stimulates the growth and secretion of each of the endocrine glands. As a result of this action the pituitary is sometimes called the "master" gland.

ENDOCRINE BALANCE. The endocrines form a very complex system, with various forms of interlocking control. Disfunction of one is quite likely to be accompanied by overcompensation from another and adjustment of the organism with its environment. For example, the pituitary first stimulates the development of the gonads and is then itself checked by the action of these same gonads.

Exercise. Exercise increases consumption of the food supply and production of waste in the cells of the tissues. This results in increased heart rate and blood pressure, increased rate and depth of respiration, and a general increase in bodily tonus. The blood, under these conditions, contributes a maximum of oxygen and food to each cell of the body. Thus general development is enhanced. Continuous exercise of specific muscles causes the cells which make up these muscles to grow, resulting in the heavily muscled arms of the boxer, the heavily muscled legs of the runner, etc. Related organs such as the heart and lungs are also likely to become enlarged with excessive exercise.

GROWTH AND DEVELOPMENT BEFORE BIRTH

The growth and development of the human being before birth takes place in the *uterus,* except for a very brief period when the fertilized cell is migrating from the *oviduct* to the uterus. A structure called the *placenta* connects the mother and child. Oxygen and food substances pass through this placenta from mother to child, and carbon dioxide and waste products pass through from child to mother. The blood streams and nervous systems of mother and child are independent. Thus the physical and mental influences of the mother are limited to the amount and kind of nourishment made available in the blood stream at the point of transfer, the placenta.

Physical Growth. Several stages of growth before birth are identified.

GERMINAL PERIOD. The first two weeks after fertilization comprise the germinal period. During this time the fertilized cell divides into two smaller cells which generally remain united. If they happen to separate at this time the result is identical twins. These two cells grow and again divide, this process continuing and the number of cells increasing in geometrical progression. During the first two weeks the fertilized cell migrates from the oviduct and becomes firmly attached to the wall of the uterus.

EMBRYONIC PERIOD. This period encompasses about the next five weeks of the organism's life. Growth generally continues by cell division and subsequent enlargement. However, differentiation of structure and function begins. The beating of the cells which later develop into the adult heart occurs about the end of the first week of this period (Pflüger, 1877).

FETAL PERIOD. This period comprises the third through the ninth month of the organism. General growth continues. Differentiation of cells becomes marked. A rapid increase in size occurs. The heart and brain grow most rapidly during the fetal period. See Williams (1931) for a summary of development during this period. Because of the rapid development of the brain, and particularly the cerebral cortex, the head of the newborn infant is approximately two-thirds of its adult size.

Development. Stimulation of the fetus as early as eight weeks of menstrual age has been shown to result in movements of the arms and the body (Yanase, 1907; Minkowski, 1920). By about twelve weeks stimulation of extremities results in some general localization of response. For example, stimulation of the palm results in partial closure of the fingers (Hooker, 1938). Other reflexes definitely established as at least partially elicited in the fetal stage are the sucking response and the eyelid reflex (Minkowski, 1922; Bolaffio and Artom, 1924). Also, shifts of position by the mother affect the labyrinth of the fetus and result in turning movements.

GROWTH AND DEVELOPMENT AFTER BIRTH

Much more fully catalogued than fetal growth and behavior are the growth and behavior of the neonate (baby), the infant, the child, and the adolescent.

Physical Growth. Growth from birth to maturity does not take place at a uniform rate. Certain structures grow rapidly at first and then more slowly; others grow very little during early years and enlarge greatly during later years. This variation is reflected in changes in relative bodily proportions of the various structures. The most noticeable external structures exhibiting these marked differences in proportion are the head, the arms, and the legs (Jackson, 1914, 1928). Internal structures may vary even more in relative rate of growth (Scammon, 1930).

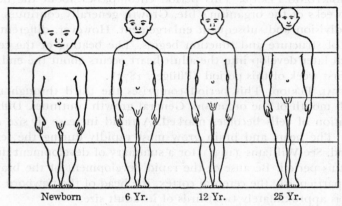

Newborn   6 Yr.   12 Yr.   25 Yr.

FIG. 18. Change in relative proportion of the human body in infancy, childhood, youth, and adult life. (From W. J. Robbins, S. Brady, A. G. Hogan, C. M. Jackson, and C. W. Green, *Growth*, Yale University Press, 1928.)

OVER-ALL GROWTH. Despite the differences in outward appearance caused by differential rates of growth in the head and neck and in the arms and legs, the general aspects of bodily growth follow this pattern: (1) rapid growth until about the fourth year; (2) relatively slow growth until about the twelfth year; (3) rapid growth until about the eighteenth year; and (4) very slow growth until maturity is reached. This pattern is characteristic of: (1) the skeleton as a whole; (2) the body musculature; (3) the blood volume; and (4) the organs of the respiratory and digestive systems.

Marked individual differences exist, and Shuttleworth (1939) has shown that the maximum growth period for an individual child may exist at almost any age. Girls are generally more mature than boys of the same age though their actual physical size is likely to be smaller except in early adolescence, where their earlier pubescence results in a temporary physical superiority.

GROWTH OF OTHER SYSTEMS. Scammon distinguishes three types of growth in addition to the general. When plotted to a common scale, the several curves are markedly different.

Neural Type. The brain and its parts, the spinal cord, the optic apparatus, and many head dimensions increase very rapidly during the first six years of life, more slowly during the next two or three years, and very little, if any, during the remainder of life. Included in this rapid early development is myelinization (outer covering) of the neurons and branching of the neurons (Flechsig, 1876; Conel, 1939).

Lymphoid Type. The lymphatic system grows very rapidly until about the twelfth year of life and then stops. In fact, parts of the system usually atrophy.

Genital Type. The sex glands and sex organs grow slightly during the first two years of life and then change little until about the twelfth year. During the next two or three years there is an extremely rapid growth. In addition, secondary sex characteristics such as pubic hair, beard in the male, enlarged mammary glands in the female, and change in voice develop very rapidly. None of the individual differences associated with growth of the various structures are more pronounced than those associated with sex. The onset of puberty may occur as early as eight or nine or may be delayed as late as the twenties.

Sensitivity. Stimuli in the form of sounds, white light, colored light, odors, solutions of sugar, salt, quinine, etc., stroking, pinching, needle pricking, water of varying temperatures, all result in an increase in the activity of the neonate. Thus, he is said to possess all the basic sensitivities, though greater stimulation may be required to produce an observable response than is required at later stages of development. Observable reaction to each stimulus applied is not universal among neonates. The conclusion stated above is established through the fact that stimulated neonates demonstrate a greater activity level than nonstimulated neonates used as controls (Pratt, Nelson, and Sun, 1930). At birth a large majority of all responses are general in nature. That is, several structures are involved in the observed activity. However, the greatest proportion of responses, both general and specific, is nearest the stimulated region.

Reflexes. During the first few days after birth the reflexes involved in feeding develop rapidly. The feeding reaction includes not only the sucking response, but the orientation of the head, lip reflexes, and swallowing (Peiper, 1936). The elimination reflexes involving both urination and defecation appear quite early (Halverson, 1940). Many infants exhibit a grasping reflex, holding a rod so tightly that they can support their own weight (Robinson, 1891; Halverson, 1937). This reflex usually disappears during the first half-year of life. Still another reflex is the plantar (Babinski) reflex in which stimulation of the sole of the foot results in movement of the toes. All these and other early reflex movements are accompanied by many diffuse general activities, and development is characterized by elimination of these extraneous movements as well as perfection of the reflexes themselves.

Locomotion. Development of locomotor habits is dependent on growth and maturation of several structures. The spine must stiffen; the bones and muscles must become strong enough to bear the infant's weight; motor and sensory nerves must mature; and the higher brain centers must mature since locomotor movements are generally voluntary.

With growth and maturation comes a sequence of activities which culminates in walking and running. The amount of time required to complete the sequence varies from infant to infant, but the sequence itself is usually followed rather closely. The major steps in this sequence are (Shirley, 1931):

> Chin up—about 1 month.
> Chest up—about 2 months.
> Sits with support—about 4 months.
> Sits alone—about 7 months.
> Stands with help—about 8 months.
> Stands holding furniture—about 9 months.
> Creeps—about 10 months.
> Walks when led—about 11 months.
> Pulls self up to furniture—about 12 months.
> Climbs stair steps—about 13 months.
> Stands alone—about 14 months.
> Walks alone—about 15 months.

Prehension. The ability to oppose thumb and forefinger in grasping small objects is one of man's major advantages over other organisms. This ability is not present at birth and usually appears in infants about the end of the first year. The development is gradual, as the following summary shows (Gesell, 1925):

No voluntary attempts to grasp objects appear during the early months of infancy.

Stimulation of the palm results in closure of the fingers, the grasping reflex. This reflex gradually disappears during the first half-year.

Both hands are moved toward an object placed before the infant about five or six months old. The object is "palmed" by whichever hand makes contact.

Later on, one hand is used instead of two, and a hand preference gradually develops.

Localization of the object nearer to the thumb and forefinger develops gradually, with the encirclement of the object still the predominant behavior.

Direct opposition of thumb and forefinger in the characteristic "pinching" position finally appears.

Vocalization and Language. Grunts, cries, vowel sounds, certain consonants, and simple combinations of consonants and vowels, all appear during the first half-year of life. These lack meaning and are really speech sounds rather than speech. Their variety is limited by such factors as lack of teeth and weakness of lip muscles.

Any one of these vocalizations may acquire meaning. A variety of expressive grunts often forms a limited vocabulary for the securing of food, attention, change of garments, etc. Speech develops from the babblings of the infant by the differentiations made by parents and others in a position to minister to the infant's wants and needs. For example, in our language the vocalization *ma-ma* is fussed over by the parents, is repeated to the infant, thus stimulating it further (the response is largely reflexive in nature), and so is finally developed into a symbolic representation which results in satisfaction of one or several of the infant's needs.

The development of language has been the subject of intensive study (Gesell, 1925; C. Bühler, 1930; Bayley, 1933; Shirley, 1933; Gesell and Thompson, 1934; C. Bühler and Hetzer, 1935; Gesell, Thompson, and Amatruda, 1938; Cattell, 1940).

The first sounds to become differentiated into words are nouns, names for things. This pattern usually begins to emerge toward the end of the first year. At about eighteen months a very rapid development of use of nouns begins, with the infant often learning the names of several things in one day. The other parts of speech gradually appear, though nouns predominate for several years.

During the second year of life the *one-word sentence* usually appears. This is a word, normally a noun, which includes the action as well as the identification. For example, "milk" may mean "I want some milk," as well as serve as the identification of the liquid in the glass.

Speech continues to develop in terms of both vocabulary and complexity throughout the childhood and adolescent stages. Some specialization usually continues throughout life. Vocabulary is one of the best indicators of mental ability as measured by our present-day intelligence tests (Terman and Merrill, 1937).

Brain injuries in certain parts of the temporal lobe produce disorders involving speech. In *aphasia* the individual loses the ability to speak words though there is nothing wrong with the vocal mechanism. In *alexia* the words can be read but have no meaning to the reader.

Gestures form an integral part of our language. Shaking the head to indicate "no," wrinkling the nose to indicate distaste, and many other gestures are language. Some of these appear to develop through attachment of meaning to reflexes. Others are definite imitations, dependent upon social structures and limited to certain cultures. Many of these occur before the infant is able to speak.

Writing is an aspect of language which develops very slowly. The child must achieve sufficient motor co-ordination to make the symbols required, and he must learn what the symbols signify. The child may learn the meaning of the symbols before he is able to reproduce them, or he may learn to copy them by rote with no meaning attached. Reproduction and interpretation are both necessary before true written language is acquired.

Emotion. Emotion in the infant appears as a state of general excitement. Differentiation of emotional patterns is dependent upon maturation of the hypothalamus and the cortex. The former appears to activate emotional activity; the latter inhibits or mediates such activity. The classification of emotions in terms of some end activity is a function of the society in which we live, and this end activity is largely learned behavior. Observation of an emotionally toned reaction without knowledge of the stimulus seldom results in proper classification.

MATURATION

Sensitivity, locomotion, prehension, speech, writing, and emotion have all been shown to depend upon maturation as well as learning. Under normal circumstances these go hand in hand. There is considerable argument as to the relative contribution of each.

Experimental Investigations of Maturation. The earliest experimenter in this field (Spaulding, 1873) worked with swallows, confined them in cages where they could not exercise their wings, and found that they flew readily when released after the time most birds fly. Carmichael (1928) placed frog eggs in two dishes, one with plain water and one with an anaesthetic. After an allotted time for maturation he found that the tadpoles in the dish of plain water swam about whereas those in the drugged water remained motionless, though apparently they had grown to the same stage of development. When plain water was substituted for the drugged water, these tadpoles swam without the more lengthy opportunity for learning.

Co-twin studies with infants, in which one infant has had no special attention whereas the other has had special training, have been attempted. The results are only partially conclusive. The studies of Johnny and Jimmy (McGraw, 1935) and of "T" and "C" (Strayer, 1930) suggest that training in motor skills and in vocabulary increases the rate of development. However, similar training given at a later stage is more efficient, as measured by the amount learned or the amount of time required to reach a given degree of mastery.

Hilgard (1932) trained a group of children in ladder-climbing while keeping a control group away from opportunity to practice the same activity. After the practice group had been trained for twelve weeks, the control group was trained for one week. At the end of the thirteenth week the two groups were identical in ladder-climbing skill.

Observations of Hopi children suggest similar conclusions. Traditional practice is to restrain movements of the infants by a binding process. Certain mothers living in the same tribe do not follow this practice. Careful observation of bound and non-bound infants shows that the average age of walking is the same for both groups (Dennis and Dennis, 1940).

Maturation Differences between Species. The development of reaction capacities is quite different in different species. The guinea pig is very nearly mature after the first day of life. The cat takes about twenty-five days to reach the same stage of maturity (Tilney and Kubie, 1931). Kellogg and Kellogg (1933) reared an ape and a child together and showed, among other things, that the ape matured much more rapidly than the child in the things which it could do. The ape's repertoire of behavior became much greater than that normally found in apes, but heredity placed a definite limit on many accomplishments, most of which the child developed without difficulty at a later stage in his maturation.

SUMMARY

All organisms are composed of cells. The number of such cells and the differentiation of them as to structure and function are determined by the gene structure. This gene structure determines the ultimate capacity of the organism. The degree to which this ultimate capacity is fulfilled is determined by food required to nourish the various cells, the hormone secretions of the endocrine glands, and exercise or training.

In the human being the organism gets its start in the uterus of the mother. Nourishment is provided through the placenta which connects mother and child. By the time of birth the organism's structures are differentiated, though sometimes in rudimentary form, and a certain amount of reception of stimuli and reaction thereto is possible. From birth onward physical growth, maturation of structure and function, and experience, all interact to enable the individual to function in his environment.

11

Learning

Modern experimental psychologists (*c.* 1920 to the present) devote more time and energy to research on learning than they do to research on any other topic in psychology. Such research has a long history. For example, Ebbinghaus (1885) systematically studied memory. Yet, it was not until psychologists accepted behavior, rather than states of consciousness, as a fit subject for study that learning became a highly important topic.

Behavior is modified through learning; of that there can be no question. However, many other factors are involved in modification of behavior—growth and maturation, drive states and emotional states, instincts and inheritance—though all these are intimately tied to learning.

The beginning student may well wonder at the tremendous amount of time devoted to the learning of white rats, chickens, monkeys, etc. and the emphasis on nonsense syllables, mazes, puzzle boxes, etc. as learning problems. His wonderment will decrease if he considers the enormous complexity of the human organism and the multitude of uncontrollable variables which surround even the simplest learning of man.

A WORKING DEFINITION OF LEARNING

Learning is the development and modification of the tendencies that govern the psychological functions (adapted from Kingsley, 1946). Such a definition does not involve commitment to any of the specific theoretical formulations of how learning occurs, nor does it exclude any. It is generally assumed that there is some concomitant change in the neural structure which parallels the modification of tendencies to action. But as Skinner (1938) has pointed out, the behavior of organisms can be studied without reference to such neural modifications. However, it must also be remembered that theories based on the study of behavior alone must not be contrary to the known facts of neural structure and function.

RESEARCH ON LEARNING PROBLEMS

The study of learning involves answering a number of questions. Hilgard (1948) raises the following: (1) the limits of learning, (2) the role of practice in learning, (3) the importance of reward, punishment, or other motives, (4) the place of understanding and insight, (5) the effect of prior learning on later learning of something else, and (6) the events of remembering and forgetting. Most of the controlled laboratory experiments have been aimed at securing evidence on one or more of these questions.

Criteria of Learning. General observation of change in the functional tendencies is insufficient for experimental purposes. Specific criteria of learning are established to define the change. The general criteria of learning are quantitative measures of *performance* (accomplishment), as indicated by *amount, time* (speed), and *errors* (accuracy). Learning is said to take place when the amount increases, the time for increase is reduced, or the number of errors is reduced. Forgetting is indicated when these measures are in the opposite direction. These general criteria are applicable to both animal and human learning. However, the ability of the human organism to verbalize has led to the use of special criteria of language learning.

RECALL. The subject (S) is required to recall or reproduce the material he has been learning.

RECOGNITION. The material which S has been learning is presented along with other material, and S is required to indicate the items he recognizes as having observed before in the experiment.

RELEARNING. In the "savings method," S is required to relearn material previously learned. The time required to relearn is compared with the time required for the original learning.

These three measures for human learning are not interchangeable, though they have been so treated by some experimenters.

Tasks for the Study of Learning. Learning tasks (materials,

problems) are samples of psychological activities which are selected by experimenters for the study of the process of learning.
A large number of materials have been standardized. The use of
such standard materials permits comparison of results from different psychological laboratories.

PROBLEM BOXES. S is placed in a situation where he must learn
certain reactions to escape confinement or secure other appropriate reward. In the learning task S may be required to pull the
correct string or strings, to manipulate latches or levers, or to
step on contacts in the floor in a certain sequence. Measures of
learning are: (1) the time required to solve the problem (a decrease in subsequent times showing the progress of learning),
(2) the number of errors committed (a decrease in errors indicating learning), or (3) some combination of the two.

MAZES. S is placed in a starting compartment from which he
must traverse a path containing cul-de-sacs (blind alleys) to get
the reward. The measure of learning may be time, errors, or
number of trials. Paper and pencil, or other "tracing mazes," are
used with human subjects.

DISCRIMINATION APPARATUS. Problem apparatus is provided in
which S must learn to make differential reactions to different
sensory stimuli. Representative tasks are turning left when confronted with a triangle and right if the stimulus is a circle, or
pressing a key with the right hand if the light is red and with the
left hand if the light is green.

DELAYED-REACTION APPARATUS. S may be placed in a "choice
situation" as a learning task, but the reaction must be delayed
for a time after presentation of the stimulus. The measure is the
maximum delay following which the learner can make the correct reaction, or the percentage of correct reactions following a
given period of delay.

CONDITIONING APPARATUS. S is placed in a situation in which
presentation of a stimulus will evoke some previously identified
response. This stimulus is presented along with some normally
inadequate stimulus. The measure is the number of presentations which will convert the normally inadequate stimulus into
one which evokes the desired response.

MEMORY DRUMS. Standard verbal materials are typed or
printed on a strip of heavy paper or cloth which is fastened
around a drum that is completely enclosed except for an expo-

sure window. As the drum revolves, succeeding items appear. The subject may be required to anticipate the next item or to associate a stimulus word with a second word. The number of trials necessary to reach a predetermined criterion level is the most frequent measure of learning.

PURSUIT ROTOR OR PURSUITMETER. S uses a jointed stylus to pursue a metal disc set flush with the surface of a turntable which revolves at a relatively high rate of speed. The target may move in a synchronous or asynchronous pattern, and speed may be varied. The measure of learning is usually the total time spent in contact with the disc during successive practice periods of equal duration.

MULTIPLE-CHOICE PROBLEMS. S is presented with a number of choices such as keys, one of which will extinguish a light. When the correct solution is found, another problem is presented. The correct choice can be determined by some principle. The measure is the number of problems necessary to learn the principle.

EVERYDAY ACTIVITIES. Human learning has also been investigated by means of such ordinary motor tasks as dart-throwing, typing, telegraphy, etc. and such symbolic or verbal tasks as learning poetry, working arithmetic problems, picture completion, and others.

GENERAL PHENOMENA OF LEARNING

The definition of learning implies progress, though the scientific usage does not necessarily imply desirable direction from the social point of view. This progress is shown graphically in a *learning curve.* This is a graph of the relationship between some measure of learning (errors, time, amount) on one axis (*ordinate*) and the number of trials or length of practice on the other (*abscissa*).

Individual and Group Curves. Plotting the progress of one or a small number of learners' responses ordinarily gives a curve which is very irregular. Wide variations and many fluctuations are characteristic of all individual curves, but a continual decrease in errors or increase in performance is shown in the curves. If the results for a group of learners are averaged, and these averages are plotted, the curve loses its irregularities and becomes smooth. See Fig. 19, p. 149.

Forms of the Learning Curve. Many attempts have been made to derive an equation for a generalized learning curve. However, the conditions of a given experiment usually control the shape of the curve found. Most curves approach one of three forms—a convex curve, a concave curve, or an S-curve. See Fig. 20, p. 150.

Convex Curves. Early practice results in relatively large increments of success (gain), and later practice is less productive of

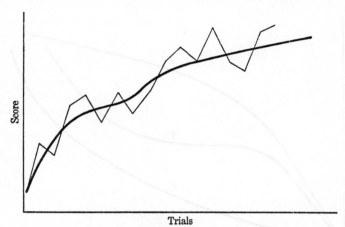

FIG. 19. Comparison of an individual learning curve (the irregular light line) and a smooth curve plotted from averages for 25 subjects.

gain. The learning curve is said to be *negatively accelerated*. This form usually appears when the subject already possesses certain skills or knowledge which may be utilized in the new task or when special motivation or interest in the task is present.

Concave Curves. Early practice results in relatively small increments of success, and later practice is more productive of gain. The learning curve is said to be *positively accelerated*. This form usually appears when the subject begins close to the zero level in skills or knowledges required and the task being studied involves later organization or synthesis of these skills or knowledges.

S-Curves. In early practice the curve is positively accelerated, shifting to negative acceleration as practice continues. An inverted S-curve, the reverse of the above, may also be found. The parts of an S-curve are likely to be separated by a *plateau*.

Plateau Phenomena. Plateaus are segments, especially in individual curves, where the curve flattens out and there is no ap-

preciable progress in learning. Various explanations have been
offered for plateaus. The first learning integrations may undergo
a period of automatization (habituation or "stamping in") ; the
intent of the learner may be changed; fatigue or boredom may
set in; new skills may be required before transition to the next
level of learning is possible; or other conditions may be aroused.
The plateau phenomena were first brought into prominence by

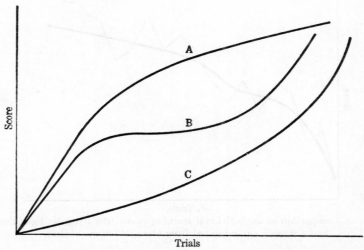

Fig. 20. Learning curves. A. Convex curve showing rapid initial learning
followed by slower later learning. B. S-curve showing rapid initial learning,
then almost no learning in terms of score, and another period of rapid learning. C. Concave curve showing slow initial learning followed by rapid later
learning.

the studies of telegraphic-skills learning by Bryan and Harter
(1897, 1899) . See Fig. 21, p. 151.

The marked deceleration which characterizes a curve approaching a high level of performance is often called the *end
plateau.* This may be due to a *physiological limit* reached by the
learner, but it is more likely to be due to realization of the goal
set by the learner. Increased motivation will often result in
higher levels of performance.

"Insight" Phenomena. In certain types of learning, notably
that known as problem-solving, the solution appears suddenly
and little or no further improvement is noted. The phenomenon

is evident in the curves of some of Thorndike's puzzle-box experiments (1911), but it was Köhler's experiments with chimpanzees (1925) which led to great interest in the problem.

CHARACTERISTIC TYPES OF LEARNING

Though the various theoretical formulations may emphasize one type of learning and attempt to subsume all others under it, it is common practice to differentiate several types of learning. Such titles as conditioning, trial-and-error learning, insight learn-

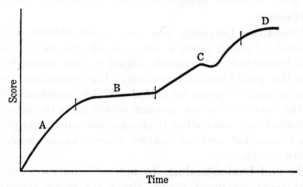

FIG 21. Learning curve showing initial spurt (A), plateau (B), end spurt (C), and final plateau (D).

ing, etc. permit grouping of research findings about a common topic. However, there is the danger that preoccupation with a particular type of learning may make the experimenter insensitive to some major differences in type.

Associative Learning. Discussion of association as the principle of learning dates from Aristotle and reached its historical peak in the work of the English associationist philosophers of the 18th and 19th centuries. The principal subject matter was "ideas," and the laws of association were *contiguity, similarity,* and *contrast.* However, no experimentation was offered in support of the discussion, and modern association theories are based on behavior rather than ideas.

Conditioning. The careful study of the association of stimuli and responses, and particularly the development of substitute stimuli, dates from the work of Pavlov, Bekhterev, and Twitmyer, about 1900. (The principles have been discussed in detail in Chapter 4.) Essentially, conditioning involves presentation of two stimuli in close temporal contiguity, one of these stimuli known to be adequate for production of a particular response and the other known to be normally inadequate. With repeated presentation the originally inadequate stimulus becomes effective for elicitation of the response. Or, in a later development known as instrumental conditioning, an inadequate stimulus is present, and the organism in its more or less random activity performs an act selected as the one to be rewarded (or reinforced in other ways); with repeated presentation the inadequate stimulus becomes effective.

Trial-and-Error Learning. The task of the learner is to select the correct response from a large repertoire of available responses. Puzzle-box experiments afford a good example of this form in the psychological laboratory. The stimulated organism performs a great amount of varied activity, eventually "hitting upon" the correct response, the one which leads to the appropriate reward. With succeeding trials the amount of inappropriate activity diminishes and the correct action occurs more quickly and more surely.

Insight and Understanding. In marked contrast to more mechanical types discussed above, there are many situations in which the solution appears suddenly (insight) or in which the organism demonstrates understanding of a problem with little or no previous experience with the exact situation. Insight and understanding are most likely to occur when: (1) problems are solvable by grasp of a general principle, relation, or method; (2) a new condition, motivation, or method of attack is introduced; or (3) the act which solves the problem is unitary, or at least simple. Insight learning is least likely to occur when the task must be accomplished by mastery of a number of part solutions.

FACTORS WHICH INFLUENCE LEARNING

There are several generally agreed-upon factors which influence learning. The way in which these interact forms the core of the problem for learning theorists.

Drive and Motivation. Activity does not occur in the absence of some drive or motive. The experiment in learning is frequently aimed at determination of the effect of different drives or motives, or at determination of the effect of different degrees or amounts of drive. It is impossible to measure drive directly. Some measure of control is usually exerted by depriving the organism of food, water, sex, etc.; applying shock or other presumably noxious stimuli; or, in the case of human beings, applying symbolic (frequently verbal) motives. Motivation of itself is insufficient for learning. There must be some reward or other reinforcement. Thus, the deprived rat gets food at the end of the maze; the child who works the arithmetic problems is praised.

The importance of motivation was first stressed by Thorndike (1898). Called the *Law of Effect*, the basic principle is as follows: "When a modifiable connection between a stimulus and a response is made and is followed or accompanied by a satisfying state of affairs, that connection's strength is increased. When made and accompanied by an annoying state of affairs, its strength is decreased." This formulation has been attacked many times, usually because of the hedonistic implications of the statements and because of the experiments which show punishment to be effective. Nevertheless, some basic relationship between motivation and reinforcement is found in almost all learning.

McGeoch (1942) has summarized the relationships somewhat as follows and identified them with representative experiments:

1. Motive-incentive conditions determine to a great degree the directional persistence (set) which is essential to learning (Moss, 1924; Warden, 1931).

2. A potential incentive (e.g., food) without a corresponding motive (e.g., hunger) is ineffective as a condition of learning (Carr, 1917).

3. Learning is slight and very slow when a motivating condition (e.g., hunger) is present but when there is no corresponding incentive (e.g., food) (Blodgett, 1929; Tolman and Honzik, 1930).

4. When an incentive object appropriate to the motive is present early in practice and is later removed, learning ceases and a disintegration of the activity already learned may occur (Sharp, 1929; Bruce, 1930).

5. There is some relationship between learning and the strength of the motives which are operating (Ligon, 1929), and between learning and the amount or intensity of the incentives (Grindley, 1929).

6. Incentives and, inferentially, motives differ widely in their influence on learning, and only sometimes are two motive-incentive conditions acting together superior to one alone (Simmons, 1924; Bunch and Magdsick, 1938).

7. Even with infrahuman organisms, symbolic incentives (e.g., coins, poker chips) may serve as determiners of learning (Williams, 1929; Wolfe, 1936; Cowles, 1937).

Repetition and Practice. Except for unitary or extremely simple activities, some repetition is usually necessary for successful performance, or for improvement and perfection of performance. But repetition of itself is insufficient. Thorndike originally posed a *Law of Exercise* which did make repetition a very important factor in strengthening connections, thus raising the probability that a given response would occur. In 1929 Thorndike reversed himself, stating that connections get established or reinforced by being rewarded, not by just occurring.

Repetition with reinforcement builds habit strength, the probability that a given response will occur again in a given stimulus situation. Further, in a complex situation where there are many elements in the response pattern, a kind of discrimination learning occurs as correct elements are rewarded more frequently and erroneous responses drop through lack of reward.

One of the more consistent findings of learning experimentation is that *distributed practice* is superior to *massed practice*. This is true for a large variety of materials and for many different time intervals of rest or substitute activity (e.g., nonsense syllables by Jost, 1897; mirror-drawing by Lorge, 1930; finger mazes by Crook, 1937; code substitution by Gentry, 1940; and many others). Many possibilities have been advanced as explanations of the phenomena—rehearsal, fatigue, interest and motivation, perseveration, and differential forgetting. Of these the last named possible factor seems to explain more of the data than do the others.

Generalization and Transfer of Training. By "transfer of training" is meant the effect of practice in one activity on accomplishment in another activity. In its earliest form transfer of training was accounted for in terms of *faculties*. The faculty psychologists held that memory, will, reasoning, etc. were in themselves strengthened by practice just as a muscle is strengthened by exercise. Experimental evidence, beginning with James in 1890, has been consistently against such an interpretation. Nevertheless, transfer effects are common. There are positive effects in which prior learning facilitates future learning and negative effects in which prior training inhibits future learning.

Most research studies have aimed at positive transfer, possibly because of the greater utility of the findings. However, one basic principle, sometimes called the *Müller-Schumann law of associative inhibition* (1894), can account for most of the negative transfer findings: If two items, A and B, have been associated, it is more difficult to form an association between either and a third item, C. Simply, it is a case of habit interference. If learning something new requires repression or extinction of previous learning, negative transfer is likely to result.

What is transferred in positive transfer is not always clear, but various experiments offer evidence for a number of hypotheses.

LEARNING TO LEARN. Practice on successive samples of the same kind of material almost invariably shows a positive effect. This is true even though specific items of the material may be affected by factors which would normally bring about negative transfer effects (e.g., learning the opposite response as the new correct response).

IDENTICAL ELEMENTS. A simple example will suffice. Practice in adding will transfer positively to multiplying because multiplication includes addition in obtaining the correct response. Thorndike (1914) proposed this as the basis of all transfer.

GENERALIZATIONS AND PRINCIPLES. The classic experiment is that of Judd (1908), who trained one group of boys in the principle of refraction while they practiced throwing darts at targets under water. A control group also threw darts but were not given the principle of refraction. When the depth of the targets under water was changed, the group which had been taught the principle adjusted more readily to the new situation. Judd emphasized determination of the principle or generalization as the major factor in transfer.

SET OR ORIENTATION. Though it is difficult to isolate and test for, transfer of set is evident in most transfer experiments. It is the directional factor which results in the individual's looking for identical elements, principles, and so on.

CROSS-MEMBER. Training one member of the body to perform a task also trains partially all other members capable of making the response. Thus, practice in throwing darts with the right hand improves somewhat the performance of the left.

Other Factors. There are several other factors which have been isolated and studied.

INTRASERIAL PHENOMENA. Many learning tasks consist of a series of parts or steps which must be learned in order. Curves of the learning of the parts or steps are customarily bow-shaped, showing that the initial and final steps are most easily learned and the middle portions learned with most difficulty.

MEANINGFULNESS. There is a direct relationship between meaning of the material to be learned and the rate of learning. Nonsense syllables are harder to learn than comparable three-letter words, just as a list of unrelated words is harder to learn than a list of related words (McGeoch, 1930).

SENSE MODALITY INVOLVED. There is little real evidence concerning the superiority of any sense modality in reception of material to be learned, except of course as particular materials restrict themselves. There is evidence that stimulation of more than one sense aids learning (Cohn, 1897; Barlow, 1928; Koch, 1930; Honzik, 1936).

WHOLE VS. PART METHODS. With material which cannot be learned with one or a few repetitions, the material may be learned in one of three ways: (1) it may be practiced as a whole unit until it is learned; (2) it may be broken into parts, with the parts combined into the whole after each is learned; or (3) it may be learned by parts with each part incorporated with all that has been previously learned as it is learned. Evidence for any one method is controversial. Woodworth (1938) gives the suggestion, after a careful review of the studies, that: "In a practical situation it is probably best to start with the whole method while feeling free to concentrate at any time on a part where something special is to be learned."

ACTIVE VS. PASSIVE LEARNING. Active participation in the learning task (recitations, verbalizations, and other activities) increases the efficiency of the learning process (Gates, 1917).

RETENTION AND FORGETTING

Any measurable degree of persistence of material learned is considered evidence of retention. There are five principal ways in which retention is measured: (1) recall, (2) recognition, (3) reconstruction, (4) relearning, and (5) transfer. These measures are not interchangeable (Luh, 1922).

Curves of Retention. Ebbinghaus (1885), studying retention of nonsense syllables by the savings method (relearning), developed a curve of retention. He found that the amount retained dropped rapidly at first, then less and less rapidly, giving a negatively accelerated curve. This curve has often been used as *the* curve of retention. Most curves of retention do show a similar form, but certain curves depart markedly.

Factors in Retention. Most of the factors found important to learning are also important for retention, but there are some additional important factors for retention.

INDIVIDUAL DIFFERENCES. More intelligent individuals usually retain more than less intelligent. Rapid learners retain more than slow learners (Gillette, 1936).

Exceptional memorizers sometimes appear. Investigation reveals that persons with this ability usually restrict their performance to some very narrow range of materials, practice at every opportunity, and operate under very high motivation.

TYPE OF MATERIAL INVOLVED. Meaningful material is retained much more easily than nonmeaningful material. Similarly, integrated habits such as perceptual-motor activities of typing or bicycle-riding seem less likely to show the sharp initial drop in retention. The evidence on superior retention of perceptual-motor activities is equivocal since it is extremely difficult to equate them with verbal-ideational tasks and to control such factors in learning as motivation and repetition.

Pleasantly toned materials are generally shown to be retained slightly better than unpleasantly toned materials or indifferent materials (Barrett, 1938; Sharp, 1938).

DEGREE OF ORIGINAL LEARNING. As original learning increases, retention increases. Thus, if repetition is continued past the point of successful response (commonly called *overlearning*), retention is increased (Ebbinghaus, 1885; Krueger, 1929).

DISTRIBUTED PRACTICE. Retention is greater where distributed practice has been used in learning (Robinson, 1921).

RECITATION DURING LEARNING. Retention is greater where recitation has been used in the learning task (Gates, 1917; Forlano, 1936).

INTENT TO REMEMBER. Learning with the intent to remember results in greater retention than mere learning with the intent to learn. This factor even persists for specific time intervals. Thus, Geyer (1930) found recall to be less when a recall test came *either* sooner or later than expected.

COMPLETED VS. UNCOMPLETED TASKS. There is some evidence (Zeigarnik, 1927; Pachauri, 1935) that interrupted tasks are recalled better than those which were completed.

Reminiscence. Under certain conditions retention curves rise for a time before the customary decrement sets in. Essentially, if practice is too brief to result in complete learning, a recall test given after the lapse of some time interval results in higher scores than a recall test given immediately after the practice period.

Ballard (1913) and Williams (1926) have found the phenomenon to persist from one to five days in the learning of meaningful materials such as long sections of poetry. Ward (1937) and Hovland (1938) have secured reminiscence for periods of two to twenty minutes in the learning of nonsense syllables. Numerous theories have been proposed to account for the reminiscence phenomenon. The best explanations seem to be those which emphasize the dissipation of interference and inhibition effects.

Qualitative Changes in What Is Retained. Meaningful materials such as pictures, stories, etc., or nonmeaningful materials which suggest meaningful relationships, tend to change organization. Details are lost but principles remain (Bartlett, 1932).

Forgetting. The most characteristic factor of forgetting is the decrement in retention which appears in time, even where such phenomena as reminiscence are found. This time element has often led to the conclusion that *disuse* was the explanation of forgetting. However, the accumulated evidence indicates that it is what goes on in the time interval, rather than the interval itself, that is important to forgetting.

INTERFERENCE OF INTERVENING ACTIVITIES. Experiments of the general type known as *retroactive inhibition studies* have shown that there are numerous specific variables involved in retention, though not all are isolated at this time. The basic experiment equates two groups in learning, permitting one group to rest while the other performs some other activity, and retesting on the original material. Decrements found are attributed to the interpolated activity. Among the best supported generalizations are: (1) the greater the degree of original learning, the less the effect of the interpolated activity; (2) with the degree of learning held constant, interference is greater with additional repetitions of the interpolated activity; (3) with the degree of original learning held constant, interference is greater with increasing amounts of material interpolated, more so than with repetitions of a smaller amount of material; and (4) the less activity intervening, the less the forgetting.

A major experiment bearing on the last-named generalization was performed by Jenkins and Dallenbach (1924). They compared recall of lists of 10 nonsense syllables after 1, 2, 4, and 8 hours of waking activity with recall after similar periods spent almost entirely in sleep. At all intervals tested, recall was greater after sleep than after waking activity, and after 2 hours of sleep no decrement of learning was found.

CHANGE IN SURROUNDINGS. It is seldom, if ever, that the exact stimulus situation is repeated whenever a response is elicited. Thus, it is often found that recall is impossible in one situation but is possible where additional cues of the original stimulus situation are present. The phenomenon is commonplace. We readily call Jones by name in his office but cannot recall the name when we meet him on the street.

CHANGE IN SET. Closely related to the stimulus situation is the set of the learner. The set operates to control the direction of attempted recall, recognition, etc. A faulty set will inhibit responses in the right direction.

PERSONALITY ADJUSTMENTS IN FORGETTING. With particular reference to the adjustments of everyday life, the psychoanalysts point to conflict and succeeding repression as an important cause of forgetting. We forget what we prefer not to remember. The concept is difficult to test experimentally, but it is certainly in accord with much everyday observation.

THEORIES OF LEARNING

Theories of learning and its relations have been advanced with varying amounts of detail. Some of these have been part of larger theories of behavior; others have been specifically concerned with one aspect of learning, a type of theory now becoming known as a *miniature system*. Ebbinghaus's papers on memory, 1885, probably represent the first miniature system.

In view of the amount of data given in the previous pages without reference to particular theory, the reader may wonder at the emphasis now being given to theories of learning. Theories are here presented from the point of view that they serve to "bridge the gaps" in knowledge. Experimentation then becomes a matter of verifying hypotheses rather than trial-and-error search for empirical relationships.

Hilgard (1948) devotes a chapter to each of nine learning theories: Thorndike's Connectionism (1898, 1911, 1913, 1928, 1932, 1935 *) ; Guthrie's Contiguous Conditioning (1935, 1938, 1942, 1946) ; Hull's Systematic Behavior Theory (1940, 1943) ; Skinner's Descriptive Behaviorism (1938) ; Current Functionalism (Woodworth, 1918, 1938; Robinson, 1932; Carr, 1925, 1930) ; Gestalt Theory (Koffka, 1924, 1935; Köhler, 1925, 1929, 1940, 1947) ; Lewin's Topological and Vector Psychology (1936, 1938) ; Wheeler's Organismic Psychology (1929, 1932, 1940) ; and Tolman's Sign-Gestalt Theory (1932).

It should not be supposed that all the systems mentioned above are completely incompatible. The same experiments frequently support more than one theorist. A brief description of the basic tenets of some of the theories, without critical comment, will serve as explanation.

Thorndike and the Laws of Effect, Readiness, and Exercise. For Thorndike, learning occurs by establishment of "bonds" or "connections" between sense impressions (stimuli) and impulses to action (responses). The most common form of learning is trial-and-error learning, or learning by selecting and connecting. The basic experiment in learning is the puzzle box, in which the animal hits upon the correct response by trying a variety of activity. This correct response is then rewarded. If the reward is "satisfying" the connection is strengthened; if the effect is "annoying" the connection is weakened. The concepts of satisfying and annoying created a storm center, particularly among those who showed the efficacy of punishment in bringing about learning. Also, as used by Thorndike, these concepts had a hedonistic

* The dates given in this paragraph represent major publications bearing on the theories listed.

ring, but his illustrations frequently indicated that an over-all satisfyingness in terms of the goal might include elements of learning which were definitely annoying. This "effect" is related to "readiness." Essentially readiness is the set, the preparation for action. Activity consonant with the set is satisfying; activity inappropriate to the set is annoying or frustrating. Finally, a connection is strengthened through repetition, the Law of Exercise. In his later work Thorndike virtually "repealed" the Law of Exercise, except as repetition was also rewarded.

Supplementing the basic structure covered by the three laws are many other principles: (1) the organism must be capable of varying its responses; (2) the total attitude or set guides learning and also determines what is satisfying or annoying; (3) there are prepotent elements which bring about selective reaction; (4) new situations are responded to in terms of similar past situations; (5) a response may be shifted to a new stimulus situation; (6) transfer of training occurs through presence of identical elements; (7) connections are more easily formed if *belongingness* exists; and (8) a rewarding state of affairs reinforces not only the connection rewarded but also any neighboring connections that happen to exist.

Guthrie and Contiguous Conditioning. Guthrie states (1935), "A combination of stimuli which has accompanied a movement will on its recurrence tend to be followed by that movement." Guthrie then goes on to explain a large number of the facts of learning with this one principle. Guthrie does not indulge in definitive experiments. *Cats in a Puzzle Box* (1946) by Guthrie and Horton represents the most thorough work in support of Guthrie's theory. The cats did indicate a large amount of stereotype behavior. For example, a cat which had escaped from the box by backing into the release pole kept on backing. According to Guthrie's theory, this was to be expected since that was the last act in the stimulus situation.

Guthrie's theory demands that a stimulus-response pattern be learned in one pairing. Improvement with practice occurs because the task is composed of a large number of habits and, though any one cue may be attached to the correct response in one trial, the mastery of all the cues and movements gives the customary learning curves.

Guthrie does not enunciate principles; he gives examples.

From these may be derived certain principles: (1) forgetting is due to new learning, to interference with old habits, since the new response must be conditioned to an old cue; (2) motivation determines the presence of movements which get associated with cues, but it does not control the direction of learning; (3) reward serves to fixate the last response, but simply because it ends the activity and prevents other acts from succeeding the appropriate one; and (4) internal stimuli and general environmental stimuli give direction to activities where organized, sequential behavior is observed.

Hull and Sixteen Postulates of Behavior. For Hull, learning is the formation of habit hierarchies. Learning takes place when a reinforcing state of affairs exists in the specific consummatory acts brought about as a result of activity initiated because of the existence of primary drives. The system is developed largely from information collected by the conditioned response paradigms (both classical and instrumental) and is strictly a mechanistic explanation. Hull's position is stated explicitly, along with a considerable amount of experimental evidence, in *Principles of Behavior* (1943). Various types of material are used in the experiments cited: mazes, Skinner boxes, nonsense syllables, classical conditioning apparatus. Both human and infrahuman subjects contribute, but the preference is probably for the white rat as the most stable subject for experimentation.

The behavioral event is a stimulus provided by the external world and a response which interplays with the events of the external world. Between these are unknowns. Hull believes that these intervening variables can be quantified through manipulation of the stimulus situation and the response situation.

Some understanding of Hull's variables may be derived from tracing the hypothetical chain between stimulus and response. Tracing this backward from response to stimulus:

> 1. In a given stimulus situation there is a *momentary effective reaction potential* which will evoke a response if it exists above the *reaction threshold*.
> 2. The *momentary effective reaction potential* is the *effective reaction potential* as modified by *oscillation*, a construct devised to account for instant-to-instant variation in the organism.
> 3. The *effective reaction potential* is the total *reaction potential* reduced by *reactive inhibition* (a condition developed through the simple act of responding to previous stimulation and

dissipated with rest) and by *conditioned inhibition* (a condition developed from stimuli associated with cessation of the rewarding state of affairs and not dissipated with rest).

4. The *reaction potential* is developed through some interaction of *drive* (a need state which varies in strength) and *generalized habit strength.*

5. The *generalized habit strength* is derived from the specific *habit strength* established by *reinforcement* of a particular *stimulus-response connection* and affected by stimuli on the same continuum as the originally reinforced stimulus-response situation.

The core of the theory is *reinforcement,* since it is only by reinforcement that habit strength develops and so makes possible the final response. In this connection, development of *secondary reinforcement* becomes highly important. All the properties of the situation associated with need reduction take on the properties of secondary reinforcement. Thus, the maze, the goal box, the specific environmental situation, all help maintain habit strength and play a major role in protracted behavior sequences.

Tolman and Purposive Behavior. The theories of Thorndike, Guthrie, and Hull have among other things in common an emphasis on the relatively mechanical, almost stupid, nature of much learning. Tolman emphasizes the goal-directed nature of behavior and gives the organism much more credit for knowing what is going on. In fact, one critic has said that Tolman left his rat "buried in thought." His system has neither the central principle of Thorndike or Guthrie nor the attempted quantification of Hull. It does have a series of concepts supported by evidence not adequately assimilated by the first three theories discussed. The principal experiment of Tolman is maze-learning by rats with behavior at the choice point as the measured response.

For Tolman, the organism does not learn a simple stimulus-response; it learns a *sign-significate.* That is, instead of learning correct movement sequences, the organism learns to follow signs toward a goal. In many instances the predicted outcome of the two types would be identical, so Tolman is forced to find situations in which differences will be shown. Three such situations have been proposed:

REWARD EXPECTANCY. If the reward used in a learning situation is changed (e.g., if a less-preferred food is substituted for a more-preferred food), the behavior of the organism changes, thus indicating a particular reward expectancy.

PLACE-LEARNING. If a maze is altered so that the path originally learned is blocked and several alternative new paths are provided, the organism will choose the path which is most directly oriented toward the goal rather than the one which is most similar to the learned path.

LATENT LEARNING. If an organism is forced through the maze in such a way that the correct path is eventually traversed but is not rewarded, little or no learning is evidenced by its performance. If reward is suddenly introduced, performance immediately shows evidence of learning. The organism is said to have demonstrated latent learning. A *cognitive map* of the situation has been established; learning and performance are not the same thing.

Tolman presents three groups of laws in *Purposive Behavior in Animals and Men* (1932). These are: (1) capacity laws, (2) laws relative to the nature of the material, and (3) laws relative to the manner of presentation. These laws are descriptive in nature rather than equational.

Tolman's capacity laws define a hierarchy of learning and learners. Only organisms can learn, and the following qualifications apply: (1) For simple sign-*Gestalt*-expectation learning of the conditioning type the organism must have the capacity for sign-learning (i.e., determining what leads to what), for discriminating and manipulating devices, and for retaining the results of earlier trials. (2) For trial-and-error learning these are needed plus the capacity for determining field relationships of alternate routes, detours, etc. In addition, ideational capacities which permit determination of these relationships without active manipulation are helpful. (3) For inventive learning all these plus creative instability are needed.

The laws relating to the nature of the material are perceptual in nature. Thus, togetherness, fusibility, and other *Gestalt* characteristics are needed to establish the sign-significate relationship.

The laws relative to manner of presentation are closely related to the empirical facts presented earlier in the chapter: frequency, recency, revival after extinction, primacy, distributed repetition, temporal relations, emphasis, motivation, etc. Two distinctions should be noted. Effect is discarded and emphasis is substituted. Effect relates to the performance observed, not to the learning. Emphasis on the learning may be provided by the effect situation. Motivation leads to activity, guided by the expectancies or cognitive structures available, not directly to acquisition.

Gestalt Theory and the Problem of Insight. The translation (1925) of Köhler's book, *Mentality of Apes,* brought into English examples of learning in animals which was far removed from the apparently stupid learning of Thorndike's cats. Almost simultaneously (1924) a translation of Koffka's *Growth of the Mind* attacked trial-and-error learning. The Gestalt psychologists placed great emphasis on the *structuring (Gestalt)* of the situation, giving examples of the greatly altered ability to perform the desired task brought about through simple changes in the observed relationships of the problem.

The Gestalt psychologists are particularly interested in perception and in explaining the present condition of the organism without reference to antecedent conditions. However, the influence of past experience on learning cannot well be denied. To account for this a *memory trace* is posited. This trace persists from a prior experience, interacts with present processes which are related, and becomes a modified trace. The trace may also undergo modification without definite interacting experience. In this case, changes will be in the direction of "good" *Gestalt.*

Koffka proposes four laws, all of which illustrate the general principle: (1) the *Law of Similarity*—the memory trace selected by the excitatory process will be one which possesses the same *wholeness* character; (2) the *Law of Proximity*—old impressions are less well organized and recalled than new ones because the recent trace is nearer in time; (3) the *Law of Closure*—reward is an end process which completes the activity and relieves tension; and (4) the *Law of Good Continuation*—learning is organization of the structure.

Such hypotheses are well suited to explanation of the phenomena of insight. However, it is difficult to establish empirical proof, largely because of the difficulty of predicting the elements of structuring which will produce insight at a given time and place. Studies of Maier (1945) on reasoning and of Katona (1940) on organization in memorizing argue well for the emphasis on structuring and organization.

Other Theoretical Positions. The five theories cited above do not nearly exhaust the formulations. However, their proponents have done the most toward working through comprehensive systems. The following others are worthy of mention.

SKINNER AND OPERANT BEHAVIOR. Skinner refuses to postulate the existence of stimuli where none can be observed. Instead, he evolves the concept that much of behavior is *operant* in nature (*emitted* rather than *elicited*). Using the *Skinner box* (his own development) he has studied the building of a *reflex reserve* (a tendency to press the lever in the box) through a variety of reinforcing situations. His findings cause serious difficulty for those who theorize a generalized relationship between habit strength and reinforcement.

LEWIN AND TOPOLOGICAL PSYCHOLOGY. Though Lewin was not interested in learning as such, several concepts of his psychology have considerable bearing on the problems of learning. Lewin's problems are strictly human problems and involve such concepts as extending and differentiating the *life-space* of the individual, using the factors of *ego-involvement* and *level of aspiration,* in interpretation of what is reward or success, and emphasizing the importance of the present.

WHEELER AND GROWTH PRINCIPLES. A hypothesis of stimulation-induced maturation is advanced as an explanation of learning. This is based on embryological studies and other studies which show that organisms grow into certain forms of behavior (e.g., the infant grows into walking and talking).

Summary of Theories of Learning. Present theories of learning have large differences in the various generalizations and laws put forward in explanation of the learning process. No one of them as yet accounts for all the problems and facts of learning.

SUMMARY

Learning may be defined as the development and modification of the tendencies that govern the psychological functions. Such learning may be studied from several points of view—the basic nature of the learning process, retention and forgetting, the limits of learning, the role of practice in learning, the importance of various kinds of motives, and the application of learned techniques or materials.

Learning takes place when for a given task or situation the amount accomplished is increased, the time required for a definite increase is reduced, or the number of errors is reduced. Forgetting is indicated when the opposite happenings occur.

Learning is studied by means of problem boxes, mazes, discrimination apparatus, delayed reaction apparatus, conditioning apparatus, memory drums, pursuitmeters, multiple-choice problems, and everyday activities.

Learning is greatly influenced by drive and motivation, repetition and practice, generalization and opportunity to transfer, and numerous rather specific factors such as meaningfulness of material, sense modality involved, and method used. The same factors influence retention of learned material.

Many different theories and partial theories have been advanced to explain learning phenomena. No one of them can account for all the phenomena and research findings. Each has value in interrelating a body of fact and in creating hypotheses and postulates to be tested in future research. Among the more widely discussed theories are those generally credited to these psychologists: Thorndike, Guthrie, Hull, Skinner, Tolman, Wheeler, Lewin, Koffka and Köhler, and Carr and Robinson.

12

Thinking and Problem-Solving

Thinking is a psychological category chiefly concerned with behavior in a problem situation. All behavior is motivated toward some objective. When this behavior is disrupted by a barrier, physical or otherwise, a problem occurs.

VARIETIES OF THINKING

The term *thinking* is sometimes used to include varieties of behavior other than problem-solving.

Autistic Thinking. Autistic thinking, often called *daydreaming,* is a means of creating a world which is more gratifying to the individual than the world of reality. In the dream world of autistic thinking, the individual's behavior appears to him to be adequate and satisfying, even though it would not be so in a realistic situation. This type of thinking is frequently employed by maladjusted persons.

Creative Imagination. The thinking process through which strikingly new ideas, concepts, inventions, or artistic works are produced is called *creative imagination.* The individuals whose new ideas or works are highly significant to society are commonly referred to as "geniuses." Many less intelligent individuals also employ creative imagination, but their products may attract little attention.

Reasoning. The psychologist is experimentally more familiar with the process known as *reasoning* than with any other form of thinking. Reasoning is the process of solving problems. Through the remainder of this chapter, the term *thinking* will be used to denote reasoning, unless otherwise indicated.

CHARACTERISTICS OF THINKING

Thinking has many characteristics in common with all other responses of the organism. Thinking differs from other behavioral categories chiefly in respect to the types of situations in which it occurs.

The Problem Situation. Thinking occurs when habitual responses are not adequate for adjustment to the prevailing situation, or when the situation does not strike the organism as one in which some habitual response would be adequate. Such a situation is termed a *problem situation*.

The individual's progress toward an objective is blocked by some unfamiliar quality of the situation. This interference with the smooth functioning of behavior may be in the form of a physical obstruction between the individual and his goal, in the form of missing elements in the conceptual sequence which would logically connect an intellectual question with its undetermined answer, or in the form of a temporary inability to perceive the similarity between the prevailing situation and some familiar situation to which adequate responses have already been established. The problem situation is an interference with progress toward a goal. Thinking results, and characteristically continues, until the interference is removed.

Thinking as Reaction. Just as all behavior is the interaction of the organism with its effective environment, so thinking is interaction with a particular kind of environment, namely, the problem situation. The behavior known as thinking or reasoning may involve reactions of muscles, both smooth and striated, in any part of the body.

Thinking as Implicit Behavior. Although thinking may involve overt reactions of the organism, thinking reactions are frequently implicit or at least abbreviated in character. Much of human thinking involves such minimal movements of the language apparatus and of other parts of the musculature that sensitive instruments are required for their detection.

Thinking as Indirect Reaction. Thinking may occur with reference to an object not present to the individual. Even if the object is present, physical contact with it, or manipulation of it, may constitute but a small portion of the individual's total behavior toward it. Direct contact may take place as a means of

examining the object thoroughly and thus gaining more complete data for indirect action. It may occur when it is necessary
to test a hypothesis which cannot be accepted or rejected without further knowledge. Direct reaction usually follows the acceptance of a finally correct hypothesis, but much of the activity
occurring during the thinking process itself is indirect or symbolic.

Thinking as Directed Behavior. Thinking is characteristically
directed toward some goal or objective. The attainment of this
objective is referred to as the solution. The individual is motivated in some direction, encounters an obstacle (the problem),
and must solve this problem in order to continue on his way.
During the thinking process there will be trial-and-error, or the
trying out of various hypotheses, many of which must be rejected. The directedness of the thinking process provides a criterion for the rejection of hypotheses, since rejected hypotheses
are those which are not compatible with attainment of the
objective.

Thinking and Logic. Thinking is behavior which occurs *within*
a problem situation. Logic, on the other hand, is a method of
proof; logic is resorted to *after* the problem has been solved,
either to prove to some other individual that the situation is
"logical" or correct, or to check the solution to the thinker's
satisfaction. Thinking is behavior of an informal sort; logic follows formal rules. Logic is a social convention to which the results of thinking must conform in order to gain acceptance, even
though the actual thinking process often bears little resemblance
to the logical proof to which its results are subjected.

METHODS OF INVESTIGATING
THE THINKING PROCESS

Experimental methods have been successfully applied to the
"reasoning" behavior of both subhuman and human subjects.

Methods in Animal Experiments. The study of problem-solving behavior in animals depends on careful control and highly
objective methods.

DELAYED RESPONSE. In this method, first used by Hunter
(1913), the animal is initially trained to go to the one of three
boxes which is lighted. After training, the animal is restrained

while one of the other boxes is momentarily lighted. After a period of delay, the animal is released to determine whether it will still go to the correct (previously lighted) box. If the delayed reaction is successful, it is presumed to be in response to some cue within the animal itself which substituted for the light stimulus during the delay.

MULTIPLE CHOICE. Yerkes (1915) developed a multiple-choice apparatus consisting of several small compartments, any given number of which could be left open during an experimental trial. In each trial the animal is confronted with three or more open compartments, one of which contains food according to a prearranged plan of the experimenter. For example, the food may always be placed in the middle compartment, in the first from the left, or in some other constant relationship to the open compartments. Solution of the problem is inferred when the animal is able to go immediately to the box containing food.

ABSTRACTION PROBLEMS. Several methods of studying the animal's ability to respond to an aspect common to many different stimuli (to perform abstraction) have been used. Fields (1932) trained rats to respond to "triangularity." Rats trained to jump to a door marked with a triangle and to avoid jumping to doors marked with other geometrical figures were able to respond correctly, regardless of the size of the triangle, its position, or its proportions. Kroh (1927) trained chickens to peck corn from triangular papers and to avoid pecking from other geometrical forms.

PUZZLE BOXES. Thorndike (1898) devised puzzle boxes as a means of studying the problem-solving behavior of cats, dogs, chicks, and other animals. The animal could escape from the puzzle box by pulling a particular string, pressing a lever, or turning a door button.

ALTERNATION MAZES. The alternation maze consists of pathways arranged like two squares adjacent to each other and with a side in common. The animal can start at one end of the pathway corresponding to the common side, and at its end can turn either left or right in order to return to the starting point. With this arrangement, the animal could theoretically run continuously around a given square or could alternate between the two squares. A "choice point" is designated as the far end of the common side. In alternation problems, the animal must learn to turn right at this choice point, then turn left at the next choice point, in order to receive a food reward upon reaching the starting point. In other words, the animal must respond alternately in a different way to exactly the same stimulus (the choice point). Successful mastery of the alternation presumably involves some symbolic activity on the part of the animal.

OTHER PROBLEM SITUATIONS. Among the ingenious problems set for animals to solve, those of Maier and Köhler are most often cited.

Maier devised several reasoning tests for rats, requiring for the correct solution the combination of separate learned experiences. One problem consisted of three tables connected by a pathway, each table top being screened so that it could not be seen from any other table top. The rat was first allowed to explore the pathway and the table tops (Experience I). It was then fed on a particular table (Experience II). For the test, the rat was placed on some table other than the one on which it had been fed. The correct solution consisted in going directly to the table on which food had last been found.

Köhler made use of three principal types of problems: detour problems, box-stacking problems, and tool-using problems. The detour problems involved placing the animal near a fence through which food could be seen but not reached. The correct solutions involved going away from the food temporarily, or detouring around some obstacle such as a building, in order to reach the food. The box-stacking problems involved placing food in view of the animal, but too high to be reached. Boxes were available, and correct solutions involved placing these under the food as a platform for reaching it. Tool-using problems involved placing the food outside the animal's cage, too far away to be reached without the aid of a stick. In more complicated problems a long stick had to be obtained through use of a shorter stick, or two sticks had to be joined together.

Methods in Human Experiments. Both objective and subjective methods are used in the study of human reasoning. Usually the objective methods are supplemented by subjective reports (introspection).

PUZZLES. Puzzles of many sorts (linguistic, logical, mechanical, mathematical, etc.) have been used in the study of human thinking. Lindley (1897) first used puzzles for this purpose. Ruger

(1910) made an intensive study of thinking by adults, using puzzles as experimental material. During puzzle solution, the subject's behavior and running commentary on what he thought he was doing were both recorded.

MULTIPLE CHOICE. The multiple-choice apparatus designed by Yerkes for human subjects consists of a number of flat keys which can be pushed out by the experimenter. The subject (S) pushes in keys, one at a time, until a buzzer sounds. This is his cue that he has located the one of several keys whose relation to the remaining keys he must discover. Problems are set by the experimenter (E), consisting of such relationships as the middle key, first key from the right, etc. Successful solution by S is indicated when he is able to push the correct key immediately without error on two or more successive trials. Objective records are kept of the specific keys pushed in before solution, and of any running comments or introspections which S may make.

ABSTRACTION AND CONCEPT FORMATION. A notable experiment on the process of abstraction in human subjects was reported by Hull (1920). Twelve series of Chinese characters, each series having a common element, were presented by means of an exposure apparatus. As a given character appeared, E pronounced the name arbitrarily assigned the element which the given character had in common with the other members of the series. S repeated the name after E, with the object of becoming able to pronounce the name in anticipation of E. Certain variations in the presentations of the characters were introduced in order to test experimental hypotheses.

TASK PROBLEMS. Maier (1933) set up tasks and gave the subject a minimum of equipment with which to accomplish the task. For example, one problem required S to tie together the free ends of two cords which were suspended from the ceiling, but which were placed so far apart that it was impossible for S to reach one while holding to the other. The solution required S to hang a weight on one cord, set it swinging, and, while holding the other cord, catch the weighted one as it came near in its pendulum motion.

PHYSIOLOGICAL STUDIES. Instruments for the measurement of action currents (galvanometers and oscillographs) have been attached to the subject during experiments with various kinds of problems. Through these it has been possible to detect implicit reactions occurring in many different muscles of the body during problem solution. This may partially explain why we become physically tired after exhaustive mental problem-solving efforts.

QUESTIONNAIRES AND ANECDOTAL STUDIES. Despite the unreliability of these methods, they are the source of most of our knowledge of creative imagination. Questionnaires answered by eminent scientists, artists, and inventors, or anecdotes reported by such individuals, have given some leads concerning the processes by which they came to make their discoveries or other creative contributions.

RESULTS OF INVESTIGATIONS OF THE REASONING PROCESS

The experiments with animals, with children, and with human adults have all contributed to an understanding of the reasoning process.

Results of Animal Experiments. The relative simplicity of many of the problems set for animals has made analysis of the activity a simple affair, but it has also left the way open for considerable controversy and for explanation of the solution in terms of several learning theories. In these animal experiments a sudden decrease in the number of errors made or a sudden drop in time per trial is usually taken as evidence of "insight" whereas a gradual decrease in errors or a gradual increase in speed is noted as characteristic of trial-and-error learning. Also, in trial-and-error learning, improved performance is achieved by a narrowing of the parts of the situation to which the animal responds. In insight learning, elements of the situation appear as relatively complete units with no prior overt responses in such a direction. For example, in detour problems, dogs would suddenly turn away from food seen through a fence and rapidly run the detour which led to the other side of the fence.

In all problem-solving behavior there are probably elements of insight and of trial-and-error. Neither type of behavior operates to the exclusion of the other. However, individual experiments sometimes show one or the other mode of response to dominate. Which type of behavior will dominate may be determined both by the nature of the problem and by the limitations of the organism.

Results of Experiments with Children. Use of children in reasoning experiments has been of great value because of the opportunity to observe differences which accompany maturation. Very young children were found to resort to trial-and-error in the solution of very simple problems such as pulling a string to get a desired toy (Richardson, 1932), stacking boxes (Alpert, 1928), or using a hoe to obtain a desired object seen through a fence (Kellogg and Kellogg, 1933). In very young children even slight modification of the problem appeared to set up a completely new learning task, whereas with older children this slight modification was accompanied by an immediate solution with no trial-and-error behavior.

Results of Experiments with Adult Human Subjects. The development of inductive thinking, or the process of abstracting and generalizing, appears to be the principal feature of adult human problem-solving. However, instances have been noted in which the correct response is given regularly even though the subject is unable to verbalize the principle used in selecting the response. Several factors have been isolated as important in successful problem-solving by adults.

Use of Hypotheses. Some form of hypothesis is usually established and maintained for a sufficient number of trials to warrant its acceptance or rejection.

Effect of Negative Instances. Smoke (1932) found that, contrary to popular belief, the pointing out of negative instances or the demonstrating of cases not conforming to the concept was of no advantage in the development of concepts.

Effect of Isolation. Hull (1920) found that development of the concept proceeded just as readily when the crucial element was surrounded with extraneous material as it did when the crucial element was presented in isolation. However, ability to define the concepts verbally was enhanced by isolated presentation.

Participant Behavior and Spectator Behavior. The actual trying out of hypotheses is referred to as participant behavior (Heidbreder, 1924). However, at times the subject utilizes spectator behavior. This involves relatively random activity during a time when all previously tested hypotheses have failed and no new hypothesis has yet suggested itself. During spectator behavior the individual makes observations of the situation, leading to the eventual formulation of still another hypothesis to be tested.

Puzzle Behavior. Typical behavior in the solution of puzzles illustrates clearly the utilization of spectator behavior. First attempts are usually quite random, one method after another being tried. The first solution is usually accidental, giving the subject little comprehension of how it came about. Analysis of the problem is made *after* a few of these accidental solutions, but seldom earlier. Analysis is generally of two types: (1) *place analysis* and (2) *detail analysis.* The part of the puzzle where success seems to have been located is usually the first part of the problem to be isolated. This place analysis eliminates many of the early ineffectual manipulations. After several trials following place analysis, more accurate and detailed analysis of the movements essential to success takes place.

THE ROLE OF DIRECTION. The selection of the correct part-responses is not sufficient for the solution of a problem. Correct direction, or the possession of the right approach, is also necessary. In fact, possession of the wrong direction can delay or completely prevent problem solution by precluding the appearance of a right direction which might develop if no prior assumption were interfering.

PHYSIOLOGICAL ACCOMPANIMENTS TO THINKING

Jacobsen (1932) demonstrated that implicit movements occur in the arm when the subject imagines moving his arm, in the eye muscles when visual imagery occurs, and in the tongue and lip muscles when verbal activity is imagined. Max (1935) showed that these action currents diminish during the transition from the waking to the sleeping state, are virtually absent during dreamless sleep, but appear with marked intensity during dreams.

In addition to the implicit movements directly related to the parts of the body included in the thinking activity, there is a heightened tension of all the visceral smooth muscles which accompanies most problem-solving behavior.

CREATIVE IMAGINATION

As noted earlier, experimentally obtained knowledge about creative thinking is almost nonexistent. Some analysis of the process is available from reports of scientists and artists on their creative activities.

Steps Involved in Creative Thought. Wallas (1926) distinguishes four stages in the creative process.

PERIOD OF PREPARATION. In this period facts and observations are gathered; the problem or objective is examined in the light of previously inadequate solutions, and all that can be learned in the same or an allied field is made a part of the individual's body of knowledge.

PERIOD OF INCUBATION. During this period the thinker may seem entirely idle respecting the problem or objective. No progress toward the goal seems to be made. Yet, the thinker may be implicitly considering and rejecting hypotheses.

STAGE OF INSPIRATION. At this stage the new creative product comes into being, as if in a sudden flash of insight. The new arrangement of materials or concepts is immediately recognized by the thinker as being significant enough to be tested or verified.

PERIOD OF VERIFICATION. If the creative product is a scientific hypothesis, it must be verified by experimental work. If it is an artistic conception, it must be executed in the artist's medium of expression. In either case, the "inspiration" may prove to be faulty, so that more preparation, incubation, and insight may be necessary before the product is finally acceptable to the thinker.

Factors Interfering with Creative Thought. In general, anything which disturbs the thinker will interfere with the coming of an inspiration or hunch. Among the circumstances which have been mentioned by creative thinkers as likely to disturb their creative activity are: (1) worry, (2) working too constantly or under pressure, (3) executive or administrative responsibilities, (4) having to get to work on time, (5) intense interest in something foreign to the problem at hand, (6) fear of interruption, and (7) quarrels or other emotional upsets.

Nervous Instability and Creative Thought. Nervous instability has been noted frequently to be associated with genius, or the intelligence level associated with distinctive output of a creative nature. Many of the great artists have shown more or less definite signs of emotional imbalance, and some have exhibited clean-cut neuroses or psychoses. The very process of creative thought as outlined previously must contribute to this since the world is not ordered for the benefit of the creative thinker. Then, too, though case-history data are voluminous, statistical analyses of the relative incidence of emotional instability are woefully lacking. The very eminence of the creative thinker causes all his minor aberrations to stand out whereas the foibles of ordinary individuals go unnoticed.

THE PERSONAL ELEMENT IN THINKING

Attention has been given to the relation of the self to perception, learning, motivation, and all the other elements which we isolate in studying the relationships of the individual with his environment. Piaget (1924) made extended observations of the thinking of young children with the following very important finding: The thinking of young children is self-centered. Seeing the relationship between themselves and other objects is easier for them than seeing the relationship between objects or persons which do not include themselves. The development of problem-solving behavior in adults follows much the same pattern. At the simplest level we must be included or at least be able to put ourselves "into the other fellow's shoes." We progress through various levels of concrete experience with the materials of the situation and, at the highest level, we are divorced from even secondary experience and work with symbols or abstractions.

SUMMARY

Thinking is implicit behavior whose existence is revealed by some explicit behavior usually observed in attacks on problem situations. There is apparently some explicit behavior involved directly, since sensitive instruments show minimal movements associated with speech and voice or show muscular movements occurring in search for and detection of objects or solutions. On the higher levels, thinking is largely symbolic and objects themselves are seldom manipulated. Thinking is rather clearly differentiated from logic since thinking itself may not be logical.

Experimental study of thinking has been largely through development of problem situations such as puzzle boxes, mazes, and other activities which require choice or plan in order to effect a solution.

13

Motivation

All behavior is motivated. The simplest and most primary motivations are essentially physiological in nature, arising from bodily needs. The more complicated are largely social in nature, developing from interrelationships among organisms. In human beings the pattern of needs, wants, and desires is so complicated that it is sometimes difficult to develop any traces between the physiological and the social.

EXPERIMENTAL INVESTIGATION OF MOTIVATION

Experimentation in the field of motivation has proceeded along five lines: (1) the investigation of animal drives, (2) the study of physiological and social drives in human beings, (3) the investigation of conscious intent, (4) the investigation of nerve stimulation and glandular activity, and (5) the clinical study of unconscious motives and wishes (psychoanalysis).

The Study of Animal Drives. It is obviously impossible to state properly that an animal is hungry or thirsty, or has some other definite physiological drive. However, it is easily possible to determine normal food intake, water intake, etc., and by a process of deprivation to create a condition which should result in hunger, thirst, etc. In the typical animal experiment, some standardized physiological condition is established and some goal object is set up. The goal object is separated from the animal by a maze, an electric grid, or some other obstruction. Differences in time required to run the maze, differences in frequency of grid crossings, etc. are interpreted as due to the physiological drives. Warden (1926) introduced the "Columbia Obstruction Method" which is quite representative of this type of experimentation. An animal (usually a rat or a monkey) was placed on one side of

179

an electrically charged grid, and the incentive was placed on the other side. The following comparable average number of grid crossings in 20-minute tests for white rats was reported by Warden and his associates (1931).

DRIVE	NUMBER OF CROSSINGS
Maternal	22.4
Thirst	20.4
Hunger	18.2
Sex	13.8
Exploration	6.0
No experimental drive	3.5

The Study of Drives in Human Beings. Experimentation on the effect of changing physiological drives in human beings involves infinitely greater difficulties than with animals. The social aspects of human motivation arise so early in life that free expression of the effect of physiological drives does not occur. Then, too, human beings are seldom subjected to the intensity of physiological motivation which can be produced in the case of animals. Occasionally, opportunities for observation occur, as in the case of groups isolated by calamity or taken from normal society as in a prisoner of war camp. Certain manifestations of the effect of physiological drives have been measured in the experimental laboratory. In otherwise healthy human beings, a state of hunger brought on by temporary food deprivation increased their total bodily activity, the strength of their grip, the speed with which they were able to solve arithmetic problems, and a variety of other activities which suggested a heightening of bodily functions.

But day-to-day activity in human beings is mediated by social motives, and it is these which really need study. To date, the standard experiment has involved use of a normal situation (classroom, work place) in which changes in incentives (goals) are made and the results are measured in terms of some output of work.

The Investigation of Conscious Intent. In human beings we find goal-directed behavior existing over long periods of time, even though the complete reward may never be obtained. The value of social incentives is probably dependent on changes in intent. Intent appears to include both motor sets and mental sets, predispositions favorable to goal-seeking behavior.

The Investigation of Nerve Stimulation and Glandular Activity. The study of the energy conditions of nerves and the secretions of glands has contributed to the knowledge of motivation. Since highly motivated behavior nearly always involves a stress situation, measurements of blood sugar, electricity given off under conditions of physiological excitation, secretions of stimulator or inhibitor glands, etc., all give some evidence on motivation.

The Clinical Study of Unconscious Motives (Psychoanalysis). The repression of highly motivated activity, primarily of a physiological kind, affects the adjustment of the individual in various ways. Society (environmental social situations) brings about changes in native reactions. The adjustments made in learned reactions may or may not be satisfactory, from the point of view of society at large. Unsocial reactions and abnormal mental activity are generally considered to be the result of lack of satisfaction in release of motivations. Psychoanalysts attempt to trace the activities of the individual back to the predisposing events which established the motivations and the consequent unstable behavior.

PHYSIOLOGICAL DRIVES

Drives based on bodily needs are observable from birth and continue throughout life. In Chapter 2 the fact was stressed that organisms maintain a dynamic equilibrium, and the satisfaction of bodily needs is implicit in maintaining that equilibrium. A brief survey of these bodily needs will establish their importance.

Hunger. The drive to obtain food has been widely studied. However, it is only recently (*c.* 1930 ff.) that the so-called hunger drive has been isolated into components which lend themselves to definitive study.

FOOD DEPRIVATION AND STOMACH CONTRACTIONS. Cannon and Washburn (1912) worked to determine what happened when subjects reported feelings of hunger. From X-ray observation of the behavior of the stomach before, during, and after eating, and from pneumographic recordings of gastric contractions on a balloon taken into the stomach, they were able to show that when the subject reported hunger pangs gastric contractions were taking place. The finding has since been verified many times, but it affords an explanation of only a portion of the drives which motivate the organism to seek and ingest food. There are desires for food which are independent of these stomach contractions. Cannon considered these cravings to have been learned and treated them as *appetite*.

Several experiments and observations, notably Hoelzel (1927) and Tsang (1938), have shown normal signs of hunger in organisms whose stomachs had been removed. Bash (1939) and Morgan and Morgan (1940) showed that rats whose nerves from stomach to brain were cut behaved normally with respect to food.

BLOOD CHEMISTRY AND HUNGER. Hunger, as demonstrated by stomach contractions and food intake, is related to blood chemistry. If the blood sugar level is reduced through injections of insulin, contractions and hunger pangs are reported (Mulinos, 1933). If glucose is injected to raise the blood sugar level, gastric contractions are inhibited (Bulatao and Carlson, 1924). A "hunger hormone" is suggested by experiments which show that blood taken from a starved dog and injected into a fed dog will bring about gastric contractions in the latter (Luckhardt and Carlson, 1915). The reverse of this was reported by Templeton and Quigley (1930), who found that blood transfused from a recently fed animal to a starved animal caused the stomach contractions in the latter to cease.

DIETARY DEFICIENCIES AND SPECIALIZED HUNGERS. Many of the peculiar childhood food choices such as chalk, dirt, salt, etc. have been found to be due to deficiencies in diet, and the peculiar food taken satisfied a definite bodily need. "Cafeteria-feeding" experiments have shown that organisms confronted with a wide variety of foods from which they may select freely will select a diet which is nutritive (for rats, Richter, Holt, and Barelare, 1939; and for infants, Davis, 1928). Such experiments cannot be performed with adult human beings because their food habits are too overlaid with social custom and with appetite patterns.

The evidence on dietary selection to care for vitamin deficiency is mixed. Wilder (1937) found that rats deprived of vitamins A or D did not appear to recognize them when given a choice of food with and without vitamins A and D. On the other hand, rats deprived of vitamin B show a definite hunger for it and seek out the most minute quantities.

SOCIAL FACTORS AND FOOD-TAKING BEHAVIOR. We have already mentioned the obvious fact that custom plays a large part in choice of food or the development of appetites, and it is also responsible for the temporal pattern of food-taking activity. Not so obvious, but easily demonstrable, are other factors. An animal, human or otherwise, who is satiated will begin eating again if a hungry animal joins him and begins eating. Or, an animal confronted with more than the customary amount of food needed for satiation will eat more than usual, even to the point of gorging (as witnessed in our annual Thanksgiving dinners).

Thirst. There are at least two elements in thirst—the sensation of thirst and the state in which the body is deprived of water. Cannon (1934) has shown a relationship between dryness of the mucous lining of the mouth and throat and the desire for ingestion of water. The fact that simply taking water into the mouth without swallowing it, chewing gum, etc. temporarily relieve the sensation of thirst supports Cannon's theory. However, animals deprived of water in varying amounts drink an amount generally proportional to the amount of deprivation (Adolph, 1941), and dogs deprived of their salivary glands drink water in about the same quantity as normal dogs (Montgomery, 1931). Also, when water was placed directly in the dog's stomach, as by a tube, the dog drank no water at all if offered water after about 15 minutes (Bellows, 1939).

Other Direct Bodily Needs. In addition to the needs for food and water, there are several other viscerogenic needs of the organism. Principal among these are breathing, urination, and defecation.

BREATHING. It is virtually impossible to measure the strength of the physiological drive for oxygen, but observation of the panic experience in threatened suffocation indicates that this is probably our strongest drive. Studies of lesser amounts of oxygen deprivation, as in ascents to high altitudes, suggest that lack of oxygen releases inhibitions to behavior generally considered unsocial.

URINATION. Normally, except as it is controlled by custom, the need is met without difficulty. However, G. S. Freeman (1938) has conducted a variety of experiments in which enforced micturition has been used as a driving stimulus, and body tonus, electric discharge, and various learning tasks have been used as criteria against which the effects were measured.

DEFECATION. Though no particular studies have been made, it is obvious that evacuative behavior is motivated in a highly complex manner. Consider cats, who must have some covering material.

Sex. The physiological drive commonly called the sex drive and generally culminating in mating behavior operates like the other physiological drives in only one respect, namely, a high state of the drive is accompanied by a high level of activity of the organism. In all other respects the sex drive operates very differently from the other physiological drives.

HORMONES AND SEX. The *ovaries* in female animals and the *testes* in male animals comprise the primary organs of sex, the *gonads*. In normal development the sex of the gonads is first determined by the gene structure, and then in later life the gonadal development stimulates the appearance of the secondary sex organs and the physical characteristics associated with differences between the sexes.

In all animals there is a period of immaturity during which the gonads are relatively nonfunctional, a period of maximum function, and a period of degeneration into nonfunctional status.

Estrogens and *progesterone* are the principal hormones of the female. The secretion of these hormones waxes and wanes on a cyclical basis related to the maturation and decay of *ova*. If pregnancy occurs, the secretion of progesterone is maintained throughout the term of pregnancy.

Androgens are the hormones of the male. *Testosterone* is the most important of these. Secretions of the androgens are not cyclical, and variation is influenced only by the activity of the pituitary gland.

SEX BEHAVIOR. Most experiments on the sex drive have been performed with the lower animals, rather obviously in view of the hedges and restrictions around even discussions of human sex behavior. In male rats a striking increase in activity is noted at a period of physiological growth which coincides with development of the gonads. In females the general activity level is somewhat raised but is more characterized by the onset of cyclical activity. During the height of the estrus cycle the female rat will revolve an activity cage as much as one hundred times as many revolutions as on an anestrus day.

Another aspect of behavior resulting from the sex drive is mating behavior. In lower animals this is highly stereotyped in both male and female. It appears without opportunity for observation or learning.

Maternal "Instinct." In lower animals of the female sex a very stereotyped behavior pattern of nest-building, cleaning, and care of the newborn, etc. is evident. In higher animals, including human beings, the behavior is more variable and less stereotyped. Apparently, hormone secretions are behind this behavior. In rats, administration of *prolactin* caused even virgins to care for newborn rats (Riddle, Bates, and Lahr, 1935).

SOCIAL MOTIVES AND HUMAN BEHAVIOR

The drives of human beings are socially controlled and channeled from birth onward. By the end of the first day of life the human infant is usually placed on some feeding schedule which is only generally related to his actual hunger pangs, and one measure of his progress is the speed with which he adapts to the customary feeding schedule of his prevailing society. Other drives are similarly modified and hedged about by social conventions until simple stimulus-response relationships are not even available in the study of the effect of primary drives on the behavior of human beings.

Since our society involves a complex interaction of individuals in which symbolic rewards generally take the place of satisfaction of the primary drives, effective training for life in this society must involve development and use of motives rather than primary drive states.

Two methods have been used to study the influence of motives. The first of these involves the use of verbal or anecdotal material; the second involves the use of the experimental method —frequently quite at variance with the carefully controlled conditions of the psychological laboratory, but nevertheless representing a real attempt to control or vary some element believed important to the direction of behavior.

Opinion Studies of Motivation. Starch (1923) secured ratings from a group of 74 men and women on their beliefs as to the importance of various drives and motives in determining their activities from day to day. With 10 as maximum and 0 as minimum he found "Appetite-hunger" to rate 9.2, "Love of offspring" to rate 9.1, "Health" to rate 9.0, and so through a long list to "Teasing," which rated 2.6.

Thorndike (1937) secured data on the amount of money spent by people of the United States for such items as clothing, laundry, life insurance, food, shelter, etc., and then had judges classify these items into "needs" such as hunger, protection, pleasure, social approval, dominance, etc. The result was the very interesting distribution of the dollar shown below.

Needs	Percentage of Total Expenditures
Hunger	11.2
Security	10.5
Protection against the elements	10.2
Approval of others	7.2
Welfare of others	7.2
Taste and smell	4.6
Protection against animals, disease	4.4
Social entertainment	4.2
Approval of self	4.0
Sight and sound	3.9
Sex entertainment	3.9
Minimizing pain	3.5
Mastery over others	3.0
Other needs	22.2

Investigators such as Blue and Russ (1942) and Chant (1932) have studied what workers want in a job. "Opportunity for advancement" quite regularly heads such lists and "Salary" is regularly much lower than might be expected from newspaper accounts of the bases of friction between labor and management.

Research Studies of Motivation. The schoolroom has provided a fertile field for studies of different kinds of motivation, due partially to the easy availability of subjects and partially to availability of a criterion of success in the form of school examinations. Industry has provided other studies, but these are usually less well controlled.

PRAISE—REPROOF. The effect of positive versus negative comment on performance has been rather thoroughly investigated with quite consistent results (Hurlock, 1925; Briggs, 1925; Laird, 1923; Gates and Rissland, 1923; Sears, 1936) . Public commendation, private reprimand, public reprimand, private ridicule, private sarcasm, public ridicule, and public sarcasm were effective in the order named. Hurlock's experiment included the finding that either commendation or reproof was superior to being ignored. Individual differences are noted, and there is some evidence that "private reproof" is most effective with high-grade students and "public praise" is most effective with low-grade students.

COMPETITION—CO-OPERATION. Competition is generally found to be superior to co-operation as a device for getting more accomplished. Triplett (1898) found that competition against individuals was more effective than competition against time. Sims (1928) found that matched pairs competing against each other achieved greater gains on substitution and reading tests than did large subgroups competing against each other. Maller (1929) established the following hierarchy of effective incentive conditions in a series of experiments:

1. Boys working against girls as individuals
2. Each pupil working to improve own score
3. Pupils working for teams
4. Pupils working in partnership
5. Pupils working for the classroom as a whole
6. Pupils working for a group arbitrarily picked by the experimenter

Though competition appears to be very effective in our society it would be a mistake to ascribe universality to this. Studies of other cultures, for example the Zuñi Indian tribe (Goldman), show that some cultures exist with practically no competition possible.

SOCIAL FACILITATION, INDIVIDUAL ATTENTION, PACING. Allport (1920) found that 14 of 15 subjects did better when working on mental tasks when they were with a group than they did when they were working on the same tasks alone. Wyatt, Frost, and Stock (1934) found that rearranging workers within a group had marked effects, a worker tending to be more effective when placed next to a rapid worker. They also found that production was much more closely related to that of the average in a group working situation than in an individual working situation. The

Hawthorne Studies (Mayo, 1933; Roethlisberger, 1943; Roethlisberger and Dickson, 1943) showed that worker performance improved as long as the group studied was given individual attention. Changes came about even in direct opposition to the
expected findings.

REWARDS, BONUSES, AND OTHER MATERIAL INCENTIVES. The
basic finding of all the studies of the effect of reward is clear.
Reward does affect behavior, but the fact that a true reward is
being offered must be evident. Lee (1932) studied the production records of young girls threading needles for older ones.
Their pay went to their parents rather than to the girls. Standard production at the start of Lee's experiment was 96 dozen
needles per day. Pay was changed from an hourly rate to a piece
rate, and the production dropped to 75 dozen needles per day.
A quota of 100 dozen needles per day was set with the provision
that the girls could quit when they reached the quota. The
average time of day at which the quota was reached became
2:30 in contrast to the 5:30 which had been the end of the standard work day.

Generally, bonuses or prizes have been directly effective, as
shown by Kitson (1922) on production of typesetters, and Mitch-
ell (1936) on wrapping of razor blades. Leuba (1930) studied
the comparative effects of a prize (chocolate bar), competition
for group captaincy, and a combination of the two with respect
to problem-solving by school children. The material reward appeared slightly better than the competition, and the combination was more effective than either used alone.

Moore (1942) summarized the results of 161 industrial firms
which had tried some form of profit-sharing plan. He reported
50 plans still active, 15 inactive, and 96 being discontinued. He
reports that the most common reason given for discontinuance
was employee apathy, a point which might well be checked
against Lee's conclusions.

KNOWLEGE OF RESULTS. Some effects of knowledge of results on
performance have already been discussed in Chapter 11. Book
and Norvelle (1922) gave school problems to two matched
groups, telling one group its score at the end of each practice
period but not telling the other though both groups were urged
to do their best. The group with knowledge of results finished
with an advantage of 16.5 per cent. Arps (1920) and Crawley

(1926) showed that physical exhaustion was apparently compounded of psychological and physiological factors. Subjects who had knowledge of the amount of "work" done on an ergograph (work-measuring apparatus) performed a greater amount of work than when they had no such knowledge. Crawley further showed that if a "goal" greater than normally expected production was established, an even greater amount of work was done.

Knowledge of results may easily be contaminated with knowledge of expected results. Baker (1937) permitted two groups of college students to see hypothetical performance curves, one of which suggested that music facilitated performance, whereas the other suggested that music interfered with performance. Each group was then further divided into two subgroups and studied with respect to their performance in solution of mental arithmetic problems under conditions of music and quiet. The order of improvement during the ten days of the experiment was as follows:

> First: Performance under quiet conditions when the hypo thetical curves suggested music was interference.
> Second: Performance with musical background when the hypothetical curves suggested music was facilitating.
> Third: Performance with musical background when the hypothetical curves suggested music was interference.
> Fourth: Performance under quiet conditions when the hypothetical curves suggested music was facilitating.

SPECIAL PROBLEMS IN STUDYING SOCIAL MOTIVATION. As shown in the Hawthorne and other studies, production criteria as a measure of the effects of motivation are likely to be misleading. Mere change is likely to bring results which might be labeled as effects of the motivational device used. But of even greater importance are items of behavior which may be missed in a production criterion alone. For example, Morgan (1916) showed that noise had little effect on speed and errors when typing performance was used as the criterion. Fortunately, suspicious of the result, he measured such factors as pressure exerted, breathing, etc. and found real effects. Other experimenters have not done so well. Consider the conclusion by one experimenter that his subjects were not affected by loss of sleep because they could be stimulated to work arithmetic problems just as well—even though the subjects became delirious during the experiment.

SUMMARY

Motivation is usually separated into two components: physiological drives and social motives. The physiological drives arise from bodily needs, and the organism is constantly developing new biological needs as it maintains a dynamic homeostasis. In human beings it is difficult to study the physiological drives since a whole pattern of socially acceptable or unacceptable behavior has been built around satisfaction of them.

There is a considerable body of knowledge about the effect of certain social motives in achieving production in factories, success in school, and a variety of other situations. Much less knowledge is available for any theoretical formulation which will explain motivation.

14

Emotion

Emotion is a disturbed psychological condition which can best be described as disintegrative activity. However, emotional activity may act as a stimulus to future integrations.

EMOTIONAL ACTIVITY

The stimulating situation in emotion is a highly complex mass of changes which take place in the environment, in the organism, and in awareness of the situation.

Aspects of Emotion. Emotion is observable in three aspects of psychological activity: (1) in explicit reactions, where behavior is random, disorganized, and frequently abortive; (2) in implicit reactions, particularly in the viscera, where circulatory, glandular, and vegetative functions are excited or inhibited; and (3) in awareness, where sensitivities localized in the viscera are prominent and where feeling (pleasantness or unpleasantness) is focal and intense.

Definition of Emotion. Emotion may be defined in terms of any one of its three aspects or a combination of them.

EXPLICIT BEHAVIOR. Emotion is disintegrative behavior and takes the form of random or abortive pattern reactions which usually run their course rapidly. Emotional patterns are generally denoted by such terms as fear, anger, etc., according to the nature of the stimulating situation. The immediate pattern reaction may develop into successive reactions such as running away from danger or fighting back. But these successive reactions may lose their disintegrative character and become efficient forms of behavior.

IMPLICIT BEHAVIOR. From the physiological point of view, emotion is the sum of a large number of circulatory, glandular, nerv-

191

ous, and muscular changes, measured by a variety of techniques. There are no characteristic physiological reaction patterns which differentiate the emotions as they are referred to in ordinary usage. Instead, there is a general physiological state which varies in degree and specificity of implicit reaction. The physiological reactions appear disintegrative since they interfere with normal bodily processes, but they are in one sense highly integrative since they prepare the individual for functioning on a higher level of efficiency after a certain time interval. In this fashion the physiological factors associated with emotion may appear as highly motivating factors in behavior.

AWARENESS. Feeling (pleasantness and unpleasantness) is focal in emotional awareness and is usually intense. Both immediate and recalled sensitivities are present.

CONTENT. Day-to-day terminology characterizes emotional behavior as anger, fear, surprise, jealousy, love, hate, disgust, grief, disappointment, and so on. These labels are generally associated with the outward appearance of the individual and are interpreted in terms of the manner in which the observer would react under like circumstances. Actions and expressions are the language of emotion, and there is a goodly amount of common meaning to these. However, research studies in which persons attempt to designate the emotion responsible for facial expressions shown in pictures give results little better than chance unless an account of the accompanying situation is also present.

THE STIMULATION OF EMOTION

The stimulating situation in emotion generally lends itself to analysis in the same manner as any other kind of stimulus situation.

Environmental Stimulation. Environmental stimuli which are sudden, unusual, and intense, such as a loud sound, a flash of light, pain, or a change in support, may be immediate causes of emotion. This is particularly evident with young children and infants, and these stimuli have sometimes been thought of as stimuli to native emotional reactions. But environmental situations, such as dark places, high places, open places, closed places, wild places, rough-looking men, animals, and so on, come through learning to be the important stimuli of emotion. For adults, the environmental stimuli of emotion often come to be words, phrases, acts of other people—things which involve dynamic awareness situations. The stimuli of emotion are primarily social in adult life.

Awareness of Environmental Stimulation. Words or acts, of other people in particular, may stimulate a succession of recalled awarenesses which build up to a highly emotional situation. The sensitivities from the environment which are often thought to be the initial cause are really unimportant. The background of recalled sensitivities is the significant cause. A chance environmental stimulus starts the emotional association processes in awareness, but in the awareness itself are the essential causative factors. Much of emotional activity in the adult is of this kind. An extreme illustration is the sensitive person by whom a casual act of another is interpreted as a slight and is magnified until the person becomes quite depressed.

Below the surface of awareness is the *emotional set,* developed because of similar situations in the past. The emotional set is a special form of the mental set, causing emotional activity. Where it begins its development in the life history is not known, but it seems that in early life, somehow, awareness activity takes a certain emotional course as a possible adjustment to an environmental situation. Later activity tends to follow the same course.

An environmental stimulus initiates emotional activity, but it may have very little to do with the course of development of the emotion. A very inconsequential sensitivity may stimulate an illogical sequence of recalled sensitivities.

Stimulation in Glandular Activity. The glandular, circulatory, and other implicit reactions in emotion, which become stimuli of further implicit emotional reactions, are caused by those stimuli already mentioned as important stimuli of emotion. Adult activity is full of emotional conditionings, and glandular innervation takes place from causes which are far removed from those which early in life caused visceral emotional patterns. Glandular stimulation is circular in nature, being affected by and affecting the dynamic equilibrium which has been mentioned earlier.

Secretions of the endocrine glands give rise to many bodily changes which emphasize our awareness that an emotional state exists.

EMOTION AND PERCEPTION

Emotion does not just happen. It is not an independent element which comes or goes at will. Emotion is initiated by certain perceptions, and accompanies the ongoing activities which are stimulated by the situation. Some emotional activity undoubtedly accompanies all action except that which is completely habitual. However, the emotional component is seldom recognized unless it is sufficiently strong to influence obviously the actions involved. Even though it does not reach the point of awareness, this emotional influence may compound itself to sizable proportions. We all know how much easier it is to work long hours on something we enjoy and how surprised we are to discover that we are suddenly fatigued after such activity. On the other hand, it is exceedingly difficult to work at something we dislike and we find ourselves restless, settling down to work only with conscious effort and intent.

Degree of Emotion. The degree of emotion which accompanies action with respect to a particular object or event is dependent upon a number of factors: (1) the degree to which the object or event is directly related to us and our own lives, (2) the imminence of the situation, (3) the expectations of society, and (4) the degree to which a ready response is available.

Learning of Emotional Activity. Most of our emotions are learned. We are born with a capacity for emotion and a physiological structure capable of handling emotionally charged situations, but the attachment of emotional behavior to particular objects or events and the type of explicit behavior to be shown are learned. A child is not born with a fear of or a disgust for snakes. Yet, such fear or disgust reactions are almost universal among adults in our society.

Explicit emotional behavior and eventually the accompanying implicit behavior develop primarily in two ways: (1) exposure to teaching by carefully prepared precept or example, and (2) participation in a particularly dramatic experience.

EFFECTS OF EMOTION

The results of emotion range from slightly increased tensions to a complete breakdown of the individual, with an actual inability to respond to the situation. What will happen depends primarily on the degree of emotion experienced and the availability of a response which will release the tension. The changes in implicit reaction have been rather carefully charted in the laboratory, but the changes in explicit reaction are less open to careful experimentation.

Physiological Reactions in Emotion. Various physiological changes have been observed and measured. The subject matter and the equipment used emphasize the number of factors associated with implicit emotional reaction.

METHODS FOR MEASURING PHYSIOLOGICAL ACTIVITY. Some of the tests follow:

1. Changes in pulse rate are measured by a *sphygmograph.*
2. Blood pressure is measured by a *sphygmomanometer.*
3. Breathing rates are measured by a *pneumograph.*
4. Glandular activity, especially of the adrenals, is measured indirectly by urinalysis or analysis of the blood.
5. Psychogalvanic responses are measured by a *galvanometer.*
6. Changes in digestive activity may be studied by X rays or by the "balloon technique."
7. Surgical techniques are involved in studies of certain glandular activities, as salivation, and in cutting nerves to eliminate from the total activity part of the stimuli or of the reaction.

FINDINGS CONCERNING PHYSIOLOGICAL REACTIONS IN EMOTION. A vast array of findings have been reported. Some of the results follow:

Changes in the Digestive Tract. Following emotional stimuli, changes in the tonicity of the stomach occur. Sometimes tonus is increased and sometimes it is decreased. The results for any one stimulus are not consistent (Brunswick, 1924). Stomach contractions and intestinal movements are decreased or stopped completely (Cannon, 1915). Salivary and gastric secretions are reduced, and other digestive activities are lessened.

Glandular Secretions. Following emotional stimulation the hydrogen-ion concentration (pH) of saliva is altered (Starr, 1922). Secretion of adrenalin is increased (Cannon, 1915). In some cases activity of the sweat glands is greatly increased, as in a "cold sweat." Glandular activity in general is thrown out of normal balance.

Cardiac Changes. Experimenters have found that following a "startle stimulus" the pulse rate decreases but heartbeat amplitude increases (Skaggs, 1926). Emotional stimuli are followed by greater irregularity of systolic blood pressure than are nonemotional stimuli (Landis and Gullette, 1925). The "flush of anger" and the "pallor of fear" are directly related to vasodilation or vasoconstriction of blood vessels leading to the head. In extreme cases blood pressure can rise so abruptly and strongly as to set in motion a chain of parasympathetic reflexes which literally bring the heart to a standstill, thereby reducing the blood pressure.

Respiratory Changes. A startle produces a sudden catching of the breath, increased breathing rate, and very irregular breathing which follows no consistent pattern (Skaggs, 1926).

Electrical Changes. Bodily resistance to the passage of a small electric current is decreased. The psychogalvanic response (P.G.R.) has been rather widely used as an index of emotional status.

Brain Waves. In nonemotional situations electroencephalograph readings show brain waves of 8 to 12 cycles per second, alpha waves. But when emotional topics are introduced, brain waves below 8 cycles per second, delta waves, appear (Hoagland, Cameron, and Rubin, 1938).

The Startle Pattern. A pattern of behavior which is described in terms of explicit response but which is definitely physiological in nature has been described by Hunt and Landis (1936). It appears as early as the fourth month of infancy and continues into adulthood. The "startle pattern" consists of closing the eyes, jerking the head, bringing the shoulders forward and raising them, bending the elbows and knees, clenching the fist, moving the upper trunk forward, and contracting the abdomen.

Social Reactions in Emotion. Considering the effect of emotion on our bodies, it would appear that the best response to emotion would be to take immediate action. If frightened, run or fight; if in love, take appropriate action; if unhappy, cry. However, society frowns upon strong emotionally tinged behavior, except in carefully prescribed situations. Even where strong behavior is accepted, the reaction must be in an appropriate direction. The soldier may show anger in war but must not show fear. If the individual is to avoid exhibiting socially unacceptable behavior, and yet reduce the emotional tensions aroused by the situation, some adjustment must be made.

Adjustment to situations which are emotionally undesirable is most likely to take one of three directions: (1) the individual tries to escape from the situation by avoiding it, either physically or mentally, (2) the individual tries to overcome the situation, or (3) the individual attempts to derive pleasure from what is normally an unpleasant situation. The last named of these is generally considered abnormal in our society, if it is recognized. The second, if successful, obviously corrects the situation. The first exists in great profusion and in many disguises. A brief definition of some of these may increase our insight into different personalities. It is perfectly natural to try to escape from thwarting situations. Whether or not this is desirable behavior depends upon a number of factors. The type of escape mechanism used is one factor, and the ability of the individual to cope with the situation if he did not try to escape is another.

MIGRATION. The simplest type of escape reaction is migration, literally running away from the situation.

RATIONALIZATION. Frequently associated with migration is the process of rationalization in which socially acceptable reasons are developed to cover the "loss of face" which might come from simple withdrawal.

DAYDREAMING. Virtually everyone daydreams to some extent, but the consistent daydreamer builds a dream world to the extent that he is quite lost to reality.

PROJECTION. In this form of escape from emotional pressure the individual blames other individuals or even inanimate objects for his misfortunes.

COMPENSATION. The individual compensates for his shortcomings in the emotionally disturbing area by diligent practice devoted to improvement in areas in which he knows he can be successful. Such an individual is then likely to label the things which he cannot do as not worth doing.

CONTROL OF EMOTION

Proper control of emotions consists largely of making personally and socially acceptable responses to emotional situations, and of minimizing emotion-arousing situations. As will be emphasized later in discussion of experimentally conditioned emotional reactions, tension-reducing behavior which is quite acceptable can be learned.

THE GENETICS OF EMOTIONAL REACTIONS

The genetic investigation of emotional reactions by experimental techniques was begun by Watson.

Unlearned Emotional Reactions. Watson (1920) concluded from his study of infants that there are three unlearned (inherited) emotional pattern reactions, which with their stimulating situations are as follows: (1) fear—loss of support or a loud noise, (2) love—stroking and petting, and (3) rage—restraining of bodily activities. Later studies by Sherman (1927) show that it is not possible to distinguish these three emotional reactions without some knowledge of the stimuli or other factors in the situation. Apparently the startle pattern of Hunt and Landis (1936) is the only truly unlearned emotional reaction which has been analyzed in men.

Cannon and Bard describe rage, fear, and pleasure reactions in dogs and cats. They are obviously distinguishable, even to laymen, but even here it is difficult to rule out the influences of the environmental situation.

Learned Emotional Reactions. The influence of learned emotional reactions (conditioning) is best illustrated by summarizing two famous experiments.

WATSON'S CONDITIONING EXPERIMENT WITH ALBERT. Albert was an 11-month-old healthy baby living in the hospital, in whom it had been found that only loud sounds and removal of support produced fear reactions. A white rat was presented together with a loud sound as an unconditioned stimulus to fear. The white rat became a conditioned stimulus to fear reactions in seven combined presentations so that instead of reaching for the rat, as he did before, Albert cried and crawled rapidly away from the conditioned stimulus. Also, a transfer of the fear reaction was made to other small animals and furry objects, such as a rabbit and a Santa Claus mask.

JONES'S UNCONDITIONING EXPERIMENT WITH PETER. Peter was a 2-year-and-10-month-old child who had been conditioned to fear a rabbit. The unconditioning method was positive, and a second conditioned reaction was established between the fear stimulus (the rabbit) and food after 120 combinations of the two stimuli. Each day the fear stimulus was brought closer to the child as he ate his meals and only removed when the child cried or asked that "Bunny" be taken away. At the conclusion of the experiment Peter patted and played with the rabbit. Jones describes Peter as a very difficult example of unconditioning. The degree of difficulty was determined by the distance the fear object needed to be away from the child so as not to cause avoiding reactions. In Peter's case the necessary distance was about 20 feet.

THEORIES OF EMOTION

Scientific thinking about emotional activity has gone through definite stages of development with respect to theoretical formulations for explanation of emotion.

The James-Lange Theory of Emotions. James (1884) in the United States and Lange (1885) in Denmark arrived independently at such similar conclusions that their views have been consolidated into what is generally known as the James-Lange theory of emotions. In this theory the emotion is the organic-kinesthetic awareness of the reaction to the original stimulus. The emotion follows the course of the original S–I–R activity; the implicit and explicit reactions to the stimulating situation are stimuli which affect proprioceptors and interoceptors and give the stirred-up nature to the emotional awareness. The order of activity is considered to be somewhat as follows: (1) the emotionally exciting situation, (2) the physiological reactions, in particular, and the explicit behavior, and (3) the awareness of physiological changes, in particular, and of other movements of the body. Emotional experience in the cortex arises from autonomic reactions to the emotional stimulus. The kind of emotional experience depends upon the type of bodily reaction brought about by the stimulus object. James emphasized the visceral elements of the reaction, whereas Lange placed emphasis on the activity of the vasomotor system.

McDougall's Aspect Theory of Instinct and Emotion. McDougall stated that emotion, as a conscious state, and instinct, as inherited reaction, were two aspects of the same activity. He listed fourteen combinations of emotions and instincts, such as: (1) instinct to escape—fear emotion, and (2) instinct to combat—anger emotion. Though no longer given any serious consideration, this theory is of historical importance since many writers on psychology in the latter half of the 19th century evolved theories relating instinct and emotion.

Cannon-Bard Theory of Emotion. Rather directly opposed to the James-Lange theory are several which relate the character of emotional experiences to the thalamus. Head (1920) was among the first leading exponents of such a thalamic theory, basing it on studies of patients with nervous injuries. Cannon (1927) and Bard (1934) proposed that nervous impulses from the stimulus situation go to an integrative center in the thalamus. From there impulses proceed directly to the brain and in the cerebral cortex determine the nature of the emotional experience. Simultaneously, impulses proceed to the effectors and bring about the explicit and implicit behavior which results from the perception of the stimulating situation.

The Cannon-Bard theory has a historical precursor in Descartes' theory of the pineal gland as the seat of the soul. But this theory is the product of experimental work, contradicting the James-Lange theory, in which the elimination of the action of interoceptors failed to remove the emotional reactions in animals. As genetically older parts of the brain were removed, beginning with the forebrain, there was no change in the emotional pattern in animals until the thalamus was removed. After removal of the thalamus, all emotional behavior ceased.

Each of the above theories was developed to clarify a certain point, and still other theories have been advanced to clarify other points, notably by Calkins (1925) and Meyer (1908). All have served their purpose, but none of them satisfy all the known conditions of emotional activity.

SUMMARY

A situation which is out of the ordinary for the individual is likely to result in emotional activity. This emotional activity in its outward appearance is generally random and disorganized, is accompanied by feelings of pleasantness or unpleasantness, and is universally associated with marked changes in the chemistry of the body. In general, the body chemistry changes are such as to prepare the body for violent and intensive action.

Emotional activity and the corresponding bodily changes may

be learned. That is, the original stimulus situation may be transferred and conditioned to a variety of stimuli, even symbolic, so that some portion of the original situation is redintegrated.

The strong physiological reactions which normally are counterparts of emotion are frequently inhibited by the culture in which we live. Behavior is thus changed, and unsatisfactory solutions are sometimes developed. If these solutions are counter to our society, the individual is termed abnormal in behavior.

Proper control of emotions consists largely of having personally and socially acceptable responses to emotional situations and of minimizing emotion-arousing situations.

Both implicit and explicit behavior under emotional conditions have been rather thoroughly charted. As yet, we have no completely accepted theory which accounts for all of these facts. The two best known and most nearly complete are the James-Lange theory and the Cannon-Bard theory.

15

Personality and Personal Adjustment

The personality of an individual is established as the sum total of all observable reactions. Although the individual's personality is no doubt with him at all times, it is demonstrated only when the individual is interacting with other individuals. Some characteristics of the individual are usually considered more important than others when personality is discussed, but the complete study must include all factors and all criteria by which an individual can be described.

Since the social aspect of personality is always the predominant aspect, it behooves us to consider what makes "personality" in the social sense. If we ask the man in the street why he thinks some individual X has a "good" personality, we usually get a listing of terms which describe different dimensions of personality. These are usually referred to as *traits,* and we find that the individual with a "good" personality has a combination of traits, to a particular degree, which attracts the observer to him. Having a "poor" personality or "no" personality means, in reality, that the observer does not like the individual or is indifferent to him.

There are large individual differences in the choice of traits and characteristics held to be admirable or likable. Sparks (1952) asked a number of men and women to rate descriptive words and phrases according to how fine, or how bad, they were if used to describe an individual. Some raters chose terms such as *alert, intelligent, has good judgment,* etc. as the finest things one could say about an individual. Others chose terms such as *strong, virile, manly,* etc. as the finest things. Still others chose *honest, truthful, trustworthy,* etc., and so on through several different constellations of terms.

The investigations of personality have most often concerned

themselves with study of traits or constellations of traits, though numerous investigators, particularly those with Gestalt leanings, have argued that this is fruitless activity.

OBSERVATION AND MEASUREMENT OF PERSONALITY

The methods of investigating personality may be classified in various ways. That given below enables easy summary of most of the techniques.

Case History. The case-history approach attempts to summarize and define an individual's personality in terms of his past actions, ancestry, experience, health record, etc. Case histories range from simple biographical sketches to highly complex interpretative materials couched in psychiatric language.

Rating. Rating scales have been used both by outside observers and as self-rating devices. They have covered the full range of psychological development from scales on which infants are rated as to explicit behavior to scales on which gerontologists have rated the adjustment of the aged. Like all other rating scales, those devoted to personality have a built-in source of difficulty. There is no norm except that derived from the generalizations of the rater himself.

Personality Tests. Numerous investigators have tried to assay personality with paper-and-pencil tests. These are somewhat different from the typical test in that they have no right or wrong answers. Rather, they have keys developed which classify the individual as in or out of the group being investigated, and individual scores on the entire test are interpreted in terms of group norms.

The best known of such tests is the George Washington Social Intelligence Test of Moss, Hunt, and Omwake (1930). It contains five fields—judgment in social situations, recognition of the mental state of the speaker, observation of human behavior, memory for names and faces, and sense of humor.

Other materials more properly classified as tests than as inventories are the Allport A–S Reaction Study (1939), the Allport-Vernon Study of Values (1931), the Root Introversion-Extroversion Test (1931), and the Pressey X–O Test (1920).

Personality Inventories. Since the Woodworth Psychoneurotic

Inventory (1917) a multitude of personality inventories have been published. The basic structure of all these is virtually identical. They are different in content, at least to the extent that they contain different items, and they are scored to reflect placement on different continua, at least to the extent that the factors surveyed are given different names.

The standard procedure is to ask questions such as "Do you have frequent headaches?" and to provide responses of "Yes," "?," and "No" from which the individual selects the most appropriate to describe himself.

The best known and most widely used inventories of this type are the Bernreuter Personality Inventory (1931), the Minnesota Multiphasic Personality Inventory (1943), the Bell Adjustment Inventory (1934), Guilford's Inventory of Factors STDCR (1940), and Thurstone's Personality Schedule (1929).

Behavior Tests. A few attempts have been made to separate what an individual says he does from what he actually does in a given situation. Marston (1925) studied the behavior of children in a museum, charting introverted and extroverted behavior in terms of distance traveled and stops made. Hartshorne and May (1928) reported a variety of studies relating to honesty and deceit behavior of children in situations where cheating could be detected by the examiner without the subject's realization that it could. Behavior tests are extremely difficult to carry out with subjects who have any degree of sophistication.

Interviews. Interviewing has traditional acceptance as a method of determining personality in business, industry, medicine, and a variety of other situations. Attempts to improve the interview have long been aimed at making it more objective, more amenable to scoring, and more reliable. Though great improvements have been noted, the major difficulty of dependence upon the judgments of the interviewer still remains. Then, too, improvements in objectivity and reliability are likely to take the form of greater restriction of content and thus, eventually, lead to less valid results.

Recently there has been a trend away from standardization of questions to be asked and standardization of the order in which to ask them. The interview is called "nondirective" because the interviewer does little more than listen and guide the conversation to this or that point. Such an interview is likely to have therapeutic values as well as informational objectives (Rogers, 1942). In the industrial situation such interviews emphasize requiring the interviewee to do most of the talking with prodding by the interviewer to stimulate thinking and problem-solving.

Free Association and Dream Analysis. This is the basic tool of psychoanalysis. The subject is encouraged to say everything which comes to mind, the analyst occasionally directing association by asking certain questions. The analysis is basically historical in nature, searching for associations and episodes which will reveal the source of development of emotional disturbances and explain the personality structure of the individual. In dream analysis the patient relates his dreams for analysis of motivations and other aspects of personality.

Projective Methods. The best known of the projective methods is the Rorschach Ink Blot Test, developed by a Swiss psychiatrist, Hermann Rorschach, and first published in 1921. The test consists of ten large white cards, on each of which is one large ink blot that appears as two relatively symmetrical halves which might arise from folding a piece of paper so that ink is smeared on each half. Some of the blocks are achromatic, appearing only in various shades of gray; others include color. The test is administered individually with the subject telling the examiner what he "sees" in each blot. Interpretation of the results is a highly skilled task, and a variety of indices result from such objective scoring as is attempted. The term "projective" is employed in describing such tests because the blot merely forms a structure on which the individual "projects" his own interpretation, since there is no basic right or wrong response to the stimulus.

A tremendous volume of research on the Rorschach has accumulated during the past twenty years; some of the most important data are found in publications of Beck (1937, 1944, 1945), Klopfer and Kelley (1942), and Hertz (1935).

Closely rivaling the Rorschach in popularity is the Murray Thematic Apperception Test (1935). In this test the subject is presented with cards which contain a picture in which the details are obvious but in which the situation is ambiguous or the action is poorly defined. The subject then builds a story about the picture, generally telling what he projects as the situation and frequently telling what events led up to the situation pictured and possibly what the eventual outcome will be. Scoring is accomplished by content analysis to determine the underlying themes, though there is also a quantitative method of obtaining a weighted count of the needs and forces affecting the examinee as reflected in projections on the hero or heroine of the picture.

A variety of other projective devices have been developed, with varying amounts of structure afforded the stimulating object or situation. Some of these are tests; among these are the Picture Frustration Test (Rosenzweig, 1944), the World Test (Lowenfeld, 1929), the Szondi Test (Szondi, about 1930), and the Incomplete Sentences Test (Payne, 1928; Thorndike and Lorge, 1941; Rhode, 1946; and Rotter and Willerman, 1947). Other projective techniques involve interpretation of such things as handwriting, expressive movement, finger painting, drawing, play, role-playing, and psychodrama.

PHYSIQUE

Physical characteristics of the individual contribute to the total personality and are designated as physique. These physical characteristics have been measured and categorized in many different ways and have formed the basis of several very ambitious theories of personality.

Measures of Structure. Measures are made of height, weight, cranial capacity, cranial shape, body size, body build, and facial angles, and numerous indices have been derived among these various measures. The results are usually summarized as types, and claims have been made that each physical type is characterized by a certain type of personality.

Theories Based on Physique. The first theory to gain wide acceptance in terms of relation between physical characteristics and personality factors was the phrenology of Gall (about 1800). Gall postulated that the mind was made up of many faculties and that these faculties had definite localization in the brain. If one faculty were present to a large degree, there would be a compensating bump on the cranium. The exterior of the skull was mapped very thoroughly, and "skull-reading" became a popular and flourishing business. Present-day experimentalists have thoroughly demolished the theory, but phrenological charts can still be found in use.

In the late 19th century Lombroso advanced the theory that certain criminal types could be identified by measurement of physical traits. This was later shown to be unsupportable by Lombroso himself and by several others. One of the most amusing experiments showed the distribution of Lombroso's pertinent physical traits to be the same among Harvard graduates as among Lombroso's criminals.

Kretschmer (1925) describes four types of personality based upon physique: the "pyknik" (short-limbed, round-bodied, stocky), the "asthenic" (long-limbed, long-bodied, slender, angular), the "hypoplastic" (underdeveloped), and the "athletic" (generally, the model individual). According to Kretschmer the pyknik personality is characterized by likelihood of reversion to extreme emotional reactions (extreme mania or depression). The asthenic is a daydreamer who withdraws from social contacts and becomes shut off from reality. The hypoplastic is likely to develop "inferiority complexes" due to his underdevelopment. The athletic is the nearly perfect individual. Kretschmer's theory was derived from clinical observations, but subsequent measurements of actual people do not confirm his theory (Garvey, 1933).

The most ambitious and most complete attempt to correlate physique with personality has been made by Sheldon and Stevens (1942). They studied thousands of photographs and developed a system by which each individual was classified according to: (1) his *endomorphy* (prominence of the abdominal region or the digestive viscera), (2) his *mesomorphy* (prominence of bone and muscle), and (3) his *ectomorphy* (prominence of fragile structure, long delicate bones, large surface area in proportion to bodily mass). A seven-point scale was used for classification of each photograph (greater accuracy was found from caliper measurements of the photographs than from measurement of the individuals themselves) for 200 young men. These same men were interviewed and rated for personality on 60 different traits. The ratings were correlated with the somatotype classifications, and the entire collection of data was factor-analyzed. Three clusters of traits were defined: (1) *viscerotonia,* in which digestive and vegetative functions predominated, (2) *somatotonia,* in which vigor and aggressiveness were noticeable, and (3) *cerebrotonia,* in which restraint and lack of social adaptation were pre-eminent. Sheldon and Stevens found extremely high correlations between their three major somatotypes and the temperament ratings: .79 between endomorphy and viscerotonia; .82 between mesomorphy and somatotonia, and .83 between ectomorphy and cerebrotonia. Other researches are needed before drawing final conclusions on the Sheldon-Stevens theory. However, the reader would do well to remember that demonstration of relationships does not demonstrate cause and effect.

CHEMIQUE

The oldest known theory of personality is a classification of temperaments formulated by the Greeks. About 400 B.C. Hippocrates laid the foundation for the doctrine of temperaments based on the humors (fluids) of the body, and the Greek physician Galen (167 A.D.) elaborated this theory as follows:

TEMPERAMENTS	HUMORS
Quick—strong (choleric)	Yellow bile
Quick—weak (sanguine)	Blood
Slow—strong (melancholic)	Black bile
Slow—weak (phlegmatic)	Phlegm

An exact balance of these four humors was said to make the correctly constituted personality.

Studies of Glandular and Other Physiological Factors. In addition to the more or less temporary changes in bodily chemistry related to emotion, glandular excesses or deficiencies can have great direct or indirect effects on the personality structure.

An excess of insulin causes fatigue, nervousness, and anxiety. Deficiencies of thyroxin, in addition to being related to mental deficiency in children, cause sluggishness and a decrease in physical vigor. An excess of thyroxin may, however, cause restlessness, nervousness, irritability, and general hyperactivity. The adrenal glands are related to cardiac activity, and increased secretion of adrenalin is characteristic of emotional activity. Pituitary activity influences growth. Nonreproductive (internal) secretions of the sex glands are responsible for the development of masculinity and femininity and may thus exert a powerful influence on the personality.

The endocrines are so interrelated in function that any condition tending to change the function of one is also manifest in the numerous functions of the others. Thus, apparently trivial changes in a single organ may be responsible for marked changes in the personality. Since the endocrines are ductless glands secreting directly into the blood stream, the circulatory system has often been called the chemical integrator of the body. It might be designated as the chemical integrator of the personality.

Chemical Contribution to Theory. There is, as yet, no theory composed basically of chemique. Chemical explanations of personality have been confined largely to specific personality qualities. Various personality differences are linked to the functioning of the endocrine glands, and definite correlations have been established between glandular activity and the personality qualities.

PSYCHIQUE

Despite the obvious presence of physical and chemical factors in determination of personality, interest in the subject has always centered in the psychological aspect. The study of the psychological factors of personality has generally followed two definite lines of development: (1) measurement of personality traits with special reference to the establishment of tests for the indication of degrees of personality differences among people generally; and (2) general observation with special reference to classifications of the symptoms and diagnoses of abnormal personality (mental disorder, mental disease).

Personality Traits. From use of the techniques for observation and measurement of personality discussed previously have come several definitions of psychological activity in personality. This psychological activity is designated by such terms as emotionality, temperament, affectivity, mental adjustment, social behavior, complexes, self-sufficiency, disposition, dominance and submission, and introversion-extroversion. This last type of designation, i.e., introversion-extroversion, has brought about some difficulties of interpretation not intended by the researchers. Though a continuum is supposed to exist with intro- and extro- at opposite poles, common usage has been to treat the concept as a dichotomy and to classify people as one or the other.

The chief result of early experimentation with personality traits and resultant classifications was the detection of atypical or potentially abnormal personalities. Recently, great advances in guidance and mental hygiene have caused the tests to be used widely under conditions involving less stress. Also, there has been more experimentation with personality tests as an aid to solution of the selection, placement, and promotion problems in industry.

The Abnormal Personality. In the investigation of the abnormal personality, testing is often impossible because the extremely abnormal person will not or cannot co-operate in the testing. Under such conditions, descriptive symptoms or categories of traits are used to classify the abnormal personality into kinds of mental disorder.

CLASSIFICATION OF ABNORMAL PERSONALITY

Mental disorders are classified as: (1) the *organic,* which are associated with a definite physical or chemical injury that is essentially causative of the disorder, and (2) the *functional,* which are psychogenic. The final causes of the functional disorders are usually traced in the life history of the individual, although organic changes accompany the development of the disorder and a hereditary predisposition probably exists.

The Organic Psychoses. All physical diseases are accompanied by some mental disturbance, and the following mental disorders are characterized by definite injury to nervous tissue: (1) general paralysis (paresis), caused by syphilis of the nervous system; (2) traumatic disorders, accompanied by delirium or loss of memory; (3) senile psychosis, the psychosis of old age; (4) arteriosclerotic psychosis, the psychosis caused by a hardening of the arteries; and (5) psychoses of brain disorders, such as tuberculosis of the brain, Huntington's chorea, brain tumor, brain syphilis, congenital brain injury. Chemical or toxic injury may cause mental disorder, as in pathological intoxication, delirium tremens, and other alcoholic psychoses, and the drug psychoses of accidental, trade, food, or habit origin. The symptoms of the organic psychoses are abnormal developments of the individual's original personality qualities which the organic injury has let loose.

The Functional Psychoses. Mental disorders which are explainable only in psychological terms are classified into the *psychoses* and the *neuroses.*

THE PSYCHOSES. The psychoses are marked mental disorders in which the normal personality of the individual is completely lost. Disintegration of personality qualities is complete, and the person is disoriented in his environment.

The manic-depressive psychoses, paranoia, and schizophrenia belong to this group. The distinguishing symptoms of the manic-depressive psychoses are psychomotor elation and depression, often with a circulatory course. Paranoia is characterized by weakness of judgment and systematized delusions. Schizophrenia shows progressively marked deterioration of intelligence accompanied by emotional disturbances, such as excitement, depression, delusions, stupor, loss of motive, and various other symptoms. It is the largest group of disorders, including more than half the patients of state hospitals.

THE NEUROSES. The neuroses are conditions of "nervousness" of apparently well people. They include neurasthenia, psychasthenia, and hysteria, which have as their symptoms various phobias or fears, obsessions, complexes, mental and physical weaknesses, tics, and psychological paralysis. The underlying psychological condition in neurosis is a conflict between goals of action.

Official Classification. The official classification of the American Psychiatric Association, which is widely used in mental disease hospitals, includes the following major clinical categories of mental disorder: (1) traumatic psychoses, (2) senile psychoses, (3) psychoses with arteriosclerosis, (4) general paralysis, (5) psychoses with cerebral syphilis, (6) psychoses with Huntington's chorea, (7) psychoses with brain tumor, (8) psychoses with other brain and nervous diseases, (9) alcoholic psychoses, (10) psychoses due to drugs and other exogenous toxins, (11) psychoses with pellagra, (12) psychoses with other somatic diseases, (13) manic-depressive psychoses, (14) involutional melancholia, (15) schizophrenia, (16) paranoia or paranoid condition, (17) epileptic psychoses, (18) psychoneuroses and neuroses, (19) psychoses with psychopathic personality, (20) psychoses with mental deficiency, (21) undiagnosed psychoses, (22) without psychoses. The last-named class is included for patients with epilepsy, alcoholism, drug addiction, psychopathic personality, mental deficiency, etc., confined to the mental disease institutions.

Descriptive Symptoms of the Abnormal Personality. The most characteristic descriptive symptom of the abnormal personality is inability to fit into social organization or to adjust to the customary ways of living. This symptom is evident in the slight eccentricities of the normal person as well as in the definitely unsocial behavior of the hobo, the criminal, and the insane.

Among the specific abnormal symptoms which may be indicated by tests or in interviews are changes or differences from the normal in visual, auditory, or organic sensitivities. Hallucinations and delusions are prominent in the abnormal personality. Hallucinations are false perceptions. "Voices" of good or evil from Heaven or Hell are common hallucinations, and "visions" are described by the abnormal person as if they were real experiences. Delusions generally accompany hallucinations. They are false beliefs. Delusions of reference, persecution, and grandeur occur in certain mental disorders, and in some they are systematized to include all of awareness. Thought is completely disoriented from reality in the systematized delusion.

Fixed ideas, obsessions, or the overweighting of an idea, doubts, and phobias, such as the fear of dirt (mysophobia), the fear of open spaces (agoraphobia), the fear of closed places (claustrophobia), and the fear of fire (pyrophobia) are common symptoms among certain mental disorders. Lady Macbeth's performance in the sleepwalking scene is an example of an obsession. The normal person frequently has mild obsessions that he will have a disease, fall off a cliff, or find someone under the bed. Abnormality is a matter of degree.

The stereotyped action carries the abnormal development of the obsession a little further, and one act may be performed throughout the whole day. In somnambulism the patient lives through a painful experience which he had forgotten, although he may appear very much like the ordinary sleepwalker.

A "flight of ideas" and retardation of thought are abnormal symptoms, and dilapidation of thought is characteristic of schizophrenia. Compulsions, as in kleptomania, negativisms, exaltation and depression, increased and decreased psychomotor activity, melancholia and stupor, amnesia, hypermnesia and paramnesia, multiple personality, emotional complexes, loss of motivation and interest, exaggerated symbolism in day and night dreaming, all these do not exhaust the list of symptoms of the abnormal personality.

The whole personality is affected in mental disorder. Physical and glandular changes take place. Clinical tests show disturbances of the major reflexes such as the knee jerk, eye reflex, or Babinski reflex, and indicate destruction of nervous tissue. Personality and intelligence tests show degrees of psychological changes. The genetic history of an abnormal personality may show a symptomatology of personality differences which classifies him as having one of the various mental disorders. Yet these symptoms are but exaggerated traits of the normal personality.

Causes of Mental Disorder. Mental disorder may be attributed to one of three things: (1) inherited predispositions or general susceptibility to disease, (2) individual conditioning factors such as age, physiological epochs, sex, and (3) environmental conditioning factors such as climate, civilization, trauma, infection, worry, fright, exhaustion. These three may, of course, work together so that a predisposed person may avoid mental disease by not being subjected to a stressful environment, or an extremely stressful environment may cause a less predisposed person to show mental disorder.

Specific mental disorders are not inherited, though the expectation that a mentally disordered person will have one or more close relatives who are also mentally disordered is considerably greater than chance. This is not surprising if the factors of inherited predisposition and greater likelihood of a similar stressful environment are considered.

Prevalence of Mental Disorder. Figures on the prevalence of mental disorders are extremely hard to accumulate. Great social stigma is still attached to mental disease though serious campaigns are under way to combat this feeling. Figures based on admissions to mental hospitals are certainly underestimates of the true state of affairs, but even these demonstrate the importance of the problem. There are more hospital beds devoted to patients with mental disorders than there are devoted to patients with physical disorders.

THEORIES OF PERSONALITY

In addition to the somatotypic theories discussed earlier, there are several psychological theories of personality which have vocal adherents.

The Behavior Theory of Watson (1924). According to Watson, personality is a development of conditioned reactions. Abnormal and normal attitudes and reactions are due to adaptive and nonadaptive conditioning of objects, activities, and persons of the environment. Though the theory is seldom set forth as such in today's writings, much of our educational theory and practice is definitely based on such a theory.

The Psychoanalytical Theory of Freud (1883). Freud held that the motivation of life is the *libido,* which is sexual energy undifferentiated from hunger at birth (sex and food-getting instincts). Libido striving is pleasure-seeking and avoidance of pain (pleasure-pain principle), which comes into conflict with social custom (gregarious instinct), leading to a recognition of reality (reality principle) and adjustment in various ways.

Repression of the primitive pleasure-pain impulses may force them into the unconscious and cause a "flight from reality" into neuroses or psychoses. Conflict between libido striving and reality determines the development of personality in a normal or abnormal direction.

Adler's Theory of Psychic Compensation (1917). At the foundation of Adler's theory is the doctrine of *Minderwertikgeit,* or organic and psychic inferiority. According to Adler, at some time before birth all organs of the body strive independently for nutrition. At birth they begin to function together according to the laws of compensation. Psychic inferiority has its basis in organic inferiority, and mind is the instrument by which compensation for organic defects, such as in vision or audition, is accomplished. When compensation is difficult the person does not take a "flight from reality" (Freud), but he builds up an avoidance in the face of reality. There is a "life plan" with avoiding tendencies and rationalizations of activity. All life begins with feelings of inferiority, and the measure of adjustment is the degree and kind of compensation effected by the individual.

Introvert-Extrovert Type Theory of Jung (1903). Best known of the type theories, Jung's classifies all persons into the "extrovert" and "introvert" personality. Libido, according to Jung, is defined as psychic energy. In the extrovert, psychic energy is directed outward toward objects, activities, and people. In the introvert, it is directed inward in phantasy, daydreaming, and thoughts about oneself.

Lewin's Topological Theory of Personality (1936). According to Lewin the interactions between an individual and his environment quite normally result in conflict. There are only three basic types of conflict: (1) approach-approach conflicts, in which the individual is motivated toward two positive stimuli of about equal strength, (2) avoidance-avoidance conflicts, in which the individual is motivated away from two negative stimuli of about equal strength, and (3) approach-avoidance conflicts, in which the field contains one positive stimulus and one negative stimulus. This last named is considered most likely to underlie anxiety and unresolved tensions.

ADJUSTMENT

The action of an organism upon its environment may be adaptive or nonadaptive. With human beings living in society this activity is called adjustment or maladjustment. The criterion of perfection of reaction is adjustment. Under conditions of civilization this criterion is defined in large measure by the rules and standards of society (folkways and *mores*), which are the social habits of groups of animals and people.

A human being or animal is said to be intelligent if he is able to adjust satisfactorily to his environment. Intelligence is thus thought of as the capacity for adjustment, and intelligence tests are regarded as measures of degrees of adjustment. This may be true for the mechanism of adjustment, but personality traits influence adjustment to a very great degree.

Maladjustment is indicated first by unusual reactions in a normal environment. Persons giving evidence of maladjustment are usually designated as abnormal: (1) if they score in the lower ranges of distribution on intelligence tests (the feeble-minded or aments), (2) if they score in the lower ranges of personality measures (the psychotic, neurotic, psychoneurotic, or insane), and (3) if their behavior differs too much from the usual or normal behavior of the other members of the social organization.

SUMMARY

Personality is a catchall term with a multitude of definitions. These generally add up to some description of the result of interaction of one human being with another. Most attempts to describe and measure personality have been in terms of traits or characteristics. Whether the whole personality can be broken down into some sum or interaction of these traits or characteristics is still a highly debatable question.

Many attempts to define and measure personality have had their beginnings in the extreme cases which are concentrated in hospitals because their unsatisfactory social adjustment has led to their institutionalization. The traits or other factors developed through such definition and measurement may not represent the extreme of any true continuum or set of continua.

A tremendous number of personality inventories and other tests have been developed in an attempt to define and measure personality. The latest development is the projective technique.

Since the dawn of recorded history, attempts have been made to associate the physical characteristics of the individual, particularly his body build, with the personality. To date, all classifications based on physique have failed to hold up under careful experimentation. However, there is clearly some relationship, though this may be that both physique and personality are related to some common underlying factor.

Those afflicted with mental disorders have been the subject of great interest to psychologists throughout the years. The prevalence of mental disorder is difficult to determine, partially because of the social stigma which is still attached to mental disease and partially because of the difficulty of making a diagnosis. Abnormality is a case of degree rather than of either—or.

Personality theorists are handicapped by the difficulty of definition. By far the most popular theory in terms of its relation to therapy is the psychoanalytical theory of Freud, though this has had many modifications since the original promulgation.

Personality description in particular is likely to fall heir to the mistake of dividing all people into two categories. People are said to be introverts or extroverts as if there were a bimodal distribution. In reality, introverts and extroverts are the extremes of a continuum and a vast majority of people are somewhere between these two extremes.

16

Tests and Testing

Little activity in the field of psychology is so exclusively the province of the psychologists as the construction of testing instruments. Historically, testing is considered to have begun with Sir Francis Galton, though tests as we know them today more properly originated with Cattell and his college entrance examinations.

Hundreds of tests have been developed as measures of various combinations of reactions (performances, capacities, aptitudes, abilities, traits, intelligence, personality, and achievement). The tremendous scope of measurement by tests is illustrated by a simple listing of the more important classifications: general intelligence, mechanical aptitude, clerical aptitude, artistic aptitude, musical aptitude, interests, personality, attitudes, temperament, and a host of proficiency and achievement tests. Though all too many people refer to tests as "those I.Q. tests," not all tests are measures of intelligence.

CHARACTERISTICS OF TESTS

Tests have certain general characteristics, some of which relate to the techniques of testing and some of which are basic requirements of all satisfactory tests.

Tests as Standardized Experiments. In the very strict sense of the word, a test is a sample of behavior taken so that the total behavior picture may be ascertained. Thus, a test is a standardized experiment. In its broadest usage, a test is a sample of behavior which either is representative of the total behavior or is in some way related to the total behavior which is to be measured or predicted. In the same way a test may be a miniature of the total behavior or it may consist of samples of primary elements which are not necessarily recognizable as combining to form the total behavior in which we are interested.

Individual vs. Group Measurement. Some tests can be given to only one individual at a time, whereas others can be given to groups of various size. In general, individual tests require much more highly skilled examiners than do group tests.

Verbal vs. Nonverbal Tests. Tests are frequently classified as verbal or nonverbal according to whether the use of language is required in the test itself. The truly nonverbal, or nonlanguage, test does not require any knowledge of language; the directions may be given by pantomime or by examples, and the subject makes his reactions by marking on pictures or performing appropriate manipulations of objects. Most tests, both individual and group, require a knowledge of language in some part of the testing, though there are a number of tests which do not have language in the test proper.

Speed vs. Power Tests. Tests may also be classified as speed or power tests. The speed tests have standard time limits. In a perfect speed test all items are of equal difficulty and the score is the number of items correctly answered in the specified time. The power tests have no time limits. The items are scaled for difficulty so that the simplest item comes first and each succeeding item is more difficult than the one it follows. The subject works until he has reached the limit of his ability, and the score is the number of items answered correctly. Many tests are a combination of speed and power. The items are scaled and arranged in order of difficulty, but a specified time limit is also established so that speed of effort is a factor in the final score attained.

Speed vs. Accuracy in Tests. Tests differ in their emphasis on speed and accuracy. In general, tests emphasizing accuracy include problems in which time is not important in the measurement.

Performance vs. Capacity for Performance. All tests are measures of reactions, measures of the performance of individuals on the problems of the test. But in some tests the end result of the testing is an estimate of how much the individual has achieved whereas in others the end result is an estimate of how much the individual can achieve. Thus we have *achievement* tests and *capacity* or *aptitude* tests. Intelligence tests are basically aptitude tests for prediction of generalized performance level.

Specific Tests, Omnibus Tests, and Test Batteries. In some testing the object is to measure a specific factor in the "purest" manner possible. In other testing the object is to measure a general or composite unit of behavior. In still other testing the object is to measure a number of factors in such a fashion that different summations can be achieved. Let us illustrate from the schoolroom situation. We may build the purest possible test of arithmetic, or reading, or spelling, or geography, or any other subject in order to measure performance in the particular subject. We may build an omnibus test in which we include materials from all the classroom subjects in order to measure generalized performance in a composite of all subjects. Or we may build a test battery which contains subtests of all subjects in order to make differential prediction of success in engineering, law, sales, etc. where certain subjects are more important than others and an appropriately weighted combination of subtest scores is more meaningful than any simple summation.

TEST CRITERIA

A "good" test must meet three major criteria. These three are: (1) reliability, (2) validity, and (3) discrimination. Each is determined by statistical methods, which have been discussed in some detail in Chapter 9.

Reliability. The reliability of a test is the degree to which it is a consistent measure of whatever it is supposed to be measuring. Other things being equal, an individual's score should be the same one day as it is the next unless some factor associated with an improved or diminished test score is present.

Validity. The validity of a test is the degree to which it is a true measure of what it is supposed to be measuring. A test for height which involved use of a yardstick would probably be fairly reliable; the results for a given individual would be much the same from day to day. But the scores, however expressed, would hardly be valid as an indication of the intelligence of the individual. Validity is the stumbling block over which many otherwise "good" tests fall. No test has inherent validity, and in many instances it is next to impossible to find some outside measure of the trait or characteristic against which to test the test.

Discrimination. The discriminative power of a test and its re-

liability usually go hand in hand. But it is possible to have a
fairly reliable test which lacks discrimination throughout the
range of scores for the purpose to which it is put. And it is quite
common to find reliable tests which have little or no discrimination at the upper or lower ranges. One would not use a butcher's
scale to weigh drugs in compounding a prescription, nor jewel-
er's scales for the weighing of coal.

TESTS OF GENERAL INTELLIGENCE

The tests first constructed were intelligence tests. They are
still the most widely used type of test despite all the research on
specific aptitudes and proficiencies. All kinds are available: individual or group, verbal or nonverbal, speed or power, and various combinations of these. The items which make up a general
intelligence test are characterized in one of two ways: (1) individuals of any prescribed social group will have equal opportunity for familiarity with the problem presented, or (2) reactions
to the items will not depend on formal education (schooling).
Capacity or intelligence is inferred from performance on these
tests.

It is much more difficult than might be supposed to meet
either of the two criteria for selection of test items for a general
intelligence test. Consider the first criterion. Almost all researchers have found that vocabulary is one of the best single indices
of intelligence. But even in such a prescribed social group as
United States school children, equal opportunity for familiarity
with any word except the very simplest does not exist. Geographical differences, familial differences, and a host of other
discounting factors immediately arise. So, at best, criterion number one is only approximated. Consider the second criterion.
Even so simple an activity as holding a pencil and making marks
is partially dependent on schooling. However, the problems of
meeting the second criterion are relatively simple as compared
to the first.

The major attempts to avoid difficulty with the first criterion
have been in the nature of dependence on nonverbal or manipulative material. But, unfortunately, the capacity which we
wish to predict from the intelligence test is usually that which
involves verbal or at least language behavior, and thus, in the

long run, the performance type of materials are usually considered valid to the extent that they predict scores made on verbal materials.

The difficulties described above have by no means rendered the intelligence tests valueless. Rather, realization of these difficulties will help us view their value in proper perspective.

Individual, Generally Verbal, Power Tests. In 1905 Binet and Simon formulated and used the first battery of tests of general intelligence. This battery was composed of 32 single tests designed to measure memory, mental imagery, imagination, attention, comprehension, esthetic feeling or appreciation, moral sentiments, and judgment, all of which taken together indicated general intelligence. A revision of the 1905 battery by Binet and Simon appeared in 1908 as the first age scale, and a second revision appeared in 1911. Huey (1910) and Goddard (1911) translated the Binet-Simon scale into English. Goddard revised the scale slightly and used it in the Vineland Training School. These translations were followed by many other American revisions, the most important of which are listed below.

Kuhlmann	1912
Yerkes, Bridges, and Hardwick	1915
Stanford Revision (by Terman)	1916
Kuhlmann	1922
Herring	1922
Yerkes and Foster	1923
Stanford Revision (by Terman and Merrill) . .	1937
Wechsler-Bellevue	1939

Of these the most widely used with children is the 1937 Stanford Revision. Two equivalent forms, L and M, are provided. Problems such as pointing to parts of the body, following simple directions, esthetic discriminations, visual discrimination of forms, counting, items of judgment and comprehension, naming colors, and repetition of syllables and numbers are included in the tests for the very early years (2–5). Problems of fact, arithmetic reasoning, visual imagery, induction, vocabulary, interpretation of fables, definition of abstract terms, repetition of digits, repetition of digits in reverse order, repetition of the thoughts of a prose passage, and reasoning are included in the higher levels (teen age through Superior Adult III).

The test most widely used with adults is the Wechsler-Bellevue

Scale of Mental Ability. It was specifically designed for use with adults rather than with children, though the adult population used in its development were patients in a mental hospital and its projected use at that time was diagnosis of mental defects and mental impairment. Norms are now available for a wide variety of groups. The test consists basically of two parts: (1) items of memory, vocabulary, reasoning, etc., which yield a verbal score, and (2) items involving pictures, manipulative materials, etc., which yield a performance score. Representative studies show that the Wechsler-Bellevue and the Revised Stanford Binet correlate approximatey .85 with each other.

A great many adaptations of the Binet or Wechsler tests have been made, both in English and in other languages. A recent example is the Saudi General Classification Test used in Saudi Arabia, which combines many of the best features of its predecessors.

Individual, Nonverbal, Power Tests. Tests involving knowledge of language would obviously be unfitted for use with foreign-speaking subjects, illiterate or semiliterate subjects, very young subjects, and certain individuals handicapped with speech or language defects. Nonverbal tests (also called performance tests) are used to test such persons. They are also used as a check on the verbal tests. The nonverbal tests involve the manipulation of objects such as fitting blocks into appropriate recesses in boards (form boards), solving manipulative puzzles, or assembling parts to construct a figure, or they consist of mazes, pictorial organization into rational series, or construction of designs.

SINGLE TESTS. Unlike the verbal scales (with the single exception of vocabulary), several of the items of the performance tests have been standardized separately and are sometimes used as a complete test for a rapid approximation of capacities under conditions where exact testing is difficult. Generally speaking, the performance-test items are scored in terms of time, errors, or some combination thereof and so give a spread of scores which the pass-fail items of the verbal test cannot do. This list gives some of the outstanding single nonverbal tests which have been used.

> Seguin Form Board (original and many revisions)
> Healy Pictorial Completion Tests

Manikin and Feature Profile Tests
Kohs Block Design Test
Knox Cube Test
Porteus Maze Test

The last-named test deserves special mention. Once hailed as a "culture-free" test of intelligence, it was widely administered to persons of other cultures in an attempt to discover racial differences. Among other things it demonstrated the existence of a variety of motivational factors indicating unreliable comparative test results between races. For example, in one aboriginal tribe where the examiner became initiated in order to get subjects, he found that after his initiation he was supposed to help his "brother," and if he knew the answer and his "brother" did not, the examiner was felt to be not playing fair.

NONVERBAL BATTERIES. Groups of form boards and other nonverbal tests have been assembled into batteries to increase reliability and scope. Healy and Fernald (1911) and Knox (1914) prepared batteries, but the earliest comprehensive intelligence battery of nonverbal materials was the Army Performance Scale (1917) developed by the psychologists in the Army in World War I. This battery included ten tests, as follows: the Knox Ship Test, the Manikin and Feature Profile Tests, the Knox Cube Test, the Goddard Cube Construction Tests, the Dearborn Form Board, Terman's Memory from Designs Test, the Digit-Symbol Substitution Tests, the Porteus Maze Test, a Picture Arrangement Test, and the Healy Pictorial Completion Tests.

Among performance scales used today are the Pintner-Paterson Performance Scale (1917), the Arthur Point Scale of Performance Tests (1928), and the Leiter International Performance Scale (1940). For measurement of young children, the Gesell Scale (1925) and the Merrill-Palmer Scales (1931) are extensively used.

Verbal Group Tests. Individual tests are limited in their use because one examiner is required for each subject to be tested. Group tests were developed by Otis and others about 1914 to overcome this difficulty. These tests usually combine the speed and power factors in measurement.

The World War I psychologists of the United States Army gave group testing of intelligence its greatest emphasis through development and use of the Group Examination Alpha. This test was composed of 212 items in 8 subtests as follows: following directions, arithmetic computation and reasoning, common sense, sameness and oppositeness of pairs of words, scrambled sentences, arithmetic completion, word relationships, and information. After World War I the test became part of the public domain. The test itself along with several minor revisions remains in use today.

There are literally hundreds of verbal group intelligence tests available today. Most of them contain about the same material as that of the Army Alpha, though there has been a gradual process of extension and adaptation of nonverbal materials for use in primarily verbal tests. No attempt to list the verbal group tests will be made, but three will be singled out for discussion.

OTIS SELF-ADMINISTERING TESTS OF MENTAL ABILITY. The basic Otis test (1922) consisted of 75 mixed items arranged in order of difficulty. Items included vocabulary, analogies, number series, proverbs, arithmetic problems, spatial relationships, etc. From this basic test, special forms for use with elementary and junior high school students have been prepared, and the Personnel Test (Wonderlic) has been derived from it.

Perhaps the outstanding thing about the Otis is its widespread use. Norms are based on over 100,000 cases, gathered from large samples but with little attempt at control of the source. In addition to the norms provided in the manual, many industrial establishments have local norms and use the Otis as a screening device in maintaining a minimum intelligence level in their plant or business.

ARMY GENERAL CLASSIFICATION TEST. Though the Army Alpha was still being used in civilian life, the Army psychologists of World War II built a new intelligence test. Four equivalent forms were provided to minimize leakage (questions becoming too widely known) and to provide for retesting with the minimum practice effect. The test was of spiral omnibus form in which three types of items (vocabulary, arithmetic, and block-counting) were alternated in ever ascending difficulty. The time limit imposed made the test a combination speed-power test.

Perhaps the outstanding thing about the Army General Classification Test was the contribution it made to study of test-score differences among occupational groups and geographical area groups, and to validation of intelligence-test materials as predictors of success in a variety of training and performance situations.

The test was taken by more than 11 million men. The Army Machine Records Unit regularly provided 2 per cent samples of test scores of this population as they were collected, and other data for research purposes. One of the most interesting of the studies using these data is that of Stewart (1947), showing the distribution of AGCT median scores according to civilian occupational group of the examinees.

THURSTONE TEST OF PRIMARY MENTAL ABILITIES (1938). This test is the best representative of a new trend in verbal group tests, building subtests which are relatively pure factorially. That is, each subtest should have a very low correlation with every other subtest. Such procedures not only enable coverage of the maximum amount of material with the minimum amount of testing effort; they provide a much sounder basis for studies of differential prediction in which the independent factors can be appropriately weighted to reflect success in different learning situations or occupations. The PMA Tests measure six primary mental abilities: Verbal Meaning (V), Space (S), Number (N), Memory (M), Word Fluency (W), and Reasoning (R). Tests used are: vocabulary and opposites (V), flags and cards (S), addition and multiplication (N), letter grouping (R), etc. Eleven tests in all are used, and two hours are required for testing the subjects.

Nonlanguage (Nonverbal) Group Tests. As with the individual nonverbal tests, the nonlanguage group tests are designated for illiterates, children, and others not possessing adequate language facilities. Again, the Army psychologists of World War I with the Group Examination Beta (1917) were the first to develop a group nonverbal test for extensive use.

Nonverbal tests for adults have diminished greatly in use as schooling has become more prevalent and the incidence of illiteracy and foreign tongue has diminished. Where nonverbal tests are required among adults, nonverbal portions of primarily verbal tests may be used, or some dependence may be placed on one or more of the nonverbal tests of special aptitude which are now quite prevalent. However, practically all group tests for the preschool and primary school levels are nonverbal tests, and each of the major test publishing houses catering to educational institutions has one or more with adequate reliability, validity, and normative data.

Tests for Exceptional Persons. Tests of intelligence have been devised for exceptional groups, notably the blind and the deaf.

THE BLIND. Irwin (1915) adapted the Goddard Revision of the Binet-Simon for testing the blind. Hayes (1930) adapted the Stanford Revision, and Sargent (1931) adapted the Otis Classification Test.

THE DEAF. The nonlanguage performance-test materials have been widely used in measuring the intelligence of the deaf.

TESTS OF EDUCATIONAL APTITUDE

General intelligence tests have been and are widely used as measures of capacity for success in school. In recent years specialization of these tests has been carried on to achieve maximum validity in the school situation.

Preschool and Primary Grades Tests. Since learning to read is the basic activity of the first years of school, research has been concentrated on the development of "Reading Readiness" tests. In general, these emphasize perceptual abilities, as ability to distinguish different letters or symbols, and background and experience factors needed to comprehend the subject matter of the projected reading.

Elementary School and High School Tests. Little attention has been given to other than general aptitude at these levels though some slight usage is being made of language aptitude tests for foreign language assignments and science aptitude tests at the high school levels. In some instances the college educational aptitude materials are given as early as the ninth grade to aid in vocational counseling toward or away from college training.

College Entrance Tests. Few tests have had as thorough and complete study as college entrance examinations. A "captive audience" is available, and a ready-made criterion of success (pass-fail or course grades) is also available.

Perhaps the best known and most widely used of the college entrance examinations are the American Council on Education Psychological Examination (Thurstone) and the Ohio College Association Examination (Toops). Each of these has a long his--

tory of use and is regularly revised to keep materials current, to avoid leakage of items, and to continue making improvements.

Tests for Professional Schools. Current emphasis in colleges is on tests for specialists in addition to the general educational aptitude materials. Among the groups for whom some form of specialized aptitude test is available are: dentists (Iowa Dental Qualifying Examination), engineers (Engineering and Physical Science Aptitude Test), lawyers (Iowa Legal Aptitude Test), nurses (George Washington University Series of Nursing Tests, and the Nursing Entrance Examination Program), pharmacists (American Pharmaceutical Association Examination), physicians (Moss Medical Aptitude Test), scientists (Stanford, or Zyve, Scientific Aptitude Test, and the Science Aptitude Test used in the Science Talent Search of Westinghouse), and teachers (Coxe-Orleans Prognosis Test of Teaching Ability, and the National Teacher Examinations).

In addition, many schools have developed local batteries, either by construction or by validation and combination of more general aptitude tests.

OTHER APTITUDE TESTS

Tests have been constructed for the measurement of specific capacities such as those for music, art, mechanical work, and clerical work. These aptitude tests are prepared as individual or group tests; they are composed of either verbal or nonlanguage materials; and they are administered as both speed and power tests. Many of the so-called special aptitude tests have so many items measuring general intelligence that they are really special extensions of general intelligence tests. However, if they are sufficiently reliable, they usually predict success in the special area somewhat better than do the general intelligence tests.

Tests of Musical Aptitude. The most important contribution to the measurement of "musical talent" is the battery of tests devised by C. E. Seashore (1919). He divided general musical aptitude into six specific capacities, namely: discrimination of pitch, discrimination of intensity, discrimination of time, appreciation of resonance, tonal memory, and memory of rhythm. The tests are administered by phonograph records. The pitch discrimination test is illustrative: two tones are played, and the subject reacts by indicating whether the second tone is higher or lower than the first. The scores on the six tests are plotted as a *musical profile*. The Kwalwasser-Dykema Battery (1927) consists of ten tests similar to the Seashore series.

Tests of Artistic Aptitude. The Meier Art Judgment Test (1940), a revision of the Meier-Seashore Art Judgment Test (1929), is a test of esthetic judgment in which the subject is asked to choose the preferred of two pictures which represent the same object with slight variations. "Correct" responses were determined by a jury of established artists and by internal analysis of the test.

The Lewerenz Tests in the Fundamental Abilities of Visual Art (1927) is a measure of creative artistic ability. It is composed of nine subtests: recognition of proportion, originality of line drawing, observation of light and shade, knowledge of subject-matter vocabulary, visual memory of proportion, analysis of problems in cylindrical perspective, analysis of problems in parallel perspective, analysis of problems in angular perspective, and recognition of color. An *artistic profile* of the nine capacities is drawn upon completion of the scoring.

Tests of Mechanical Aptitude. Tests of mechanical aptitude fall into two major classifications: (1) performance tests of manual dexterity, and (2) paper-and-pencil tests on mechanical relationships and mechanical knowledge. Since our modern civilization depends quite heavily on mechanical activity, great attention has been given to development of tests for measurement of the capacity for successful mechanical work. A number of standard tests of both types is available and, in addition, numerous industrial establishments have specialized tests fitted to their own operations.

PERFORMANCE TESTS OF MANUAL DEXTERITY. Various performance tests to measure hand, wrist, finger, and composite manual dexterities have been built. Some of the more widely used are described below.

Minnesota Rate of Manipulation Test (1931). A form board containing 60 holes and 60 identical discs are provided the examinee. The examination consists of some version of placing the discs in the holes. Different problems are possible with the same board, with standard norms provided for each condition. The problems may involve one-hand placement, two-hand placement, turning and placement, etc.

O'Connor Finger and Tweezer Dexterity Tests (1928). A plate with 100 holes and a tray of metal pins are provided the examinee. In the finger dexterity test the subject must pick up three pins at one time and insert them in a hole. In the tweezer dexterity test a slightly larger pin is used, and the subject must pick up one pin at a time with a pair of tweezers and place it in a hole. Score is in terms of the time required to fill the holes.

Purdue Pegboard (1943). A board with two rows of $\frac{1}{8}$ inch holes down the middle and 4 shallow cups at one end are provided the examinee. Fifty metal pins, 20 metal collars, and 40 metal washers are also provided. Five different scores are developed from these materials: (1) placing pins in the holes one at a time with the right hand, (2) same with the left hand, (3) same with both hands simultaneously, (4) the sum of these three scores, and (5) assembling pin, washer, collar, washer, using right, left, right, and left hands.

Minnesota Mechanical Assembly Test (1930). This is an expanded version of the Stenquist Mechanical Assembly Test (1923). It consists of 33 compartments each of which contains a mechanical object to be assembled—such as a wooden spring-type clothespin, a push-button doorbell, a hose-pinch clamp, an expansion nut. A time limit is provided for each task, and scores are assigned for completed objects and partially completed objects.

Pilot Selection Tests of Performance Nature. During World War II a tremendous amount of research on manipulation, dexterity, and co-ordination tests was performed toward the end of improving the selection of flying cadets. Complete descriptions cannot be given here, but some of the titles are suggestive of the content: rotary pursuit test, lathe-type two-hand co-ordination test, stick and rudder test, rudder control test, discrimination-reaction time test.

PAPER-AND-PENCIL MECHANICAL APTITUDE TESTS. The development of "mechanical aptitude" tests has been in large measure due to the necessity of selecting men for "mechanical" jobs, rather than to the desire to demonstrate a "mechanical" capacity per se. Tests now marketed under the general heading of me-

chanical aptitude cover such subjects as spatial relations, mechanical information, comprehension of physical and mechanical
principles, and nonverbal reasoning. The following are the more
widely used paper-and-pencil mechanical tests.

O'Rourke Mechanical Aptitude Test (*1926, 1940*). The
O'Rourke test contains two parts: (1) a series of pictures in
which the subject matches tools and objects to demonstrate
which are used together, and (2) a multiple-choice verbal test
involving tools, materials, and mechanical procedures.

Bennett Test of Mechanical Comprehension (*1940*). This is a
pictorial type of test in which the possible effect of various
combinations of physical and mechanical forces is shown and the
subject is asked questions which permit him to show his knowledge of the correct principle. Thus, a question may show two
arrangements of friction belts and ask which will turn the drive
wheel in a given direction. Three forms (AA, BB, CC) are provided for men, with AA being the simplest and CC the most
complex. Form W1 is provided for women and utilizes house-
hold items to a great degree.

Minnesota Paper Form Board, Likert-Quasha Revision (*1934*).
This test is representative of a variety of spatial visualization
tests. The disarranged parts of a geometrical figure are shown,
and the subject is asked to assemble these mentally and to indicate which of five possible pictures represents the figure made
by the disarranged parts.

MacQuarrie Test for Mechanical Ability (*1925*). The Mac-
Quarrie Test is characterized by its breakdown into seven subtests which are supposed to reflect basic elements of mechanical
aptitude. The seven are: tracing, tapping, dotting, copying, location, block, and pursuit.

Tests of Clerical Aptitude. Just as is true of mechanical aptitude tests, the extensive development of clerical aptitude tests is
a function of the need for improved selection of personnel for
the large number of clerical jobs in our society. The most consistent finding of all the clerical aptitude tests is the importance
of a factor of perceptual speed and accuracy, with particular
emphasis on numbers and names. The best known of the clerical
aptitude tests is the Minnesota Clerical Test (1933, 1946). Two
parts are provided—a numbers part in which pairs of numbers
are given, some identical and others slightly different, and a

names part in which pairs of names are similarly arranged. The task of the examinee is to indicate for each pair whether the two items are the same or different. The test is completely a speed test.

TESTS OF PROFICIENCY

Tests of proficiency are principally divisible into two types: (1) tests which measure educational achievement, and (2) tests which measure job proficiency.

Educational Achievement Tests. Educational achievement tests are available for virtually all levels in our educational system and for virtually all types of subject matter. In general, they are well constructed and well standardized, though variations in the curriculum may partially invalidate the test norms in any given local situation. The following account indicates their extremely wide scope.

PRIMARY AND ELEMENTARY GRADES. Here we find such tests as the Gates Reading Tests, Metropolitan Achievement Tests, Stanford Achievement Tests, and several specialized tests for spelling, handwriting, arithmetic, and other subjects.

HIGH SCHOOL. Most of the high school tests are for the purpose of predicting probable success in college, at least with respect to subject-matter requirements. Among these are the Iowa Placement Examination, a higher form of the Stanford Achievement Test mentioned above, the Co-operative Achievement Tests, and the Test of General Educational Development. The last-named test was constructed during World War II for the United States Armed Forces Institute. After the war a passing score on this test was widely accepted by colleges and by industry as showing the equivalent of a high school education.

COLLEGE. Many graduate schools require the Graduate Record Examination as a prerequisite for entrance. This test surveys the major subject-matter areas taught in college, and extensive norms are provided.

Job Proficiency Tests. Job proficiency tests are now available for a variety of occupations. The earliest tests were for the relatively standard operations of typing and stenography. These were tests of skill, and few tests have been developed in like manner for other occupations except for use in individual industrial plants. The knowledge aspect of job proficiency has been more thoroughly covered, and tests for bookkeepers, accountants, electricians, welders, and several other occupations are available.

INTEREST MEASURES

All the measures which we have discussed previously have one thing in common—they are measures of capacity or demonstrations that a certain capacity has been used. It is axiomatic in use of tests for guidance or employee selection that tests are generally more valid in indicating those who will not succeed than those who will succeed. The rationale is simple: You cannot carry 12 quarts of water in a 10-quart pail, but merely having a 10-quart pail does not mean that you will carry 10 quarts of water. The difference between full and partial realization of capacity is generally attributed by testers to differences in interest or personality. Both have been the subject of unceasing research.

Data on interests have been collected in a variety of ways, and Super (1947) differentiates four types of interest as evidenced through the data collections: (1) expressed, (2) manifest, (3) tested, and (4) inventoried.

Dozens of interest inventories can be purchased, but two stand out in terms of frequency of use and in the fact that their authors have continued unceasingly their research in the field and with their respective forms. These two are the Strong Vocational Interest Blank (1927, 1938) and the Kuder Preference Record (1939, 1943, 1948).

Strong Vocational Interest Blank. For men the blank consists of 400 items, each of which must be answered as *like, dislike,* or *indifferent to.* Items included are names of occupations, school subjects, amusements, hobbies, pastimes, peculiarities of people, ratings of abilities and personal characteristics, names of well-known people, etc. Actual job activities are conspicuous by their absence. Keys were constructed by comparing the responses of men in a given occupation, e.g., architects, with those of a composite which represented men in general. The same set of items is scored with over 40 different keys, and the scores are compared with normative data for each occupation. A profile of interest-occupation relationship is drawn. A woman's form is also available which can be scored for about 20 occupations.

Kuder Preference Record. The Preference Record consists of a number of triads, blocks of three items each, in which the respondent must select one as preferred most and one as preferred least. Items reflect nine basic interests: mechanical, computational, scientific, persuasive, artistic, literary, musical, social service, and clerical. The items included in the Kuder are descriptions of activities such as "visit a museum," "sell tickets to a dance," etc. The scores are plotted as a profile of the nine interest areas. Basically, the Preference Record gives an indication of the relative strength of each of the areas within an individual. The Strong might be said to give an indication of comparisons between groups of individuals.

PERSONALITY MEASURES

Personality is the other great unknown affecting the difference between capacity and realization. The methods used to assess personality have been discussed in Chapter 15.

TEST SCORES AND NORMS

Test scores are expressed in a variety of ways, the variation usually being fitted to the purpose for which the test was intended.

Raw or Point Scores. Results may be expressed as the number of items answered correctly, with some correction for guessing applied if the test is true-false or multiple-choice. Raw scores are of little value by themselves unless some specified criterion score or passing mark is the only point of reference to be used.

Mental Age. Many revisions and adaptations of the Binet-Simon Examination (and a few other tests) are arranged as age scales and produce scores expressed as mental ages (M.A.). This concept was devised by Binet and first used in his 1908 revision.

The test questions are classified according to their difficulties into age groups so that they can be answered correctly by about 75 per cent of children of the corresponding chronological age (C.A.). Each question gives a certain number of months' credit, usually 2 months since there are 6 questions per year in most groups. A mental age score of 6 years 6 months indicates that the child who obtained it has solved correctly the questions (or equivalents) usually solved by average children six and a half years old.

The mental age has serious limitations when applied to children with chronological ages of 13 years or more because of much conflicting evidence about the age of mental maturity and related issues.

Intelligence Quotient (I.Q.). The ratio of the mental age to the life age or chronological age is called the Intelligence Quotient (I.Q.). It was suggested as an index of brightness by Stern in 1912. The actual I.Q. is computed as M.A./C.A. $\times$ 100, to get rid of decimals. Thus, I.Q.'s of more than 100 indicate that the child is progressing mentally more rapidly than average, and I.Q.'s below 100 indicate that the child is progressing more slowly than average. The concept has had such wide usage that it has created grave errors. Like the M.A. it has little utilitarian value for teen-agers and adults. Also, the ease with which people were categorized from the ratio as geniuses, imbeciles, borderlines, etc. resulted in many social and educational actions which were later deemed unwise. As a result, I.Q. is less widely used in the educational work of professional testers with individuals and groups.

Norms. Group standards based on the population with which we wish to compare the tested individual are by far the preferred basis for interpretation of test results. Several systems are available.

PERCENTILE NORMS. Many test scores are converted to percentiles and thus expressed as a number from 1 to 100. The interpretation is made that the examinee's score exceeds that of the appropriate percentage of individuals with whom he is being compared. Thus, a percentile score of 87 would mean that the individual involved scored higher than 87 per cent of those with whom he is being compared.

SIGMA OR STANDARD SCORE NORMS. Using the mean and the standard deviation as reference points, a hypothetical normal curve is constructed and the individual's score is reported as so many standard deviation units above or below the average (mean) of the group with which he is being compared (see Chapter 9). Since standard deviation units are both plus and minus, the possibility of error in interpretation is sometimes resolved by converting the scores to a scale which will eliminate fractions and negative numbers. For example, the true mean and standard deviation of the Army General Classification Test were converted to 100 and 20, respectively. This made an average score equal to 100 and a score which was one standard deviation above the average equal to 120.

GRADE NORMS. Educational achievement tests are frequently expressed in terms of progress through school grades, Thus a Metropolitan Achievement Test Score of 2.3 would indicate that the child was equivalent to the average of those pupils three-tenths of the way through the second grade.

AGE NORMS. Similarly, average scores for various ages are called *age norms*. Many intelligence tests scored on a point or other basis are eventually expressed in terms of age norms, and I.Q.'s may be computed from these data.

SUMMARY

A test is a sample of behavior taken so that an estimate of the total behavior of the trait, characteristic, or skill under consideration may be estimated.

Tests are generally classified according to type, subject matter, or some combination of the two. Thus we have group tests and individual tests. We have intelligence tests, achievement tests, personality tests, various aptitude tests, and a number of inventories or questionnaires which laymen seldom think of as tests. Often a third classification is employed, performance tests versus paper-and-pencil tests.

A good test must be reliable and valid. It must be a consistent measure of whatever it is measuring, and it must have a demonstrated relationship between the sample behavior of the test situation and the total behavior of the individual. Validity is always "for what?" and a test may be reliable without being valid.

Test scores are meaningless without standards for comparison. Among the most widely used standards are mental age and intelligence quotient for tests of intelligence, percentile norms and sigma or standard score norms for a wide variety of tests, and grade norms for achievement tests.

17

Individual Differences

In studying the behavior of organisms it is customary to seek generalizations. Thus, we study the number of times a female rat will cross a charged electric grid to get to her young; or, we list the number of words which a nine-year-old boy can define. But organisms are perverse objects for study and definition. The particular female rat may cross 10 times in one 15-minute period, 19 times in another, 16 times in another, and so on. And a second female rat, tested under what seem like the same conditions, may give figures of 18, 15, 24, and so on. There are intra-organism variabilities and interorganism variabilities, and both must be considered in the study of individual differences.

We are inclined to forget both kinds of differences in our casual thinking about individuals and to focus attention on similarities. To be sure, all normal individuals have two arms, two legs, one nose, etc. But concentration on differences quickly leaves the impression that people are not alike; in fact, they are not even similar.

Individuals differ with respect to almost any human attribute we are to measure. They differ, of course, in physical dimensions. They differ in strength and patterning of their needs. They differ in the keenness with which their senses function and the way in which their intellectual and physical functions are integrated.

DISTRIBUTION OF INDIVIDUAL DIFFERENCES

Virtually all measures of individuals, whether they be physical, mental, emotional, or some other, show the characteristic involved to be distributed according to the normal probability curve.

The normal curve is bell-shaped and bilaterally symmetrical

on each side of its *central tendency,* the *mean.* Just as many persons are above the average as are below it. Starting with the lowest score there is a gradually increasing number of persons making each next higher score until the average score is reached. Then the number of persons making each next higher score gradually decreases until the highest score is reached.

Individual differences are ranged along *continua* of the measurement scale, not classified into categories of description such

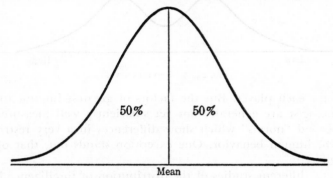

Mean
FIG. 22. Normal probability curve.

as are used in everyday life. If customary classifications of hot-cold, tall-short, light-dark, introvert-extrovert, rich-poor, strong-weak, etc. actually applied, the distribution of scores would be bimodal. See Fig. 23, p. 238.

Even where persons are not dichotomized, they are likely to be distributed in groups by the man in the street rather than ranged along a continuum. His data would be charted on a multimodal curve.

Intraindividual Differences. One measurement of one individual is merely an estimate of his status or his performance. Thus, if we score an individual on dart-throwing proficiency, any one trial is an estimate, and numerous trials are necessary to establish his true proficiency. If we make a distribution of these numerous trials, we find that the scores distribute themselves about his mean, or average, performance in a normal probability curve. Through application of appropriate statistical methods (see Chapter 9) the frequency with which he will attain any given score can be determined. With similar data on another individual, the frequency with which one would surpass the other in competition could be determined, and interindividual differences could be tested.

Interindividual Differences; Distribution of Intelligence. Differences among individuals have been widely studied by a variety of disciplines and for a variety of reasons. Thus, clothing manufacturers may keep elaborate records on size of neck, length of arm, etc. Baseball men may keep voluminous indices of perform-

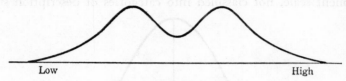

Low   High

FIG. 23. A bimodal curve.

ance for each player. But the factors of greatest interest to the psychologist are generally not yet sufficiently well measured to go beyond "norms" which show differences in a very restricted area of human behavior. One exception stands out, that of *intelligence.*

Many different studies of the distribution of intelligence have been made. The results are remarkably similar, and differences noted can usually be explained by checking the inclusiveness of the sample. Most results are expressed in terms of I.Q.'s, and a considerable body of interpretive literature has grown up to define the behavior indicated by each I.Q. level. Results are generally as follows:

I.Q. RANGE	PER CENT OF TOTAL
Below 70	1
70–79	5
80–89	15
90–109	58
110–119	15
120–129	5
130 and over	1

INTERPRETATION OF INTELLIGENCE–TEST DIFFERENCES

Interpretation of the different I.Q. levels should be restricted to mean or typical behavior. Obviously, a variety of adjustive and social factors are operating, and motivational or environmental differences materially affect any predictions.

Feeble-mindedness. According to I.Q. level, those individuals below 70 are potentially feeble-minded (aments). Whether they require institutional or other specialized care depends in large part upon the general social situation in which they find themselves. For example, a man with an I.Q. of 65 might find it possible to maintain adequate economic and social adjustment as a sheepherder in Wyoming but find it impossible to exist as an independent human being in the complex industrial environment of a large city.

The intelligence of feeble-minded individuals is frequently overrated by normal persons. Many simple activities are performed just about as well by aments as by normal people, and the limited number of such activities is often overlooked. Motor skills and memory activities are particularly likely to bring about such an overestimation.

Within the feeble-minded group, three distinct classifications are made.

IDIOTS. Idiots are the lowest in intelligence, having I.Q.'s below 20 and, as adults, mental ages of less than 3 years. The idiot is incapable of learning to any noticeable degree. He requires close supervision and care in such simple habits as eating, dressing, and cleaning himself. His behavior is on a very primitive level, and he seldom acquires coherent speech.

IMBECILES. Imbeciles are higher in the scale of intelligence than idiots. They have I.Q.'s between 20 and 50 and adult mental ages of 3 to 8 years. The imbecile cannot learn to read, spell, or do arithmetic. He seldom acquires much of a speaking vocabulary. With very careful instruction he may learn simple motor tasks.

MORONS. Morons are the highest of the feeble-minded. They have I.Q.'s of 50 to 70 and, as adults, mental ages of 8 to 11½ years. The high-grade moron can usually complete the first three or four grades of elementary school but fails frequently and is considered stupid by his teachers and fellow students.

Borderline. According to I.Q. level, those individuals between 70 and 79, as the term implies, are of such inferior intelligence that their adjustment is borderline. Their educational capacity is about the seventh grade level, attained by much special instruction and with numerous failures. They are quite capable of following routine if sufficient patience is exerted to establish it, and many borderline individuals are found in the routine activities of modern industry. There is some evidence that for the work situation itself they may be better fitted and better adjusted than individuals of higher intelligence.

Backward, Retarded, or Low Average. All these terms have been used to define the group with I.Q.'s between 80 and 89. This group can learn all the basic skills—reading, writing, and motor activities—but frequently with some difficulty. In the school situation more difficulty is encountered in developing motivation. The great increase in compulsory schooling in this country has created problems in curriculum development to fit this group. The typical college preparatory course is of little interest or pertinence.

Normal or Average. The vast bulk of the population, 50 per cent or more, falls into this category, with I.Q.'s of 90 to 109. Individuals in this group have the capacity for relatively easy accomplishment of all the skills demanded in everyday life. They form the backbone of the skilled labor, clerical, and general storekeeper population of the country. Most of them finish high school, and a substantial percentage start college. College work is usually difficult, particularly if there are any deficiencies in background preparation or motivation. On the other hand, many are highly successful, and some men and women of this group are found in the professions.

Accelerated or High Average. The group with I.Q.'s of 110 to 119 is not nearly so well defined as its counterpart on the opposite side of the average group. As we pointed out in the discussion of testing, much of the development and interpretation of test results has been in connection with school work. Much more attention has been given to special schools, special techniques, and special curricula for the below-average group than has been given to the above-average group. For the above-average group it has been a "survival of the fittest" if the members wished higher education. In general, the I.Q. group 110–119 includes large numbers of college graduates, many of whom have careers in business and technical work.

Bright or Superior. The group with I.Q.'s of 120 to 139 includes the largest number of those with the capacity for reasonably easy accomplishment of the schooling necessary for professional and scientific work. The intelligence of this group is usually underrated by normal people because the superior group is seldom challenged to do what they are really capable of doing.

Very Superior, Genius, or Near-Genius. Those with I.Q.'s of 140 or over were classified as "Geniuses" in the early days of intelligence-testing. Much confusion existed between capacity and performance. In the average school situation the educational quotient (E.Q.), derived by dividing the mental age (M.A.) into the educational age (E.A.) computed from performance on school achievement tests, almost invariably shows these individuals to be the lowest in the class in living up to capacity. The explanation is simple. Few schools have procedures or materials which fit these individuals' education. Thus, excellence in learning, if it occurs at all, is likely to appear in areas where the individual can strike out on his own without support of teachers or school.

An interesting exercise in intelligence-testing was performed by Terman and Cox (1925). They took biographical data from the histories of 282 famous people of history and fitted them into modern-day intelligence scales. The following list is a sample of their results.

NAME	I.Q.
Galton	200
Goethe	180
Voltaire	170
Longfellow	150
Jefferson	145
Franklin	145

Terman (beginning in 1925 and continuing publications through 1947) made a longitudinal study of gifted children, all of whom had I.Q.'s of 140 or above. Among his very first findings was disproof of popular opinion that the gifted child was queer, weak, sickly, etc. Actually, the superior children were taller, heavier, in better health, and better adjusted socially than were their normal counterparts in the same city. Among his later findings were data which showed that his gifted group made highly successful educational, personal, and vocational records when compared with the general population.

GROUP DIFFERENCES IN INTELLIGENCE

Society is formed of many social groups, and the question of group differences in intelligence has received considerable attention from psychologists. Overlapping of groups is common, and often the ranges of different social groups are equal where the average scores for the groups differ. Although groups differ, there are greater differences among the individuals in each group than exist between groups. Thus, groups themselves can hardly serve to categorize any particular member of the group.

Sex Differences. No appreciable sex differences in intelligence exist. Girls get higher intelligence-test scores than boys until the age of about 13. The curve of intellectual development parallels closely the curve of physical development, which shows girls to be more mature than boys until the teens. Some differences in type of materials do appear to exist. Males generally excel, as a group, in skill with numbers and spatial relationships. Females excel in memory and verbal materials.

Observations which show more noted personages and more commitments to feeble-minded institutions among males have little validity. Consider the relative opportunities for women to excel as scientists, musicians, military strategists, political figures, etc., even in today's relatively emancipated times. Or, consider the pre-eminent role of the male as the breadwinner and the relative ease with which the less intelligent female can find a supporter in our society.

Race and Nationality Differences. One of the most highly controversial subjects in the history of intelligence-testing is that of the existence or lack of existence of race or nationality differences. The basic argument is whether or not differences found through use of tests are sufficiently great to be significant when allowances are made for the admitted deficiencies of the studies reported. These deficiencies are three in number: (1) tests developed for use with individuals of one race or cultural group are not always equally applicable to measurement of other groups; (2) some racial groups are at a disadvantage because of language deficiencies (or, as we mentioned earlier, for a variety of other reasons associated with valid test results) ; and (3) the subjects tested may not be representative samples of the group being considered.

In studies of race or nationality differences, the findings are generally more easily accounted for in terms of environmental influence than in terms of inborn characteristics. Perhaps the best generalization is that people are much the same all over the world.

Occupational Differences. Surveys of the intelligence of persons engaged in the various occupations have invariably shown that the professional groups score high, the skilled trades and technical and clerical occupations score in the middle, and the unskilled trades, tradesmen, and laborers score low. The Army Alpha Test of World War I and the Army General Classification Test of World War II both revealed tremendous differences in median or average score for the various occupations and also a wide range of test scores among the members of any given occupation.

Socioeconomic Status and Intelligence. The average intelligence of children from homes of superior social and economic status is higher than that of children from average homes. Children from distinctly inferior homes are about the same amount lower in intelligence than those from average homes. Again, the problem of the effect of intelligence on provision of a particular socioeconomic status versus the effect of existence of a particular socioeconomic status on contact with those things which make up intelligence tests must be considered.

Geographical Location and Intelligence. Reports indicate slight differences in intelligence level of children in various sections of the country. There also is reported a slight superiority of urban over rural children. However, even the most careful standardization and selection of test items cannot eliminate all discrepancies in applicability of materials.

Delinquents and Criminals. A popular notion, supported by earlier investigations, is that a large proportion of delinquents and criminals are mentally deficient. Such studies were usually made on the inmates of institutions and suffer greatly from two defects: (1) it seems likely that a greater percentage of the less intelligent offenders are apprehended, and (2) of those apprehended, only a portion are incarcerated and thus afford an experimental group which is definitely a biased sample. And, again, even though test results were to reflect differences in fully adequate samples, the interrelationships of socioeconomic status, race, etc., all affect the results.

OTHER INDIVIDUAL DIFFERENCES IN PSYCHOLOGY

The application of all the measuring instruments discussed in previous chapters verifies the fact that significant differences in individuals appear in almost every trait, characteristic, or behavior pattern. Attempts have been made to define groups or types in many of these. Basic findings are always the same. First, whatever is being measured exists in some kind of continuum, not in some series of discrete classifications. Second, where group differences have been found in averages, the distributions about those averages overlap considerably. One example will suffice to illustrate the point thoroughly.

Terman and Miles (1936) constructed an index in which each item showed a significant difference in response by men and by women. When a total index score was computed from the entire list of items, the average was significantly different for men and women. But, the most masculine women (in terms of the index) scored well above the average for men, and conversely.

SUMMARY

Though it is customary to seek generalizations in the study of behavior of organisms, all organisms are characterized by variability. This variability is of two types—intraorganism variability and interorganism variability.

The normal probability or Gaussian curve results from tabulation of most measures of individuals, whether these measures be of physical, mental, emotional, or other characteristics.

Measurements are generally distributed along a continuum from a very small amount of the characteristic in question to a very large amount of the characteristic. This is contrary to popular thinking in which the extremes are likely to be used as the descriptive terms, e.g., tall-short, strong-weak, rich-poor, introvert-extrovert, etc. If popular thinking were correct measurements would result in a bimodal distribution. Where popular opinion makes a concession to the unsatisfactoriness of its concept, the concession is usually a very small one involving the admission of an average or middle group.

Individual differences in intelligence, measured in terms of I.Q., show a range from feeble-minded to very superior. Group differences in intelligence have been studied in terms of sex, race and nationality, occupation, socioeconomic status, and geographical location. Interpretation of the results must be qualified by recognition of wide variability among individuals within the group, and of overlapping among groups.

Concluding Formulation:
Principles of Behavior

In the introductory chapter the science of psychology was defined as the facts of relationships between living organisms and their environment. Science itself was defined as a unit of systematized facts or knowledge. In the sixteen chapters intervening between the introduction and this conclusion a vast number of facts have been presented. Some of these were presented as straight empirical results, relatively discrete findings which were not integrated into theoretical formulations. Others were presented as evidence for or against a theory which attempted to organize the knowledge of a particular aspect of behavior. All are important. A theory may be of incalculable value in giving direction to research, but in the long run it must be supported by a factual structure. Or, to be somewhat of a purist since the theory cannot actually be proved, a theory must not be contradicted by fact. An isolated empirical fact, independent of theory, may sometimes have considerable value in prediction and control of behavior, particularly if it has rather wide application, but in the long run its value will be strictly limited unless generalizations can be made and theory can be established.

The reader may have been somewhat disturbed at the apparent lack of acceptance of theories discussed throughout the text, or by the listing of as many as seven different theories to explain what are essentially the same phenomena. The strongest endorsement in the text is probably that accorded the duplicity theory of visual sensitivity (von Kries, 1894). Yet, modern psychologists and physiologists are not completely satisfied with this theory, and new research experiments are even now being designed to test it. Modern physical and chemical science continually open the way to new techniques and new measurements which permit more thorough tests of the postulates by which psychological theory must be bound. What then has the science of psychology to offer as evidence that it helps explain the relationships between living organisms and their environment?

Psychology has fully demonstrated the existence of the Stimulation-Integration-Reaction (S–I–R) paradigm. And in the demonstration the knowledge of the three elements of the paradigm has been remarkably extended. The changes in the environment of the individual, both explicit and implicit, which serve as stimuli are more and more carefully defined. The specialized sensitivities through which the stimuli are received are better and better charted in terms of physiological make-up and neural functioning. The structure of the integrating mechanism has been more completely set down, and great strides have been made toward an understanding of at least the mechanical and chemical nature of the neural impulses themselves. Better differentiation of the reactions, taken together with better knowledge of and ability to control stimulation, has resulted in improved bases from which to infer the integrative functioning. Thus the experimental psychologists have been delving deeper and deeper into molecular aspects of behavior and have given us insight into why certain behavior must develop as it does.

In the meantime, certain practitioners of psychology have developed a large catalogue of behavioral instances from which they can show expectation of certain reactions if certain stimuli are administered under particular conditions. Many of those who helped compile this catalogue were not even interested in why the events came to pass as they did. Nevertheless, they contributed a statistical approach to behavior which permitted some prediction and control of behavior. Many examples of this —prediction of success in college from intelligence-testing, prediction of emotional and personal adjustment from knowledge of family background, prediction of reaction under different motivational conditions, etc.—have been cited in the text.

The point of view of this book is eclectic, not an eclecticism growing out of an unwillingness or inability to adopt a theoretical position and maintain it, but rather an eclecticism growing out of the belief that all schools of psychology have a positive contribution to make to the understanding and prediction of the behavior of organisms.

In restating this point of view, we shall cite briefly the kind of contribution certain types of psychological investigation can make to developing the science of psychology.

All organisms exist in a state of dynamic equilibrium. Each organism seeks to maintain that status which gives maximum satisfaction to its needs and presents the least threat of future deprivation or lessening of such satisfactions. Certain needs are physiological in nature, and all probably have a physiological basis. However, with the exception of certain primary drive states, needs are primarily social, and threats come from the activities of the society in which the organism operates. Whether man is viewed as an automaton in whom all activity is derived from a series of conditioned responses, or viewed as a creature with a complex series of instincts and habit patterns which develop and mature at the appropriate time, makes little difference except as it leads researchers to devise experiments to prove particular points. It is the same behavior which is being investigated and with the same end result. All the learning theorists must account somewhere for the fact that motivational factors influence the end result. All those who would attempt to explain personality must recognize the importance of childhood experience in the manifest personality of the adult.

Let us consider a very homely example of expressed behavior for demonstration. A psychologist sat in a cafeteria group where one member of the party had selected buttermilk as his luncheon drink. Another member of the party said that he could not drink buttermilk except when he was ill and at that time he enjoyed it. He then jokingly asked the psychologist how he would explain such a phenomenon. The psychologist asked if the man could recall an illness from which he had derived pleasure or avoided something distasteful and during which he had had a diet of buttermilk. The response was instantaneously in the affirmative, that he had been ill with scarlet fever as a child and had consumed large quantities of buttermilk during an extended period of convalescence in which he had missed school and had been showered with attention and gifts. Of course, that is only a part of the final story which might have emerged and certainly does not answer the question of why buttermilk was avoided when the subject was not ill. But it will serve as a point of departure. What might different psychologists do with that bit of behavior? What are some of the factors involved?

Among the points which the physiological psychologists might study would be possible differences in selectivity of the taste buds during conditions of illness and health, emotional or disturbed reactions when confronted with the buttermilk stimulus as measured by electrical changes in skin resistance, chemical composition of the blood, etc., amount of deprivation of water which would be needed before the individual would take the buttermilk in order to get the water contained therein, and a variety of other studies. The psychologist interested in learning might want to find out how many presentations of buttermilk in a situation which would normally evoke the dislike reaction, together with presentation of some other stimulus which had been shown to evoke a pleased or like reaction, would be necessary to change the original dislike to like; or the learning psychologist might want to know the extent of transfer or spread of this dislike reaction: Does it include highly similar foods such as cottage cheese? The analytic psychologist would see this as an excellent opportunity to find out much more about the influence of childhood experiences on this man's adult behavior and personality. The social psychologist could use the knowledge of this dislike for buttermilk as the basis of experimentation in group conformity: What happens to the behavior of this individual if his peers all drink buttermilk and put pressure on him to do likewise?

And so throughout all the subinterests which make up the field of psychology we would find the applicability of one bit of behavior to study and conclusions regarding the source, effect, modifiability, and involvement of this one bit of behavior. Naturally, trained psychologists select the behavior they wish to study more carefully, and some situations are better controllable or give more easily measured results than others. But any aspect of behavior is fertile ground for the tools of the psychologist.

Selected References

CHAPTER 1: The Study of General Psychology

Boring, *A History of Experimental Psychology* (1950), 1–777.

Boring, *Sensation and Perception in the History of Psychology* (1942), 1–96.

Brill (Ed.), *The Basic Writings of Sigmund Freud* (1938), 933–977.

Dennis, *Current Trends in Psychology* (1947), 1–225.

Dennis, *Readings in General Psychology* (1949), 1–525.

Dennis, *Readings in the History of Psychology* (1948), 1–587.

Dewey, *How We Think* (1933), 1–301.

Garrett, *Great Experiments in Psychology* (1951), 1–337.

Guilford (Ed.), *Fields of Psychology* (1950), 1–779.

Heidbreder, *Seven Psychologies* (1933), 1–450.

James, *Psychology: Briefer Course* (1892), 1–478.

Köhler, *Gestalt Psychology* (1947), 1–369.

McDougall, *Outlines of Psychology* (1923), 1–456.

Seashore (Ed.), *Fields of Psychology* (1942), 1–643.

Titchener, *A Textbook of Psychology* (1910), 1–565.

Watson, *Psychology from the Standpoint of a Behaviorist* (1929), 1–458.

Woodworth, *Contemporary Schools of Psychology* (1948), 1–279.

CHAPTER 2: Stimulation, Integration, and Reaction

Boring, *Sensation and Perception in the History of Psychology* (1942), 1–96.

Freeman, *The Energetics of Human Behavior* (1948), 34–64.

Hull, *Principles of Behavior* (1943), 16–56.

Stevens (Ed.), *Handbook of Experimental Psychology* (1951), 121–235.

Stone (Ed.), *Comparative Psychology* (1951), 30–61; 239–281.

CHAPTER 3: Nervous Integration

Freeman, *Physiological Psychology* (1948), 8–238.

Guilford (Ed.), *Fields of Psychology* (1950), 670–694.

Lashley, *Brain Mechanisms and Intelligence* (1929), 1–186.

Lickley, *The Nervous System* (1931), 1–35.

Pintner *et al.*, *Psychology of the Physically Handicapped* (1941), 37–71.

Stevens (Ed.), *Handbook of Experimental Psychology* (1951), 50–153; 811–1236.

Stone (Ed.), *Comparative Psychology* (1951), 292–315.

CHAPTER 4: Development of Reaction

Britt, *Social Psychology of Modern Life* (1949), 83–111.
Crafts *et al.*, *Recent Experiments in Psychology* (1950), 14–39.
Dennis, *Readings in General Psychology* (1949), 249–267.
Hilgard and Marquis, *Conditioning and Learning* (1940), 26–74.
Hull, *Principles of Behavior* (1943), 50–101.
McDougall, *Outlines of Psychology* (1923), 43–120.
Shaffer, *The Psychology of Adjustment* (1936), 22–82.
Stevens (Ed.), *Handbook of Experimental Psychology* (1951), 154–208.
Stone (Ed.), *Comparative Psychology* (1951), 330–361.
Watson, *Psychology from the Standpoint of a Behaviorist* (1929), 186–223; 262–299.

CHAPTER 5: Sensation and Perception

Boring, *The Physical Dimensions of Consciousness* (1933), 1–251.
Boring, *Sensation and Perception in the History of Psychology* (1942), 3–96.
Lickley, *The Nervous System* (1931), 100–137.
Postman and Egan, *Experimental Psychology* (1949), 9–31.
Titchener, *Textbook of Psychology* (1910), 46–193.
Woodworth, *Experimental Psychology* (1938), 392–449; 684–712.

CHAPTER 6: Vision and Visual Phenomena

Bartley, *Vision: A Study of Its Basis* (1941), 1–350.
Boring, *Sensation and Perception in the History of Psychology* (1942), 97–311; 588–602.
Chapanis *et al.*, *Applied Experimental Psychology* (1949), 67–117.
Evans, *An Introduction to Color* (1948), 1–340.
Postman and Egan, *Experimental Psychology* (1949), 105–216.
Stevens (Ed.), *Handbook of Experimental Psychology* (1951), 811–984.
Woodworth, *Experimental Psychology* (1938), 539–683.

CHAPTER 7: Audition and Auditory Phenomena

Boring, *Sensation and Perception in the History of Psychology* (1942), 312–436.
Chapanis *et al.*, *Applied Experimental Psychology* (1949), 189–263.
Postman and Egan, *Experimental Psychology* (1949), 51–84.
Stevens (Ed.), *Handbook of Experimental Psychology* (1951), 985–1142.
Wever, *Theory of Hearing* (1949), 1–484.
Woodworth, *Experimental Psychology* (1938), 501–538.

CHAPTER 8: Our Other Senses

Boring, *Sensation and Perception in the History of Psychology* (1942),
437–573.

Moncrieff, *The Chemical Senses* (1946), 1–424.

Postman and Egan, *Experimental Psychology* (1949), 33–50; 85–104.

Stevens (Ed.), *Handbook of Experimental Psychology* (1951), 1143–
1236.

Woodworth, *Experimental Psychology* (1938), 450–500.

CHAPTER 9: Collection, Analysis, and Interpretation of Data

Andrews, *Methods of Psychology* (1948), 1–716.

Garrett, *Statistics in Psychology and Education* (1947), 1–465.

Greene, *Measurements of Human Behavior* (1952), 1–790.

Kelly (Ed.), *New Methods in Applied Psychology* (1947), 17–42.

Lundberg, *Social Research* (1942), 1–44; 113–133.

Peatman, *Descriptive and Sampling Statistics* (1947), 1–577.

Snygg and Combs, *Individual Behavior* (1949), 245–279.

Thorndike, *Personnel Selection* (1949), 32–184.

Traxler, *Techniques of Guidance* (1945), 20–67.

Watson, *Readings in the Clinical Method in Psychology* (1949), 1–740.

CHAPTER 10: Birth, Growth, and Maturation

Baldwin, *Physical Growth of Children from Birth to Maturity* (1921),
1–411.

Beach, *Hormones and Behavior* (1948), 1–368.

Carmichael (Ed.), *Manual of Child Psychology* (1946), 43–369.

Cole and Morgan, *Psychology of Childhood and Adolescence* (1947),
1–416.

Gesell *et al., The Child from Five to Ten* (1946), 1–475.

Gesell *et al., The First Five Years of Life* (1940), 1–393.

Guilford (Ed.), *Fields of Psychology* (1950), 68–169.

Snyder, *The Principles of Heredity* (1946), 1–450.

Stevens (Ed.), *Handbook of Experimental Psychology* (1951), 236–386.

CHAPTER 11: Learning

Cantor, *Dynamics of Learning* (1946), 1–282.

Carmichael (Ed.), *Manual of Child Psychology* (1946), 370–449; 791–
844.

Crafts *et al., Recent Experiments in Psychology* (1950), 264–334.

Dunlap, *Habits: Their Making and Unmaking* (1949), 1–394.

Freeman, *The Energetics of Human Behavior* (1948), 173–201.

Guthrie and Horton, *Cats in a Puzzle Box* (1946), 1–67.
Hilgard, *Theories of Learning* (1948), 1–409.
Hilgard and Marquis, *Conditioning and Learning* (1940), 1–429.
Hull, *Principles of Behavior* (1943), 1–422.
Koffka, *Principles of Gestalt Psychology* (1935), 1–720.
Köhler, *Gestalt Psychology* (1947), 1–369.
Lewin, *Principles of Topological Psychology* (1936), 1–231.
McGeoch and Irion, *Psychology of Human Learning* (1952), 1–596.
Skinner, *The Behavior of Organisms* (1938), 1–457.
Thorndike, *The Fundamentals of Learning* (1932), 1–638.
Tolman, *Purposive Behavior in Animals and Men* (1932), 1–463.
Wheeler, *The Science of Psychology* (1940), 208–275.

CHAPTER 12: Thinking and Problem-Solving

Carmichael (Ed.), *Manual of Child Psychology* (1946), 423–441.
Carr, *Psychology* (1925), 189–215.
Crafts *et al.*, *Recent Experiments in Psychology* (1950), 404–439.
Dewey, *How We Think* (1933), 1–301.
Hilgard and Marquis, *Conditioning and Learning* (1940), 228–254.
James, *Psychology: Briefer Course* (1892), 151–175.
Maier and Schneirla, *Principles of Animal Psychology* (1935), 444–479.
Titchener, *Textbook of Psychology* (1910), 428–470; 505–549.
Watson, *Psychology from the Standpoint of a Behaviorist* (1929), 341–377.
Wertheimer, *Productive Thinking* (1945), 1–224.

CHAPTER 13: Motivation

Freeman, *The Energetics of Human Behavior* (1948), 129–172.
Fryer and Henry (Eds.), *Handbook of Applied Psychology* (1950), 03–99.
Hull, *Principles of Behavior* (1943), 226–257.
McGeoch and Irion, *The Psychology of Human Learning* (1952), 194–238.
Roethlisberger and Dickson, *Management and the Worker* (1942), 1–615.
Ryan, *Work and Effort* (1947), 1–323.
Snygg and Combs, *Individual Behavior* (1949), 52–77.
Stevens (Ed.), *Handbook of Experimental Psychology* (1951), 435–472.
Stone (Ed.), *Comparative Psychology* (1951), 65–94.
Symonds, *Dynamic Psychology* (1949), 11–41.
Viteles, *Motivation and Morale in Modern Industry* (1953), 3–510.
Young, *Motivation of Behavior* (1936), 1–317; 388–432.

CHAPTER 14: Emotion

Cannon, *Bodily Changes in Pain, Hunger, Fear, and Rage* (1929), 1–404.

Carmichael (Ed.), *Manual of Child Psychology* (1946), 732–790.

Dollard *et al., Frustration and Aggression* (1939), 1–201.

Freeman, *The Energetics of Human Behavior* (1948), 202–235.

Ruckmick, *The Psychology of Feeling and Emotion* (1947), 1–529.

Snygg and Combs, *Individual Behavior* (1949), 105–175.

Stevens (Ed.), *Handbook of Experimental Psychology* (1951), 473–516.

Young, *Emotion in Man and Animal* (1943), 1–422.

CHAPTER 15: Personality and Personal Adjustment

Brill (Ed.), *The Basic Writings of Sigmund Freud* (1938), 1–1001.

Freeman, *The Energetics of Human Behavior* (1948), 236–274.

Guetzkow (Ed.), *Groups, Leadership, and Men* (1951), 1–293.

Horney, *The Neurotic Personality of Our Time* (1937), 13–299.

Klopfer and Kelley, *The Rorschach Technique* (1942), 319–405.

Lewin, *A Dynamic Theory of Personality* (1935), 1–286.

Maslow and Mittleman, *Principles of Abnormal Psychology* (1941), 1–638.

Murphy, *Personality* (1947), 1–999.

Murray, *Explorations in Personality* (1938), 1–761.

Rogers, *Counseling and Psychotherapy* (1942), 1–450.

Stagner, *Psychology and Personality* (1948), 1–465.

Stein, *Manual for the Thematic Apperception Test* (1948), 1–91.

Symonds, *Dynamic Psychology* (1949), 1–413.

White, *The Abnormal Personality* (1948), 1–613.

CHAPTER 16: Tests and Testing

Adkins *et al., Construction and Analysis of Achievement Tests* (1947), 1–292.

Cronbach, *Essentials of Psychological Testing* (1949), 1–475.

Dorcus and Jones, *Handbook of Employee Selection* (1950), 1–349.

Fryer and Henry (Eds.), *Handbook of Applied Psychology* (1950), 135–194; 469–509.

Greene, *Measurements of Human Behavior* (1952), 1–790.

Lawshe, *Principles of Personnel Testing* (1948), 1–227.

Stead and Shartle, *Occupational Counseling Techniques* (1940), 1–273.

Strong, *Vocational Interests of Men and Women* (1943), 1–746.

Super, *Appraising Vocational Fitness* (1949), 1–727.

Thorndike, *Personnel Selection* (1949), 1–358.

CHAPTER 17: Individual Differences

Anastasi and Foley, *Differential Psychology* (1949), 1–894.

Fryer and Henry (Eds.), *Handbook of Applied Psychology* (1950), 49–132.

Guilford (Ed.), *Fields of Psychology* (1950), 331–412.

Heath, *What People Are* (1945), 1–135.

Tyler, *The Psychology of Human Differences* (1947), 47–65; 241–255.

Wechsler, *The Measurement of Adult Intelligence* (1944), 19–48.

Examinations

The examinations which follow will indicate to the student how well he has mastered the content of general psychology. The tests are arranged according to the chapters of the text. They have been prepared upon the content of the chapters and their reference readings.

Scoring keys for these chapter tests will be found on pp. 283–288. The scoring keys facilitate self-correction. They make it possible for the student to compare right and wrong answers, to correct his misconceptions, to acquire new information, and to review facts already known to him.

The purpose of the tests is to inform the student of his level of knowledge in their several areas. Where numerous incorrect answers are made to the items of a chapter test, the student should review all content in the area of the chapter by rereading the chapter and several of its references. Where errors are made in answer to only a few items, the student might study the parts of the chapters and readings dealing with the topics on which items have been missed.

TESTING PROCEDURE

Three kinds of items are included in the tests: True-False, Multiple-Choice, and Completion items. These are illustrated as follows:

F _____ 1. William James was an exponent of the genetic method.

This is a "true-false" item. It has been marked "F" for False, in the margin. If it were true, "T" would have been placed in the margin.

c _____ 2. (a) Galen, (b) Kant, (c) Gall, (d) Hobbes, (e) Galton, related the "faculties" to definite cranial areas.

This is a "multiple-choice" item. The correct choice among the five alternatives has the letter (c) before it in the question, and "c" has been placed in the margin.

___Spinoza___	3.	The theory that the mind and the body are but different aspects of the same substance was first
___Double aspect___	4.	advocated by (1). This view is now known as the (2) theory.

This is a "completion" item. Note that the number of words required to complete the sentence is indicated by the figures in the parentheses. The correct answers have been placed in the margin opposite the numbers for the item.

The total score is the number of correct answers filled in at the left.

Test for Chapter 1

_____ 1. According to the doctrine of physical monism, mind and body are one.

_____ 2. According to (a) Plato, (b) Aristotle, (c) Hippocrates, (d) St. Augustine, (e) the Stoics, emotion or bodily feeling was a bad moral influence on mental life.

_____ 3. For Aristotle, associations were made by (1), (1), and
_____ 4. (1).
_____ 5.

_____ 6. Hippocrates expressed the view that different feelings are due to the bodily humors.

_____ 7. The earliest appearance of the notion that extreme degrees of emotion are the same as mental disease appeared with (a) Hippocrates, (b) Galen, (c) St. Augustine, (d) Kraepelin, (e) Plato.

_____ 8. The theory of psychophysical dualism maintains that only sensations and ideas are real.

_____ 9. An enlarged special area of the cranium is indicative of high development of a psychological faculty.

_____ 10. Psychophysics deals with the relationship between psychology and physics.

_____ 11. Psychology as an experimental science is about 100 years old.

_____ 12. Traditional structural psychology analyzed the introspective reports of conscious activity into elements.

_____ 13. Early studies in psychology were directed toward the determination of general laws.

_____ 14. The aim of functional psychology is to understand by introspective study the conscious dimensions of sensitivity.

_____15. ⎫
_____16. ⎬ The doctrine of mental faculties classified mind into such
_____17. ⎭ departments as (1), (1), and (1).

_____18. By universal determinism is meant: (a) In no case may we interpret an action as the outcome of a high psychical faculty if it can be interpreted as the outcome of one lower in the psychological scale. (b) Every effect has a cause. (c) Every law of nature is simply a description of a high correlation. (d) Every event is intelligible only as a direct effect of an active universal soul.

_____19. Any person whose knowledge of human nature is great may properly be called a psychologist.

_____20. A conception that cannot be isolated and shown to exist cannot be studied experimentally.

_____21. The correlation method was invented by (a) Galton, (b) Hall, (c) Cattell, (d) Wundt.

_____22. The founder of the first psychological laboratory was (a) Galton, (b) Hall, (c) Cattell, (d) Wundt.

_____23. (1) introduced the use of the introspective method.

_____24. The first intelligence test was constructed by (a) Aristotle, (b) Binet, (c) Thorndike, (d) Terman, (e) James.

_____25. Scientific psychology differs from common sense psychology chiefly in the kinds of problems it attempts to solve.

_____26. If an expectant mother decides that she would like her child to be a musician, she can influence its later development by thinking about it before the child is born.

_____27. The receding chin denotes lack of will power but is compensated for in man by the growth of the cerebrum.

_____28. Brunettes are more emotional than are blondes.

_____29. Most artistic people possess long, slender fingers.

_____ SCORE
(Number of correct answers)

Scoring Key on Page 283

Test for Chapter 2

_____ 1. Psychological stimulation is received by (1).

_____ 2. S–I–R means stimulation, impulses, and responses.

_____ 3. There are two parts of every receptor: sensitive cells and reacting cells.

_____ 4. Not all physical changes in the environment serve as stimuli for psychological activity.

_____ 5. The psychological stimulus is always a total situation.

_____ 6. The formula S–I–R means that stimulation usually, but not always, leads to some sort of integrated response.

_____ 7. The receptors involved in stomach-ache are among those called (1).

_____ 8.⎫
_____ 9.⎪ Specialized functions of protoplasm on the psychological
_____10.⎬ level are (1), (1), (1), and (1).
_____11.⎭

_____12. All psychological stimuli are energy changes in the explicit environment.

_____13.⎫ There are probably many (2) not within the range of
_____14.⎭ any of our (1).

_____15. Changes in muscular movements are sensed by means of exteroceptors.

_____16. The stimulus excites receptors, which in turn excite nerves, and these in turn arouse effectors.

_____17.⎫ An effector is a number of specialized contractile or
_____18.⎭ glandular (1) which function as a (1) in the reaction of an organism.

_____19.⎫ Muscles are of two kinds: (1) and (1).
_____20.⎭

_____21.⎫ Effectors are classified as (1) or (1) according to their
_____22.⎭ action upon the environment.

_____23. The (2) contract and expand more rapidly under stimulation than do other effectors.

_____24. The objective evidence of the activity of effectors is called (1).

_____25. The major physiological system of integration in the human body is the (2).

_____26. Chemical integration is through the (2).

_____27. Integration refers to consciousness as well as to nervous activity.

_____28. The simultaneous pattern reaction functions usually as a separate and distinct unit of behavior, as in the reflex.

_____29. What we "see, hear, and feel" depends not only on our sensory equipment but also upon our past experiences.

_____30. Psychological activity, whether thinking or acting, is in relation to a goal.

_____ SCORE
(Number of correct answers)

Scoring Key on Page 283

Test for Chapter 3

_____ 1. The structural unit of the nervous system is the (a) synapse, (b) reaction arc, (c) axon, (d) neuron.

_____ 2.⎫
_____ 3.⎪ The four principal parts of a nerve cell are (1), (1), (1),
_____ 4.⎬ and (2).
_____ 5.⎭

_____ 6. The functional juncture of two or more neurons is called a (1).

_____ 7. ⎫
_____ 8. ⎭ Nervous impulses are said to vary in (1) and (1).

_____ 9. The functional unit of the nervous system is the (2).

_____ 10. ⎫
_____ 11. ⎪
_____ 12. ⎬ The five lobes of the cerebrum are (1), (1), (1), (1), and (3).
_____ 13. ⎪
_____ 14. ⎭

_____ 15. Afferent impulses traverse fibers entering the (1) horn of the cord.

_____ 16. ⎫ The nerve fiber, the (3), and the (2) compose the neuro-
_____ 17. ⎭ muscular unit.

_____ 18. The principal path of communication from higher to lower co-ordination centers is the (a) spinal lemniscus, (b) pyramidal tracts, (c) columns of Goll and Burdach, (d) medial lemniscus.

_____ 19. The "motor area" is located in the (a) cuneas, (b) ascending parietal convolution, (c) superior temporal convolution, (d) precentral gyrus.

_____ 20. That part of the brain which acts as a relay station for all afferent tracts (except the olfactory and vestibular) and passes these sensory impulses on to the cerebrum is the (a) cerebellum, (b) precentral gyrus, (c) thalamus, (d) cuneas.

_____ 21. The largest interlobular fissure of the brain is the (a) fissure of Rolando, (b) parietal-occipital fissure, (c) fissure of Sylvius, (d) longitudinal fissure.

_____ 22. "It is the great center for the proprioceptive reactions of the body much as the cerebrum is for the exteroceptive." The reference is to the (a) pons, (b) thalamus, (c) cerebellum, (d) corpus callosum.

_____ 23. The white matter of the nervous system is due to the (a) function of conduction, (b) synapses present, (c) medullary sheaths, (d) structure of nerve cell.

_____ 24. All (1) have the possibility of contact with all effectors by means of the nervous system.

_____ 25. The frequency with which a neuron discharges is determined primarily by: (a) the refractory period of neuron excitation, (b) the intensity of the stimulus, (c) synaptic growth through learning.

_____ 26. No nerve impulse is initiated in the central axis.

_____ 27. Comparative embryological studies indicate that complexity of behavior is due to (a) lowered threshold, (b) lowered synaptic resistance, (c) increased neural connections.

_____ 28. The autonomic system (a) functions independently of the central system, (b) co-ordinates the skeletal muscles, (c) controls bodily posture and equilibrium, (d) maintains tonus of the unstriated effectors.

_____29. The pathway the nerve impulse will take through the nervous system is determined by (a) the length of the central axis from where the impulse enters, (b) the thalamus, (c) synaptic resistance, (d) the cerebellum,

_____30. The theory that neural impulse diverts into its pathway neural impulses of other pathways is (a) the drainage hypothesis, (b) the all-or-none law, (c) the wave motion theory, (d) Bell's law, (e) the membrane hypothesis.

_____31. The four language centers (speaking, writing, hearing, reading) are found in (a) the cerebellum, (b) both hemispheres of the cerebrum, (c) the spinal cord, (d) the thalamus.

_____32. The notion that a stimulus may be dammed up somewhere in the central nervous system and is released upon the appropriate occasion is erroneous.

_____33. The theory that after training neural impulses tend to follow one common pathway is the (a) wave motion theory, (b) explosion fuse theory, (c) electrical energy theory, (d) drainage theory.

_____34. The term *polarized neuron* refers to (a) a difference in electrical potential between the two ends of the neuron, (b) a neuron that will conduct in one direction only, (c) a neuron connected in some way with a nerve net, (d) a neuron of the central nervous system.

_____SCORE
(Number of correct answers)

Scoring Key on Page 283

Test for Chapter 4

_____ 1. Since the knee jerk is a simple reflex, it cannot be inhibited or reinforced in any way.

_____ 2. Swallows kept in a cage until after the customary time for flying fly immediately upon being released.

_____ 3. The pupillary reflex is aroused without consciousness by external stimulation.

_____ 4. The repertoire of vocal sounds of a normal French baby is different from that of a baby of a Chinese parent.

_____ 5. Glandular responses may be conditioned to external stimuli.

_____ 6. As a general rule, learned and inherited reactions are independent in development.

_____ 7. In evolutionary development, the effectors appeared before the receptors.

_____ 8. In general, motor activity occurs in large muscular patterns rather than as single reactions.

_____ 9. A successive reaction develops when the goal cannot be immediately achieved by a simultaneous pattern reaction.

_____10. Reaction time for warm receptors is (a) greater than, (b) the same as, (c) less than reaction time for cold receptors.

_____11. Instinctive reactions are successive reactions which have been organized largely as a result of heredity.

_____12. The complexity of the behavior is the essential difference between the instinct and the reflex.

_____13. Most reflexes are subject to modification with environmental stimulation.

_____14. Even if the bird-environment be changed, the young bird invariably has the song of its own species.

_____15. The response to a present stimulus may be partly due to the responses that have just been made to other stimuli.

_____16. Spontaneous activity is usually the result of energies present in the external environment.

_____17. Smooth-muscle effectors are relatively slower in losing tension than are striated-muscle effectors.

_____18. Conditioned reactions cannot be established through the autonomic nervous system.

_____19. Prenatal development of reactions is wholly in maturation.

_____20. An action potential can be generated in a resting muscle.

_____21. Feeble-minded children are not conditioned as readily as youngsters with normal mental endowment.

_____22. Foreign peoples speak their own languages without training.

_____23. High efficiency of reactions is not achieved without exercise under environmental stimulation.

_____24. Smooth muscles show tonic but not phasic contractions.

_____25. The knee jerk is (a) a cortical reaction, (b) an automatic reaction, (c) a spinal reflex, (d) an intended reaction.

_____SCORE
(Number of correct answers)

Scoring Key on Page 284

Test for Chapter 5

_____ 1. All environmental stimuli are equivocal in degree in causing sensitivities or affectivities.

_____ 2. } In the human being, the accessory apparatus of receptors for (1) and (1) is more extensive than for any other
_____ 3. } sense.

———— 4. ⎫
———— 5. ⎬ Quantitative dimensions existing for all sensitivities are
———— 6. ⎭ (1), (1), and (1).

———— 7. Protensity describes the spatial characteristics of the sensitivity.

———— 8. The integration of sensitivities into meaningful wholes is not possible without past experience.

———— 9. Motion and change of position are perceived through all departments of sensitivity.

————10. Stratton's famous experiment with inverted lenses shows, for the sensitivity of vision, the effect of (a) relative size, (b) distinctness, (c) brightness, (d) superposition, (e) past experience.

————11. "Local sign" is a motor perception.

————12. The less intense a sound or odor, the greater the distance at which the stimulus is localized.

————13. FIGURE is to GROUND as PERIPHERY is to FOCUS.

————14. Concrete imagery develops with age and by most adults is used more than verbal imagery.

————15. Many of our preferences, as for colors, tones, and odors, are inherent in the organism; they are innate or inherited characteristics of the race.

————16. The range of affective experiences is just as great for the ditch-digger as for the millionaire.

————17. Illusions are errors of perception.

————18. The tendency of sensitivity under stimulation to return to equilibrium is called (1).

————19. The minimum stimulus capable of causing sensitivity is called the (a) absolute threshold, (b) differential threshold, (c) physiological limit, (d) j.n.d., (e) subliminal limen.

————20. In all sensitivities, "fatigue" equals "adaptation."

————21. Synesthetic sensitivities are awarenesses in a sensitivity department other than the one being stimulated.

————22. Wide differences in training exist where wide group differences in affective values of colors are found.

————23. Attending to pleasantness eliminates the pleasantness.

————24. Movement and change of stimuli are effective determiners of the direction of attention.

————25. Weber's Law is a general statement of the relationship between intensity and protensity of sensitivity.

————26. The most acceptable theory of sensitivity intensity is the volley theory.

————27. The Heuristic Hypothesis states that affectivities are functions of sense-organ activities which are described as bright and dull pressures when the subject introspects on the sensitivities.

————28. In determining the recall value of events and ideas, the

following influence appears to be the least important:
(a) incentive effect, (b) affective value, (c) overlearning,
(d) completion of task.

_____SCORE
(Number of correct answers)

Scoring Key on Page 284

Test for Chapter 6

_____ 1. The point at which the optic nerve enters the retina is called the (2).

_____ 2. Cutting one lateral branch of the optic nerve on the side of the optic chiasm nearest the brain affects the sensitivity of only one retina.

_____ 3. The law of the visual angle operates exactly in brightness sensitivity.

_____ 4. The shortest wave lengths of the spectrum stimulate vision of (a) gray, (b) red, (c) purple, (d) black, (e) violet.

_____ 5. The range of visual adaptation in the rods is about (1) times as great as in the cones.

_____ 6.⎫
_____ 7.⎬ Three qualitative dimensions of visual sensitivities are
_____ 8.⎭ (1), (1), and (1).

_____ 9. Of the most saturated hues, the one of least relative saturation is (a) red, (b) yellow, (c) blue, (d) green, (e) gray.

_____10. The negative afterimage can be used to determine the complementary of a given hue.

_____11. Visual intensity appears to be synonymous with (1) of achromatic sensitivity.

_____12. Moving stimuli are observed most readily at the periphery of the retina.

_____13. Stationary "visual movement" is dependent upon successive stimuli the rate for which is about 24 per second.

_____14. A visual afterimage is twice the size of the sensitivity when projected on a screen twice the distance from the point of stimulation.

_____15. The shift in the relative brightness of colors with changes in the illumination is called (a) Purkinje, (b) Müller-Lyer, (c) Hering, (d) Helmholtz, phenomenon.

_____16. "Aerial perspective" means that near objects are (a) larger, (b) superimposed, (c) closer, (d) clearer.

_____17. The Poggendorf illusion relates to the incorrect perception of (a) figure and ground, (b) aerial perspective, (c) areas, (d) small angles.

_____18. The mixture of any two colors which are not complementary produces a color sensitivity of intermediate hue.

_____19. If one fixates a traffic light for a long time, the color of the light gains in saturation.

_____20. Colored hearing is a form of synesthesia.

_____21. Placing a red area next to a green area of the same brightness makes it (a) brighter, (b) darker, (c) more saturated, (d) less saturated, (e) bluish.

_____22. Double images have a confusing effect on distance perception.

_____23. Visual hues at the ends of the spectrum are usually more pleasant than those in the middle.

_____24. An eidetic image is produced by mixing complementary colors.

_____25. In estimating space, a one-eyed person cannot make use of (a) accommodation, (b) parallax, (c) perspective, (d) convergence, (e) shadows.

_____26. According to the Young-Helmholtz theory of color vision, there are only three elemental colors.

_____27. The duplicity theory states that the only function of the rods is in achromatic vision.

_____SCORE
(Number of correct answers)

Scoring Key on Page 284

Test for Chapter 7

_____ 1. The nonperiodic sound waves stimulate sensitivities of noise.

_____ 2. The lowest audible tone has a stimulus frequency of about (1) d.v. per second.

_____ 3. Before air waves can affect the auditory nerve fibers, they must give rise to vibrations of liquids.

_____ 4.⎫
_____ 5.⎬ Three qualitative dimensions of auditory sensitivities are
_____ 6.⎭ (1), (1) , and (1) .

_____ 7. If one end of the auditory nerve of a cat is connected to a radio loudspeaker, it will be found to reproduce words spoken into the cat's ear.

_____ 8. With overtones eliminated, all musical instruments would sound alike.

_____ 9. Irregular or very brief vibrations are heard as noise.

_____10. Dischords have as high a pleasantness-unpleasantness value as chords among (a) kindergarten children, (b) college students, (c) average adults, (d) those untrained in music.

_____11. The difference between two adjacent notes on the piano is the smallest difference that can be discriminated by most human beings.

_____12. A third tone, of definite pitch, called a (2) can often be heard when two tones are sounded together.

_____13. A dog can distinguish between a metronome beating 1000 strokes per minute and one beating at the rate of 94 strokes.

_____14. The number of beats per second is the sum of the frequencies of two fundamentals.

_____15. Practice is unlikely to increase one's accuracy in discriminating pitches.

_____16. Familiarity is likely to increase the pleasantness-unpleasantness value of any musical composition.

_____17. Intensity, pitch, or temporal accentuations are necessary for the perception of rhythm.

_____18. The differences in people's voices are due to differences in (1).

_____19. The decibel is about equal to the (2) of intensity discrimination in audition.

_____20. Sounds are localized most accurately when they are (a) in front of the head, (b) at either side of the head, (c) behind the head, (d) in the median plane.

_____21. Timbre depends upon (a) amplitude of sound wave, (b) wave length of the fundamental tone, (c) pitch and intensity of the fundamental tone, (d) complexity of the wave form and the presence of overtones.

_____22. (a) Intensity, (b) time, (c) phase differences of vibrations, is (are) most important in auditory space sensitivity of high tones.

_____23. The auditory intensity threshold is almost exactly constant for different frequencies within the range of 32 to 10,000 cycles.

_____24. Beats are related to changes in the amplitude of sound waves.

_____25. Tonal islands are points in the scale of auditory pitch where discrimination is difficult.

_____26. Fourier's Theorem states that a clang can be analyzed into fundamental tones and overtones.

_____27. According to Helmholtz's theory of audition, we are able to distinguish one pitch from another because certain fibers of the basilar membrane respond to one pitch and others respond to other pitches.

_____SCORE
(**Number** of correct answers)

Scoring Key on Page 285

Test for Chapter 8

_____ 1.

_____ 2. The four elementary taste sensitivities are (1), (1), (1),

_____ 3. and (1).

_____ 4.

_____ 5. Taste receptors are activated only by dissolved substances.

_____ 6. A subliminal salt stimulus applied to one side of the tongue is not sensed, but if a sugar stimulus is applied to the other side the salt will then be tasted. This is an example of adaptation.

_____ 7. In everyday life, it is relatively easy to stimulate the taste receptors without stimulating other senses as well.

_____ 8. Odors and tastes may be internally stimulated.

_____ 9. For cane sugar the threshold at the tip of the tongue is lower than it is at the edges of the tongue.

_____ 10. Of 90 possible chemical elements, it appears that about (a) $33\frac{1}{3}$ per cent, (b) 50 per cent, (c) $16\frac{2}{3}$ per cent, are smell stimuli.

_____ 11. An olfacty is the (1) of an odor stimulus necessary at threshold sensitivity.

_____ 12. The complex perception of a hot cup of coffee "fixed to taste" includes (a) 2, (b) 4, (c) 6, (d) 8, (e) 10, sense qualities.

_____ 13. Pain follows overstimulation of any sense organ.

_____ 14. Hair bulbs are probable receptors of (2).

_____ 15. The probable receptors for cutaneous pain are (3).

_____ 16. It is possible to stimulate the skin simultaneously at two points so close together that they cannot be discriminated as two points but only as one.

_____ 17. Pain sensitivity adapts faster than pressure sensitivity with equal stimulation.

_____ 18. Two-point pressure discrimination varies with the distance of the area from its axis of locomotion.

_____ 19. The theory of the temperature gradient states that the degree of flow outward from the body of heat determines the intensity of temperature sensitivity.

_____ 20. The theory of the pressure gradient states that pressure sensitivity diminishes and increases with the steepness of the deformation created in the skin surface by a mechanical stimulus.

_____ 21.

_____ 22. Kinesthetic sensitivities are localized in the linings of the

_____ 23. (1), (1), and (1).

_____ 24. Nausea is a complex awareness, but necessarily there is pressure or pain sensitivity localized in the throat.

_____25. The threshold of kinesthetic sensitivity of movement in the joints is greater than 5 degrees.

_____26. Rotary movement is sensed when (a) the speed of rotation becomes constant, (b) greatest movement of the body is attained, (c) otolith receptors of the vestibule are stimulated, (d) there is a change in acceleration of rotation.

_____27. The illusory movement of the environment experienced after bodily rotation is called (a) nystagmus, (b) labyrinthine fatigue, (c) visual vertigo, (d) the Müller-Lyer illusion.

_____28. Kinesthesis of the ciliary muscles may be distance cues when related to visual cues.

_____29. Wetness is an elemental cutaneous sensitivity.

_____30. Equilibrium sensitivities are usually fairly focal in awareness.

_____ SCORE
(Number of correct answers)

Scoring Key on Page 285

Test for Chapter 9

_____ 1. The family-history method is appropriate in studying whether or not feeble-mindedness and genius run in families.

_____ 2. Doubtful reports of discrimination can be ignored without influencing the results in the summation of data from an experiment.

_____ 3. In the "order of merit method" each stimulus is presented as one member of a pair of stimuli and the subject indicates which of the two he likes better.

_____ 4. One should expect a bell-shaped curve in a distribution of measures of any personality trait.

_____ 5. An apparatus used to measure time in sigma (milliseconds) is called a (1).

_____ 6. A rating scale is a device gauging ability under comparable estimation conditions.

_____ 7. On reaction time tests, 68 per cent of the men exceed the median of the women. This means that (a) 68 per cent of the men are better than 50 per cent of the women, (b) 18 per cent of the men are better than 50 per cent of the women, (c) 32 per cent of the men are better than 50 per cent of the women.

_____ 8. Unrelated individuals resemble each other to a degree represented by a correlation coefficient of (a) —1.0, (b) —.50, (c) 0.0, (d) +.50, (e) +1.0.

_____ 9. A correlation of —1.00 between card-sorting and ability to solve multiple-choice problems would mean (a) that those who did the best in one act did the best in the other, (b) that there was no relation between the acts, (c) that those who did the best in one act did the worst in the other.

_____10. The reliability of a test refers to (a) whether or not it measures what it is supposed to measure, (b) whether it is consistent in measuring something, (c) whether it is a speed or power test, (d) whether or not it is equally applicable to different groups.

_____11. Test validation is based on (1) of successful performance.

_____12. The "halo effect" tends to cause ratings on different traits to cluster around the favorable extreme.

_____13. The interquartile range is a measure of central tendency.

_____14. The mean is that average above which and below which 50 per cent of the scores fall.

_____15. In administering a genuine power test, (a) no time limit is used, (b) a specific time is allowed, (c) time used to complete the test is scored.

_____16. The sigma is computed from the (a) mean, (b) median, (c) mode.

_____17. A skewed curve has 50 per cent of the measures on both sides of the (a) mean, (b) median, (c) mode.

_____18. The formula for the critical ratio has for its denominator (a) $\sigma_{(dist)}$, (b) $\sigma_{(m)}$, (c) $\sigma_{(diff)}$.

_____19. Correlations are high between performance before and after practice.

_____20. The coefficient of variation (V) is used as an index of relative variability between two or more measures of variability.

_____21. The Standard Deviation (σ) of a normal distribution shows the range of the middle 57.5 per cent of the measures.

_____22. Standard scores are not directly comparable for different tests.

_____23. A negative correlation is of the same value to the psychologist as a positive correlation of the same size.

_____24. A (1) is any increase in magnitude of stimulus above the absolute threshold that is sensed as a change.

_____25. The product-moment coefficient of correlation (r) is computed by the formula:

$$\text{(a) } 1 - \frac{6\Sigma D^2}{N(N^2 - 1)}, \qquad \text{(b) } \frac{\Sigma xy}{N\sigma_x\sigma_y}.$$

_____ SCORE

(Number of correct answers)

Scoring Key on Page **286**

Test for Chapter 10

_____ 1. In the evolutionary development of organisms, the effectors appeared before the receptors.

_____ 2. The elaboration of the cerebrum parallels an important progressive development in animal behavior from the relatively invariable to the variable.

_____ 3. The mother's hereditary influences continue to affect the child until birth.

_____ 4. The brain of a highly skilled juggler cannot be distinguished from the brain of one entirely unskilled in manual acts.

_____ 5. According to Kretschmer, the ideal physical type is the "pyknik."

_____ 6. Resemblance in mental traits increases in proportion to the increase of blood resemblance.

_____ 7. Biologists today believe that the reason the present-day giraffe has long legs and a long neck is that its ancestors for many generations stretched themselves to reach the foliage of trees.

_____ 8. Correlation for twins in intellectual traits averages about (a) .50, (b) .23, (c) 1.00, (d) .78, (e) .60.

_____ 9. A dominant characteristic is one that is in the soma as well as in the germ plasm, whereas a recessive characteristic appears only in the germ plasm.

_____ 10. According to the principles of Mendelian heredity, grandchildren cannot resemble their grandparents if the grandchildren do not resemble the parents.

_____ 11. The most common physical defect determining learning is in (a) hearing, (b) vision, (c) tonsils, (d) adenoids, (e) hookworm.

_____ 12. Studies of identical twins reared apart show that their environments do not produce any great differences between them.

_____ 13. Removal of diseased tonsils results usually in an increase in I.Q.

_____ 14. Duct glands secrete their products to one particular part of the body whereas endocrine glands secrete directly into the blood stream and therefore all over the body.

_____ 15. The secretion of the (a) thyroid, (b) parotic, (c) pituitary, (d) thymus, (e) adrenal, gland prepares the body for activity.

_____ 16. Children naturally fear snakes.

_____ 17. Activity of the first ten days in the life of the child is determined essentially by (a) interoceptive, (b) proprioceptive, (c) exteroceptive, stimulation.

_____ 18. In general, we may say that the fetus and the newborn infant are radically different in their behavior because re-

actions appear soon after birth which are entirely different from any appearing in the fetus.

_____19. A newborn infant is just as readily pacified by an artifi-
cially produced soothing sound as by the mother's voice.

_____20. Walking in the child is primarily the result of (a) matu-
ration, (b) experience, (c) learning, (d) imitation,
(e) parental guidance.

_____21. Maturation of reactions is completed at birth, and any
further development of the reaction is due to stimulation.

_____22. Learning differs from maturation in that (a) maturation
is only acquisition, (b) maturation is only reproduction,
(c) maturation is modification of reaction through previous practice, (d) maturation is change in behavior
through physiological growth.

_____23. Rigid specific training may accelerate the process of matu-
ration, at least temporarily.

_____24. Emotional maturity refers to whether an individual has
experienced all the emotions life offers.

_____25. The rate of mental decline is the same for all healthy in-
dividuals.

_____ SCORE
(Number of correct answers)

Scoring Key on Page 286

Test for Chapter 11

_____ 1. Learning occurs only when the organism has reached an
appropriate level of maturation.

_____ 2. Retroactive inhibition influences in similar degrees both
recall and recognition.

_____ 3. The problem-box experiment was introduced into animal
psychology by (a) Watson, (b) Thorndike, (c) Köhler,
(d) Yerkes, (e) Gesell.

_____ 4. The nonsense-syllable technique was introduced into experimental psychology by (a) Jones, (b) Watson, (c) Ebbinghaus, (d) Wundt.

_____ 5. The process of learning may involve reacting in one way
to a stimulus and later reacting in a different way to the
same stimulus.

_____ 6. Passive learning, in general, is superior to recitation.

_____ 7. The zero point of learning is the beginning point in most
curves of learning.

_____ 8. Reinstatement of learning is known as (a) retention.
(b) recognition, (c) reproduction, (d) trace.

_____ 9. The correlation between overlearning and retention is
(a) negative, (b) zero, (c) high and positive, (d) low
and positive.

_____10. The learning curve (a) is the same for all types of learning, (b) is always a steady curve upward, (c) always shows a rapid rise at first, (d) varies with the type of learning, (e) contains no plateaus.

_____11. Learning is less efficient when the learner is not allowed to know the results of his efforts than when he has such knowledge.

_____12. Fewer artificial associations are formed by the whole method of learning than by the part method.

_____13. The fact that training in mirror-tracing with the right hand transfers to the left hand is called (a) transfer of training, (b) cross-education, (c) formal discipline.

_____14. Sudden decrease in time or in errors in a learning curve has been taken to indicate (a) trial-and-error learning, (b) insight, (c) completed learning, (d) memory.

_____15. Mere repetition produces fairly efficient learning.

_____16. One learns more efficiently by intense application for a long period of time than he does by intense application for the same time distributed over short periods.

_____17. No learning will take place if there is no "effect."

_____18. All types of imagery may be used in learning, but one type is usually favored.

_____19. If two associations are of equal strength but of different age, the older will lose strength more slowly with the further passage of time.

_____20. The "savings method" measures (a) the number of repetitions necessary for relearning, (b) the time saved by using the part-whole method of learning, (c) the saving effect of repetition.

_____21. The curve of forgetting, where there is little overlearning, indicates that most of our forgetting takes place very soon after learning.

_____22. We retain only those responses which lead to the reward and eliminate all those which result in punishment.

_____23. The reason that a habit such as ball-tossing is retained better than a habit such as nonsense-syllable memorizing is that the former is a motor co-ordination and the latter is a verbal acquisition.

_____24. The frequency theory requires for learning that correct reactions occur more often than incorrect reactions.

_____25. The forgetting of a habit is not simply a fading out, but is largely the result of the activities interpolated between the original acquisition and the attempted reproduction.

_____SCORE
(Number of correct answers)

Scoring Key on Page 286

Test for Chapter 12

_____ 1. The exact motor movements of the tongue have been found to be duplicated in thought and speech of the same words in about 50 per cent of the observations.

_____ 2. A congenital deaf-mute cannot learn to reason abstractly.

_____ 3. The substitution of symbols for objects is an important characteristic of the process of thinking.

_____ 4. Most thinking by the average man is actually in terms of language, either written or oral.

_____ 5. The ability to combine separate experiences to make a new form of response is a kind of thinking found only in human beings and apes.

_____ 6. No man can become a great thinker unless he uses imagery in thinking.

_____ 7. Watson explained thinking as (a) subvocal speech, (b) language, (c) symbolism, (d) a conditioned reflex.

_____ 8. The first advocate of the school of imageless thought was (a) Wundt, (b) Spearman, (c) Titchener, (d) Kulpe.

_____ 9. An essential start in a thinking process is (a) trial-and-error, (b) insight, (c) a ready response, (d) a goal, (e) imagery.

_____ 10. Elimination of error, trial by trial, occurs in both reasoning and learning.

_____ 11. The absence of minimal motor responses during "thinking" is proof that thinking is performed in the nervous system.

_____ 12. A successive awareness (thinking) and a successive reaction (acting) differ in (a) integration, (b) degree of consciousness, (c) temporal relations, (d) method of observation, (e) presence of a goal or purpose.

_____ 13. Productive or creative imagination is found in dreams.

_____ 14. Group thinking may intensify an error if (a) the group is too large, (b) a majority agrees on the same wrong answer, (c) personal errors are equally distributed, (d) the problem is very abstract.

_____ 15. Ability to state an opinion indicates that reasoning behavior has been used in connection with the problem.

_____ 16. The report of the awareness situation is a full and complete statement of a thinking activity.

_____ 17. Two men theoretically of equal language ability would have equal ability in problem-solving.

_____ 18. Reflective thinking is less controlled than creative thinking.

_____ 19. Ideas and generalizations are retained longer than specific facts.

_____ 20. Thinking is any sequence of directed awarenesses. This definition can be supported with experimental facts.

_____21. Working together, on the average, results in greater efficiency in free associations.

_____22. All psychological activity, whether thinking or acting, involves without exception a succession of events.

_____23. Attitudes are nonaffective logical awarenesses.

_____24. Reasoning is not a trial-and-error process; it is a straightforward analysis of a situation.

_____25. Insight is the solution of a problem by thinking which does not depend upon past experience.

_____SCORE
(Number of correct answers)

Scoring Key on Page 287

Test for Chapter 13

_____ 1. When a person goes through the same performance "day in and day out," he can be said to be unmotivated.

_____ 2. The motivation for shelter in primitive man was (a) the gregarious instinct, (b) the temperature drive, (c) the desire for a family, (d) the instinct of constructiveness.

_____ 3. When an organism reacts in a manner to remove the drive, it does so as the result of learning.

_____ 4. In male rats, the (a) sex, (b) thirst, (c) exploratory, (d) temperature, drive results in the largest number of grid crossings in the obstruction apparatus.

_____ 5. A drive once aroused usually results immediately in (a) specific organic or kinesthetic sensitivity, (b) intentional directed motivation, (c) general abortive activity, (d) emotional reactions.

_____ 6. Motive is distinguished from drive by the amount of conscious direction present in the activity.

_____ 7. A development of reactions so that incentives remove drives always results in greater socialization.

_____ 8. Conditioned reactions are always formed under conscious motivation.

_____ 9. The fact that any person exhibits a certain amount of general activity every moment of his life may be attributed to the ever-changing and ever-present tissue conditions.

_____10. Social motives, e.g., ideals and ambition, have been traced in their development from the fundamental tissue conditions of the organism.

_____11. Ordinary noises interfere with efficiency in mental work as a rule.

_____12. To work for group benefit (group competition) is a stronger motive than to work for self-benefit (individual competition) .

_____13. The essential incentive difference between rewards and punishments is their long-period effect.

_____14. Experiments have shown that the more severe the punishment up to the point the worker "cannot take it," the more rapidly will errors be eliminated in the task.

_____15. Experimental results on social facilitation demonstrate that one accomplishes more by work at home than in class.

_____16. The evidence is conclusive that praise is superior to reproof in increasing effort in work with all children.

_____17. If both a negative and a positive valence are present, the positive valence dominates.

_____18. Shift of mental set is more detrimental to efficiency in complex than in simple performances.

_____19. When two incentives, such as rivalry and reward, are present, one may expect an effect in performance that is additive of their individual effects.

_____20. A set toward a goal is present in both action and thinking.

_____21. Tasks completed in performance, but unsatisfactorily so to the worker, are more likely to be recalled later than tasks voluntarily left uncompleted.

_____22. Any incentive presented to a group of workers will affect the poorer workers more than the better workers.

_____23. Intentionally selected exteroceptive stimuli in the satisfaction of a motive are called (a) instincts, (b) incentives, (c) sets, (d) drives, (e) tissue conditions.

_____24. The pleasantness or unpleasantness of particular incentive stimuli is due to training.

_____25. Holt's Theory of Neurobiotaxis is a theory of (a) emotions, (b) feelings, (c) learning, (d) motivation.

_____SCORE
(Number of correct answers)

Scoring Key on Page 287

Test for Chapter 14

_____1. During emotional excitement there is (a) increase in glycogen in blood, (b) increase in imagery, (c) decrease in breathing rates, (d) decrease in blood supply to skeletal muscles.

_____2. The physiological changes in such dissimilar emotions as rage and fright may be the same.

_____3. The most infantile fear stimulus is (a) the dark, (b) a snake, (c) a rough nurse, (d) falling, (e) slapping.

_____4. Using cats as subjects (with X-ray techniques), the peristaltic action of the stomach during or following an emotion was found to be (a) facilitated, (b) greatly retarded, (c) slightly retarded, (d) very greatly increased, (e) unaffected.

_____ 5. Emotions are expressed in much the same manner in all people over the world.

_____ 6. Emotional reactions, such as fear, anger, and joy, are not subject to conditioning processes after the manner of simple reflexes.

_____ 7. An "emotional state" can be produced in an individual by injection of adrenalin.

_____ 8. The overt reaction made in an emotion is a reliable indicator of the kind of emotion felt by the individual.

_____ 9. Introspective studies of emotion indicate that emotional awareness is (a) clear, (b) full of many kinds of imagery, (c) disintegrative, (d) goal directed, (e) nugatory.

_____ 10. The facial expressions of emotions of adults are more variable and less stereotyped than those of children.

_____ 11. Systolic blood-pressure curves are sensitive indicators of emotion.

_____ 12. The word association (free association) test is used to discover (a) tonicity, (b) complexes, (c) ideas, (d) empathy, (e) glycosuria.

_____ 13. The inspiration-expiration ratio is (a) lower, (b) higher, (c) the same, before a false answer to a question is given than after the true answer has been given.

_____ 14. During emotional states, the "skin resistance" (a) is lower than during normal states, (b) is often lower and often higher than during normal times, (c) is higher than during normal times.

_____ 15. Children have a native fear, dread, or repulsion for strange-looking things.

_____ 16. A state of frustration is a state of excessive emotional activity on the part of an organism.

_____ 17. The emotions of infants can be accurately classified by experts by studying cinema records of their reactions.

_____ 18. Fear of the dark is an example of conditioning.

_____ 19. Although experiments have shown that the hunger cry of the newborn is actually different from an anger cry, many persons are unable to detect the difference if they do not know the actual cause in each case.

_____ 20. Temper tantrums often are due to inherited emotional instability.

_____ 21. The distinction between fear and anger is based on differences in (a) native behavior, (b) explicit activity, (c) implicit activity, (d) amount of adrenalin secreted.

_____ 22. When an actor expresses emotion, he (a) merely allows his natural unlearned expressive movements to occur freely, (b) reduces the natural expressive movements,

(c) uses characteristic modifications of natural expressive movements, (d) builds up a new set of expressions.

—————23. The best method for unconditioning a fear response is to condition a new and appropriate response to the fear stimulus.

—————24. Cannon's work with emotion was mainly a study of (a) the striped muscles, (b) heart action, (c) glands of internal secretion, (d) fetal kittens.

—————25. According to the James-Lange theory, the first phase of emotional activity is (a) the emotion, (b) the sensitivity of environmental stimulus, (c) the sensitivity of internal turmoil, (d) the explicit response to the stimulus.

——————————————SCORE
(Number of correct answers)

Scoring Key on Page 287

Test for Chapter 15

—————1. When two motives are not in accord, we always have a (a) neurosis, (b) conflict, (c) repression, (d) phobia.

—————2. The activity of a person who meets an obstacle may be increased not only in vigor but also in variety.

—————3. That a given situation is not equally frustrating to all people depends chiefly on (a) differences in their motives, (b) the overt pressure of other persons, (c) intelligence differences, (d) the implicit attitudes.

—————4. Social frustrations of the individual (a) are regarded as abnormal social occurrences, (b) always bring about maladjustive responses, (c) are independent of habit formation, (d) evoke adjustments of various qualities and kinds, (e) cause repressions as a rule.

—————5. The thwartings least likely to result in unfortunate substitute adjustments come from (a) material frustration, (b) social frustration, (c) emotional frustration, (d) frustrations of inadequacy.

—————6. Overlapping of distributions of personality measures for different groups is commonly found.

—————7. Glandular disorders may cause remarkable changes in the personality.

—————8. Chemical explanations of personality have been confined largely to specific personality qualities.

—————9. The whole personality changes markedly from one hour to the next.

—————10. All persons who score above the tenth percentile in any personality trait should have psychiatric attention.

—————11. Attitudes are permanent predispositions to react in characteristic ways.

_____12. Attitudes appear only after a long and gradual process of accumulation of specific experiences.

_____13. Hallucinations are real perceptions.

_____14. The factor most likely to be responsible for delinquent conduct is (a) presence of a step-father, (b) small stature, (c) emotional instability, (d) too much spending money.

_____15. Daydreaming is (a) always a helpful practice, (b) always a harmful practice, (c) usually a defense mechanism, (d) a sure sign of mental illness, (e) a mark of genius.

_____16. The results of the testing with the masculinity-femininity test showed that the differences between men and women are due to training.

_____17. The normal person frequently has mild obsessions.

_____18. An individual who ranks a 50 percentile in introversion is an introvert 50 per cent of the time and an extrovert the other 50 per cent.

_____19. According to Adler, feelings of inferiority are the most important motivators of behavior.

_____20. A hysterical disability in a man is nothing more than pretending that his arm, for example, is paralyzed, although he knows it really is not.

_____21. In the "conflict" type of frustration, the social factor (a) is represented in overt group pressure, (b) operates through the individual's attitudes and habits, (c) is frequently present in group attitudes, (d) is due to the individual's feelings.

_____22. A symptom of overcompensation is (a) anxiety, (b) cruelty, (c) boasting, (d) depression.

_____23. Delusions of persecution and grandeur are symptoms of (a) hysteria, (b) paresis, (c) manic-depressive psychosis, (d) paranoia, (e) involutional melancholia.

_____24. From one's intelligence it is impossible to draw valid conclusions regarding his standing on other personality traits.

_____25. The child's feeling states have little to do with his observed personality.

_____SCORE
(Number of correct answers)

Scoring Key on Page 288

Test for Chapter 16

_____ 1. Most of the general intelligence tests now in use stress (a) linguistic ability, (b) mechanical ability, (c) mathematical ability, (d) social adaptation.

_____ 2. The first group test of intelligence was the (a) Pintner-Paterson, (b) Stanford-Binet, (c) Army Alpha, (d) Otis Self-administering, (e) Kuhlman-Anderson.

_____ 3. A performance test means (a) a power test, (b) a test not involving the use of language, (c) a test of mechanical skill, (d) a test of special abilities.

_____ 4. Normal intelligence is indicated by an I.Q. of (a) 102, (b) 70, (c) 132, (d) 68, (e) 161.

_____ 5. A test to discover whether one would make a good plumber is called (a) an intelligence test, (b) an aptitude test, (c) a performance test.

_____ 6. Gesell's scale is designed for (a) those above the level of the Binet, (b) college students who cannot pass the entrance test, (c) very young children, (d) same as the Binet level.

_____ 7. If a child passes a test at the five-year level of the Stanford-Binet, he has done something that 100 per cent of the children at that age can do.

_____ 8. Modern psychologists consider (a) 14 years, (b) 18 years, (c) 21 years, to be about average mentality as measured by intelligence tests.

_____ 9. Intelligence tests may be said to best indicate one's (a) social intelligence, (b) academic ability, (c) earning capacity, (d) ability to solve problems.

_____10. Motor abilities are highly correlated.

_____11. The Binet-Simon Tests are best suited to (a) adults, (b) people between the ages of 16 and 20, (c) children between the ages of 3 and 12, (d) occupational groups of all ages.

_____12. For the great mass of children, the I.Q. remains fairly constant from year to year.

_____13. Clerical aptitude tests usually measure (a) skill in arithmetic, (b) manual dexterity, (c) typing ability, (d) ability to notice details.

_____14. Tweezer dexterity tests usually measure (a) artistic ability, (b) mechanical skill, (c) manual aptitude.

_____15. An achievement quotient is related to the intelligence quotient.

_____16. Assume two tests of general ability X and Y. Test X is better standardized than is Test Y if (a) the items of X were more carefully selected than those of Y, (b) X was applied to a number of highly selected groups of individuals, whereas Y was applied to a heterogeneous group, (c) X was standardized by use of a larger number of unselected people than was Y, (d) individuals score higher on X than on Y.

_____17. Place the following items in order of succession for planning an occupational selection test: (a) validation of tests, (b) establishing reliability of criteria of vocational success, (c) selection of test materials, (d) job analysis, (e) item analysis, (f) establishing critical scores, (g) selection of criteria of vocational success.

_____18. An older child and a young child of the same mental age may have the same I.Q.

_____19. In individual testing, (a) the test is given as directed and takes no account of special conditions, (b) literal form and established standards must be used but results are interpreted in the light of special conditions, (c) no training is necessary if one reads the directions given for the test, (d) the examiner may force the subject to work.

_____20. The mental age of a child indicates (a) his mental maturity, (b) his rate of mental development, (c) his brightness, (d) his special abilities.

_____21. A test norm for any age is (a) the average score for children of that age, (b) the highest score for that age, (c) the lowest for that age, (d) the range ratio for that age.

_____22. Children of unusual mental capacity, on the average, are physically superior to normal children.

_____23. The two-factor theory conceives of intelligence as consisting of general ability and of specific abilities in various fields.

_____24. A useful intelligence test for the deaf is the (a) Pintner-Paterson, (b) Stanford-Binet, (c) Army Alpha, (d) Herring-Binet, (e) Kuhlman-Anderson.

_____25. According to test results, the teens are the period of most rapid growth in intelligence.

_____SCORE
(Number of correct answers)

Scoring Key on Page 288

Test for Chapter 17

_____ 1. The universal belief of mankind that one race is superior to another is pretty good evidence that such superiority is a fact.

_____ 2. Feeble-mindedness is indicated by an I.Q. of (a) 98, (b) 105, (c) 136, (d) 42, (e) 153.

_____ 3. The more intelligence one has, the better adjusted he will be in any vocation.

_____ 4. Individuals of the same age differ greatly in every trait that has been measured.

_____ 5. Resemblance in mental traits increases in proportion to kinship.

_____ 6. Individuals whose general scholastic averages are equal show approximately equal proficiency in all subjects.

_____ 7. Genius and feeble-mindedness differ quantitatively rather than qualitatively.

_____ 8. The best capacities of the individual are usually about (a) 3, (b) 6, (c) 9, (d) 12, times his worst.

_____ 9. A true statement is that: (a) Occupations differ widely in their intelligence requirements. (b) The median intelligence of various occupational groups is almost the same. (c) The distribution of intelligence in an occupational group is narrow.

_____ 10. If some children of a very intelligent family were reared in a very poor environment, the probable result would be (a) feeble-mindedness, (b) a slight decrease in I.Q., (c) a great change in I.Q., (d) no change in I.Q.

_____ 11. A congenital deaf-mute can learn to generalize from experience.

_____ 12. The correlation between character traits and the size and shape of the features is zero.

_____ 13. An idiot may eat garbage probably because normal (a) gustatory sensitivity is impaired, (b) olfactory sensitivity is impaired, (c) food discriminations have not been learned.

_____ 14. There are no mental traits unique either to male or female.

_____ 15. At least 75 per cent of juvenile delinquents are defective mentally.

_____ 16. Hookworm seldom affects mental development.

_____ 17. Children are more accurate reporters of events than adults.

_____ 18. The faster worker is more accurate than the slower worker.

_____ 19. Interests are usually (a) permanent throughout life, (b) grouped according to social background, (c) prognostic of vocational success.

_____ 20. Older men are (a) more certain than, (b) as certain as, (c) less certain than, younger men regarding the validity of their judgments of psychological qualities, although the actual validity of their judgments is about equal.

_____ 21. In repetitive simple industrial operations, boredom (feelings of fatigue) is greater for workers of high intelligence.

_____ 22. Mental disease appears far more frequently in family groups than chance would warrant.

_____ 23. Children in institutions for the feeble-minded are somewhat larger than average.

_____ 24. Traits of sibs correspond more closely than do those found in fraternal twins.

_____ 25. There is less difference between the dullest and the ablest child at 6 than at 16.

_____SCORE

(Number of correct answers)

Scoring Key on Page 288

Scoring Key—Test for Chapter 1

1. F
2. a

(Any Order) { 3. Contiguity
4. Similarity
5. Contrast

6. T
7. b
8. F
9. F
10. F
11. T
12. T
13. T
14. F

(Any Order) { 15. Intellect
16. Emotions
17. Will

18. b
19. F
20. T
21. a
22. d
23. St. Augustine
24. b
25. F
26. F
27. F
28. F
29. F

Scoring Key—Test for Chapter 2

1. Receptors
2. F
3. F
4. T (Any Order)
5. T
6. T (Any Order)

(Any Order) { 7. Interoceptors
8. Sensitivity
9. Reaction
10. Integration
11. Learning (Development)

12. F
13. Environmental changes
(Energy changes)
14. Receptors
15. F
16. T

17. Cells (Fibers)
18. Unit (Whole)
(Any Order) { 19. Striped (Striated)
20. Smooth (Unstriated)
(Any Order) { 21. Explicit
22. Implicit
23. Striped muscles
(Striated muscles)
24. Reaction (Response, Behavior)
25. Nervous system
26. Circulatory system
(Blood stream)
27. T
28. F
29. T
30. T

Scoring Key—Test for Chapter 3

1. d

(Any Order) { 2. Axon
3. Dendrite
4. Nucleus
5. Cell body

6. Synapse
(Any Order) { 7. Intensity
8. Frequency
9. Reflex arc
(Reaction arc)

(Any Order) { 10. Frontal
11. Temporal
12. Parietal
13. Occipital
14. Isle of Reil

15. Dorsal
(Any Order) { 16. Motor end plate
17. Muscle fiber
18. b
19. d

283

Scoring Key—Test for Chapter 3 (*continued*)

20. c	28. d
21. c	29. c
22. c	30. a
23. c	31. b
24. Receptors	32. F
25. a	33. d
26. T	34. b
27. c	

Scoring Key—Test for Chapter 4

1. F	14. F
2. T	15. T
3. T	16. T
4. F	17. T
5. T	18. F
6. F	19. F
7. T	20. T
8. T	21. T
9. T	22. F
10. a	23. T
11. T	24. F
12. T	25. c
13. T	

Scoring Key—Test for Chapter 5

1. T	15. F
(Any Order) { 2. Audition	16. T
3. Vision	17. T
4. Intensity	18. Adaptation
(Any Order) { 5. Protensity (Duration)	19. a
6. Extensity	20. F
7. F	21. T
8. T	22. T
9. F	23. T
10. e	24. T
11. F	25. F
12. T	26. T
13. F	27. T
14. F	28. b

Scoring Key—Test for Chapter 6

1. Blind spot (Optic disc)	5. 100
2. F	(Any Order) { 6. Hue (Chroma)
3. F	7. Brightness (Brilliance)
4. e	8. Saturation

Scoring Key—Test for Chapter 6 (*continued*)

9. e	19. F
10. T	20. T
11. Brightness (Saturation)	21. d
12. T	22. F
13. T	23. T
14. F	24. F
15. a	25. d
16. d	26. T
17. d	27. T
18. T	

Scoring Key—Test for Chapter 7

1. T	14. F
2. 10 to 20	15. F
3. T	16. F
(Any Order) 4. Pitch	17. F
5. Octave (Tonality)	18. Overtones (Partials)
6. Volume	19. Differential limen
7. T	20. b
8. T	21. d
9. T	22. a
10. d	23. F
11. F	24. T
12. Combination tone	25. F
(Difference or summa-	26. F
tion tone)	27. T
13. T	

Scoring Key—Test for Chapter 8

(Any Order) 1. Sweet	16. T
2. Sour	17. F
3. Salt	18. T
4. Bitter	19. T
5. T	20. T
6. F	(Any Order) 21. Muscles
7. F	22. Tendons
8. T	23. Joints
9. T	24. T
10. c	25. F
11. Area	26. d
12. d	27. c
13. F	28. T
14. Cutaneous pressure	29. F
15. Free nerve endings	30. F

Scoring Key—Test for Chapter 9

1.	T	14.	F
2.	F	15.	a
3.	F	16.	a
4.	T	17.	b
5.	Chronoscope	18.	c
6.	T	19.	T
7.	a	20.	T
8.	c	21.	F
9.	c	22.	F
10.	b	23.	T
11.	Criteria	24.	J.n.d.
12.	F	25.	b
13.	F		

Scoring Key—Test for Chapter 10

1.	T	14.	T
2.	T	15.	e
3.	F	16.	F
4.	T	17.	a
5.	F	18.	F
6.	T	19.	T
7.	F	20.	a
8.	d	21.	F
9.	T	22.	d
10.	F	23.	F
11.	c	24.	F
12.	F	25.	F
13.	F		

Scoring Key—Test for Chapter 11

1.	T	14.	b
2.	F	15.	F
3.	b	16.	F
4.	c	17.	T
5.	T	18.	T
6.	F	19.	T
7.	F	20.	a
8.	c	21.	T
9.	d	22.	F
10.	d	23.	F
11.	T	24.	T
12.	T	25.	T
13.	b		

Scoring Key—Test for Chapter 12

1. F	14. d
2. F	15. F
3. T	16. F
4. T	17. F
5. F	18. F
6. T	19. T
7. a	20. T
8. d	21. T
9. d	22. F
10. T	23. F
11. F	24. F
12. d	25. F
13. T	

Scoring Key—Test for Chapter 13

1. F	14. F
2. b	15. F
3. T	16. F
4. b	17. F
5. c	18. F
6. T	19. F
7. F	20. T
8. F	21. T
9. T	22. T
10. F	23. b
11. F	24. T
12. F	25. c
13. T	

Scoring Key—Test for Chapter 14

1. a	14. b
2. T	15. F
3. d	16. T
4. b	17. F
5. F	18. T
6. F	19. T
7. T	20. F
8. F	21. b
9. c	22. c
10. F	23. T
11. T	24. c
12. b	25. b
13. a	

Scoring Key—Test for Chapter 15

1.	b	14.	c
2.	T	15.	c
3.	a	16.	T
4.	d	17.	T
5.	a	18.	F
6.	T	19.	T
7.	T	20.	F
8.	T	21.	b
9.	F	22.	a
10.	F	23.	d
11.	T	24.	T
12.	T	25.	F
13.	F		

Scoring Key—Test for Chapter 16

1.	a	14.	c
2.	c	15.	T
3.	b	16.	c
4.	a	17.	d, g, b, c, e, a, f
5.	b	18.	F
6.	c	19.	b
7.	F	20.	a
8.	a	21.	a
9.	b	22.	T
10.	F	23.	T
11.	c	24.	a
12.	T	25.	F
13.	d		

Scoring Key—Test for Chapter 17

1.	F	14.	T
2.	d	15.	F
3.	F	16.	F
4.	T	17.	F
5.	T	18.	T
6.	F	19.	b
7.	T	20.	a
8.	a	21.	T
9.	a	22.	T
10.	b	23.	F
11.	T	24.	F
12.	T	25.	T
13.	c		

Index

Index

Abnormal psychology, 210–213; beginnings of, 6; field of, 11
Absolute threshold, 57
Abstraction, 173, 175. *See also* Conceptual thinking, Generalization.
Accommodation, 82
Achievement tests, 218; educational, 231; job, 231–232. *See also* Tests.
Acromegaly, 135
"Act" psychology, 5
Acuity: tactual, 110; visual, 81
Adaptation: emotional, 196–197; gustatory, 106; olfactory, 104; pain, 109; pressure, 109; temperature, 109; visual, 75, 78–79
Adjustment, 202–216; to emotional situations, 196–197
Adkins, 255
Adler, 10, 214
Adolph, 183
Adrian, 39, 98
Afterimages, 75
Age, changes in hearing with, 100–101
Aguilonius, 83
Alexia, 142
Allen, 106
All-or-none principle, 21, 39
Allport, 187, 203
Alpert, 175
Amatruda, 141
Aments, 239–240
Anastasi, 256
Andrews, 253
Angell, 8
Anger, 191, 192, 198, 199. *See also* Emotion.
Animism, 1
Anosmia, 104–105
Aphasia, 142
Apparent movement, visual, 87–88
Aptitude tests, 218; artistic, 228; clerical, 230–231; educational, 226–227; general, 220–226; mechanical, 228–230; musical, 227–228; special, 227–230. *See also* Tests.
Aquinas, 2
Arachnoid, 30
Aristotle, 2
Aristotle's illusion, 110
Army: Alpha Test, 223–224, 243; General Classification Test, 224–225, 234, 243; Performance Scale, 223
Arp, 188
Arthur, 223
Artistic aptitude tests, 228
Artom, 137
Association, free, 205

Associationism, 2–4, 151
Associative areas, 37–38
Asthenic type, 207
Athletic type, 207
Attention, 60–63
Attributes of sensation, 59–60, 64, 67; auditory, 94–96, 102; cutaneous, 107–108; definition of, 59–60; gustatory, 105; olfactory, 103; visual, 72–73
Aubert, 79
Audiogram, 100, 101
Audition, 90–102; apparatus of, 92–94; area of brain for, 37; phenomena of, 94–96; principal functions of, 90; and space perception, 98–100; stimulation of, 90–92; theories of, 97–98, 102; threshold of, 95–96
Autistic thinking, 168. *See also* Daydreaming.
Autokinetic movement, 88
Average error, method of, 58
Avoidance conditioning, 48
Awareness, 54, 66–67, 192; emotional, 193, 199. *See also* Consciousness.
Axis. *See* Central axis.
Axon, 28, 34, 35, 39. *See also* Neuron.

Babinski reflex, 140, 213. *See also* Reflex.
Bain, 4, 5
Baker, 189
Baldwin, 253
Ballard, 158
Bard, 198, 200
Barelare, 182
Barlow, 156
Barrett, 157
Bash, 182
Basilar membrane, 93–94, 97–98, 100, 101. *See also* Receptors.
Bates, 185
Bayley, 141
Beach, 253
Beats, 96
Beck, 205
Behavior tests, 204
Behaviorism, 5, 8–9
Bekesy, 97
Bekhterev, 151
Bell, 4, 204
Bellows, 183
Belongingness, 161
Bennett, 230
Berkeley, 4
Bernard, 5
Bernheim, 6

291

Reasoning, 55, 154, 168–169; problems, 172; results of investigations on, 174–176
Recall, 146, 157, 158, 159. *See also* Learning.
Recalled sensitivities, 65–66, 67. *See also* Sensitivity.
Receptors, 18, 19, 22–24, 34, 36–37, 38, 40, 41, 44, 54; adjustments of, in attention, 60–61; auditory, 92–94; chemical, 107; classification of, 20; cutaneous, 107; definition of, 19; equilibrium, 111; gustatory, 106; kinesthetic, 110–111; olfactory, 92–94; structure of, 19–20; visual, 69–72
Recognition, 146, 157, 159. *See also* Learning.
Redintegration, 53, 65, 201
Reflex, 44, 139–140; arc, 40–41, 44; Babinski, 140; conditioned, 45; definition of, 44; eyelid, 44; grasping, 140; knee jerk, 44, 213
Reid, 4
Reinforcement, 163, 166
Reliability: coefficient of, 127–128; definition of, 127, 219
Reminiscence, 158
Remmers, 119
Repetition, 154, 164, 167. *See also* Learning.
Retention, 156–159, 167. *See also* Learning.
Retina, 70–72. *See also* Receptors.
Retinal: disparity, 82; image, 81–82; zones, 76
Retroactive inhibition, 158–159
Reward conditioning, 48
Reward-punishment, 188. *See also* Incentive.
Rheobase, 55
Rheotropism, 44
Rhode, 206
Rhodopsin, 79, 81
Rhythm, 64
Ribot, 6
Richardson, 175
Richter, 182
Riddle, 185
Rissland, 187
Robbins, 138
Robinson, 140, 157, 160, 167
Rods and cones, 71, 80–81, 89
Rods of Corti, 36
Roethlisberger, 188, 254
Rogers, 205, 255
Rolando, fissure of, 31–33, 37
Root, 203
Rorschach, 115, 205; test, 205
Rosenzweig, 206
Rotter, 206
Rubin's vase, 84
Ruch, 14
Ruckmick, 255
Ruger, 172
Russ, 186
Rutherford, 98
Ryan, 254

Saint Augustine, 2
Sarcolemma, 22
Sargent, 226
Scammon, 138, 139
Schizophrenia, 211

Schneiderian membrane, 36, 104, 113
Schneirla, 254
Schools of psychology, 13, 20–21; classification of, 7–10
Schwann, sheath of, 27
Science, definition of, 1
Scientific method, 14–15, 114–130; experimental, 117–118; statistical, 119–127
Scotopic vision, 79, 81
Sears, 187
Seashore, 227, 228, 251
Secondary sex characteristics, 139
Seguin, 6, 223
Semicircular canals, 36, 92–94, 111, 113
Sensation, 54–55; attributes of, 59–60; auditory, 94–96; cutaneous, 107–109; definition of, 54; gustatory, 105; olfactory, 103; visual, 72–73. *See also* Sensitivity.
Sensitivity, 18, 19, 21, 25, 54; and adaptation, 63; auditory, 94–102; chemical, 106–107; classification of, 54; cutaneous, 107–110; equilibrium, 111–112; gustatory, 105–106; individual differences in, 66; kinesthetic, 110–111; neonate, 139–140; noise, 90; olfactory, 103–105; organic, 112; recalled, 65–66; visual, 72–89
Sensory areas in brain, 37–38
Set, 65, 155
Sex, 139, 180, 184–185, 186, 213; hormones, 184; index of, 244; intelligence differences in, 242
Shaffer, 252
Sharp, 153, 157
Shartle, 255
Sheath of Schwann, 27
Sheldon, 207
Sherman, 198
Sherrington, 110
Shirley, 140, 141
Shuttleworth, 138
Sign-*Gestalt*-expectation, 164
Significance, 126–127; measures of, 123–125
Similarity, 64, 151; law of, 165
Simmons, 154
Simon, 6, 221
Sims, 187
S–I–R formula, 17, 247; in emotion, 199
Skaggs, 195, 196
Skill: achievement tests of, 231–232; aptitude tests of, 228–231; individual differences in, 243
Skinner, 145, 160, 166, 167, 254
Skinner box, 48, 162, 166
Smell, 103–105, 113. *See also* Olfaction, Sensitivity.
Smoke, 175
Smooth muscles, 23, 44
Snyder, 253
Snygg, 253, 254, 255
Social facilitation, 187–188
Social motivation, 185–189
Social psychology, 5, 9, 12, 249
Sociometric status, 243
Somatotonia, 207, 208
Somatotypes, 1, 206–208
Somesthetic area, 37
Somnambulism, 212